The Memphis Red Sox

The Memphis Red Sox
A Negro Leagues History

KEITH B. WOOD

Foreword by Leslie Heaphy

McFarland & Company, Inc., Publishers
Jefferson, North Carolina

This book has undergone peer review.

LIBRARY OF CONGRESS CATALOGUING-IN-PUBLICATION DATA

Names: Wood, Keith B., author.
Title: The Memphis Red Sox : a Negro Leagues history / Keith B. Wood.
Description: Jefferson, North Carolina : McFarland & Company, Inc., Publishers, 2024 | Includes bibliographical references and index.
Identifiers: LCCN 2024013796 | ISBN 9781476693767 (paperback : acid free paper) ∞
ISBN 9781476652276 (ebook)
Subjects: LCSH: Negro leagues—Tennessee—Memphis—History—20th century. | Memphis Red Sox (Baseball team)—History—20th century. | Baseball—Social aspects—Tennessee—Memphis—History—20th century. | Racism in sports—Tennessee—Memphis—History—20th century. | African American baseball players—Tennessee—Memphis—History—20th century. | Memphis (Tenn.)—Race relations—History—20th century. | BISAC: SPORTS & RECREATION / Baseball / History | HISTORY / African American & Black
Classification: LCC GV863.T2 W66 2024 | DDC 796.35709768/19—dc23/eng/20240412
LC record available at https://lccn.loc.gov/2024013796

BRITISH LIBRARY CATALOGUING DATA ARE AVAILABLE

ISBN (print) 978-1-4766-9376-7
ISBN (ebook) 978-1-4766-5227-6

© 2024 Keith B. Wood. All rights reserved

No part of this book may be reproduced or transmitted in any form or by any means, electronic or mechanical, including photocopying or recording, or by any information storage and retrieval system, without permission in writing from the publisher.

Front cover: Casey Jones (far right) of the Memphis Red Sox is greeted by his teammates after a home run in Martin Stadium (Withers Collection Museum and Gallery)

Printed in the United States of America

McFarland & Company, Inc., Publishers
Box 611, Jefferson, North Carolina 28640
www.mcfarlandpub.com

To Zachery Kerr:
Hey, cat, thanks for opening
my eyes to this story.

Table of Contents

Acknowledgments	viii
Foreword by Leslie Heaphy	1
Introduction	3
1. Early Professional Blackball in Memphis	11
2. "Take Me Out to the Ballgame"—Martin Stadium at Lewis Park	19
3. Black Owned and Operated	49
4. The 1938 Championship Season	79
5. Boss Crump Ejects J.B. Martin	104
6. The Boys of Summer	119
7. Barnstorming	150
8. Winterball	163
9. The Final Outs	171
Epilogue	190
Chapter Notes	195
Bibliography	217
Index	221

Acknowledgments

Special thanks to: University of Memphis's Steve Ross for his interest in this project and for granting access to the hours of video interviews. John Haddock, whose passion for Negro leagues baseball includes an extensive collection of Red Sox memorabilia. Jim Cushing in the University of Memphis Special Collections for my numerous requests to sift through VHS tapes. Curt Hart for sharing a number of radio interviews with former Negro leaguers.

Delores Brown, the daughter-in-law of iconic Red Sox catcher/manager Larry Brown, is a true gem, and her help in getting this story told was immeasurable. Connor Scanlon, at the Withers Collection in Memphis, not only provided initial images to aid in the research phase but also aided in working with the Withers family to get this story told pictorially.

I am grateful to the History Department at the University of Memphis for continuing to challenge me as an academic. Aram Goudsouzian for his willingness to review, critique, and make suggestions for improving the scholarship found in the following pages. I would also like to thank Wayne Dowdy, in the Memphis and Shelby County Room at the Memphis Public Library, for his help throughout the years on various projects, including this one.

A special thanks to Jim Gates in Cooperstown at the National Baseball Hall of Fame for welcoming me to the Symposium on Baseball and American Culture. Cassidy Lent's assistance at the Hall during the latter stages of this project has been priceless. I am grateful to William Simmons and Leslie Heaphy for publishing presentations on the Memphis Red Sox in the early stages of this project as editors of academic journals on baseball.

Finally, I am deeply grateful for the love, support, and encouragement from my wife Sheri and our three boys: Cameron, Chandler, and Carson.

Foreword

by Leslie Heaphy

I have had the pleasure of knowing Keith Wood for many years. I got to know Keith because of my own work on the Negro leagues and my interest in the history of the Memphis Red Sox in particular. I have written a number of books and articles about the Negro leagues and as a result am familiar with the literature. A book on the history of the Memphis Red Sox and the Martin family is long overdue.

I met Keith at the annual Cooperstown Symposium on Baseball and American Culture after we chatted by email for some time. That first meeting was such a pleasure as I learned about Keith's background and why he was interested in the subject of the Martins and the Red Sox. Keith is a resident of Memphis and so this history is personal. Not only has he taught in the city, but he has researched its sports history for more than a decade, publishing both articles and a book, *Memphis Hoops: Race and Basketball in the Bluff City, 1968-1997,* along the way. He is an expert on the subject, and as the editor of *Black Ball*, I have had the privilege of publishing some of his work.

In this new book, Keith sets out to tell the story of black baseball in Memphis, though the Red Sox are the primary focus. Wood is careful to position this history within the larger context of the life of blacks in the city. Readers will learn about the history of Martin Stadium, one of a few black-owned stadiums in the United States, but also of the Martins themselves. The story of their Red Sox helps fill a gap in the literature of black baseball, which tends to focus on the teams playing in the North.

Wood walks us through the history of the Red Sox, following their triumphs and challenges. As a team in the Negro Southern League, they never quite achieved the status of the major teams from the North such as the Homestead Grays, Kansas City Monarchs and Pittsburgh Crawfords. Their best season came in 1938 and ended with a championship,

Foreword

but the Red Sox fought against, and were hobbled by, the racial prejudice in Memphis every year. They received uneven press coverage, had trouble arranging for quality visiting opponents, and generally suffered under Memphis politics and politicians. Local political figure Boss Crump, for instance, ran Memphis and expected loyalty from those who wanted to accomplish anything in the city. When J.B. Martin refused to go along, he was eventually run out of the city.

Keith Wood also does a wonderful job of introducing his readers to many of the great players who found a home with the Red Sox. He does this not through a litany of player biographies but by weaving their stories—and in particular those of Larry Brown, Verdell Mathis, and Joe B. Scott—into the larger, thematically organized story of the team. Readers learn from them what it was like to play throughout the segregated South as the Red Sox barnstormed across the country.

Though the Red Sox are not often recognized as central to the history of the Negro leagues, Wood demonstrates that they were in fact one of the most stable teams over their forty-year existence. With their own stadium and black ownership, they navigated the challenges thrown their way to become an important piece in the full story of black baseball. Keith Wood is the right person to tell their compelling story.

Leslie Heaphy, an associate professor of history at Kent State University at Stark, is the president of the International Women's Baseball Center, vice president of SABR and editor of the book series Black Ball: New Research in African American Baseball History.

Introduction

The role of black professional baseball in Memphis in the early twentieth century provides a unique look into black life in the city. Professional baseball's acceptance of Jim Crow norms in the late 1880s gave rise to the Negro leagues. Black businessmen employed Booker T. Washington's philosophy of building a segregated enterprise within the fabric of the national economy. Washington's philosophy emerged from his 1895 *Atlanta Compromise Speech,* where he offered that "in all things purely social we can be as separate as the fingers, yet one as the hand in all things essential to progress."

Pioneers such as Frank Leland, Rube Foster, C.I. Taylor, and Edward Bolden emerged as leaders in the growth of black professional baseball nationally. Historian Michael Lomax reminds us that the Negro leagues inform us of how African Americans endeavored to compete within the framework of the United States economy. They also represented the overall pursuit of freedom and self-determination. African Americans made it clear that despite their exclusion from mainstream America, they would develop their institutions and shape their sporting patterns.[1] As professional leagues in black baseball emerged, the Great Migration of African Americans north to larger urban cities increased opportunities for these black businessmen to capitalize on the black professional game. In Memphis, a migration of rural blacks into the city provided similar population growth.

Baseball became a part of the city's social fabric for black Memphians as the club provided the potential for self-organization, creativity, and expression. Red Sox games at Martin Stadium provided a reprieve from the grim conditions faced by Memphis's black working class. Through identification with the Red Sox, black fans fostered a sense of racial pride. In large Southern cities like Memphis, the Negro leaguer was a celebrity, performing before large, though almost exclusively black, crowds.[2] The men who played for the Red Sox became symbols of

Introduction

African American competence and achievement. Moreover, the black ownership group of the organization maintained a level of respectability and business acumen common in many of the more prominent Northern Negro leagues organizations.

Despite the failure of numerous black businesses in the 1920s and 1930s in the city, the Red Sox organization became a symbol of black economic success. The Negro leagues were among the most significant black businesses in the United States before the breakdown of segregation, and in their prime, they were a multi-million dollar operation.[3] Martin Stadium was a crucial component in their portfolio; black-owned parks were a rarity among Negro leagues organizations. The stadium provided a safe space for black political assertion during a tenuous era of racial relations in the city. Renovations to Martin Stadium during the Second World War established the park as one of the elite black-owned facilities in all American sports. Black ownership of the playing venue allowed the Red Sox to avoid the booking issues faced by other Negro leagues teams.

Historically, pundits of Negro leagues baseball labeled them as little more than booking agencies. However, their elevation by Major League Baseball's Commissioner Rob Manfred in 2020 provided the type of racial uplift men like Foster, Taylor, Bolden, and the Martins sought through black Organized Baseball. Moreover, the economic success of the Fosters, Boldens, and Taylors required interracial cooperation in their respective cities. The Martins were the same here in Memphis. Whichever iteration of the Negro Southern League, Negro National League, or Negro American League to which the Red Sox belonged, their economic success depended on their success barnstorming the region and playing against local semi-pro teams. Many of those games were against white teams.

As problematic as it was to follow league games in the media, discovering records of barnstorming games remains even more precarious. Nevertheless, these barnstorming tours allowed the Martins to meet payroll and keep the team economically viable. During these barnstorming games, victories against white semi-pro teams undermined segregation and slapped Jim Crow in the face. Communication with black fans became a critical factor in the success of Negro leagues teams, as Negro newspapers gained traction throughout black America.

Unlike their Northern counterparts in Chicago and Pittsburgh, who relied on the *Defender and Courier*, the Red Sox saw limited coverage in the *Memphis World*. Like so many other black newspapers of

Introduction

the era, the *World* published once a week. Without the more extensive circulation and budget of Northern counterparts like *The Defender* and *Courier,* the *World's* coverage of the Red Sox remained limited. Likewise, coverage in the white newspapers, the *Commercial Appeal,* and the *Press-Scimitar* was limited. As historians continue to explore the histories of Negro leagues teams, finding accurate statistics and coverage remains a daunting hurdle. Yet, the story of the Red Sox remains as integral to the narrative of Memphis in this era as do the stories of the American Giants to Chicago, the Homestead Grays to Pittsburgh, or the Hilldale Athletic Club to Philadelphia.

Within a stringent Jim Crow society, the Martins carved out a space for the economic success of the Red Sox. Yet, unlike their Northern counterparts who dealt with de facto segregation, the Martins faced racial animus entrenched in the segregationist laws of the South. The realities of Jim Crow forced Red Sox owner J.B. Martin to sell off his share of the team to his brothers and relocate to Chicago in 1940. The long shadow of police chief Clifford Davis, an avowed member of the Ku Klux Klan, along with political boss Edward Hull Crump, forced Martin's departure following a political dispute with Crump. Unjustly labeled as frugal by many who played for the Martin brothers, they ran a tight payroll similar to the likes of Rube Foster with his Chicago American Giants. Players may have jumped and left for higher salaries with other clubs up North or East, only to find that their new owners came up short on payroll occasionally. This was something that never happened with the Martins.

Black Diamonds, Blues City: Stories from the Negro Leagues' Memphis Red Sox, a documentary produced by University of Memphis professor Steven Ross, sought insights into Memphis's symbolic meaning and value as a Negro leagues baseball city during Jim Crow. As a grass-roots analysis, it located the main points of intersection between black professional baseball and the South in the four decades that spanned the modern Negro leagues era. It analyzes the racial dynamics in the city through the lens of the Memphis Red Sox, a black-owned and -operated organization that stood as a pillar of success.

Baseball provides a vehicle to examine the racial inequalities and issues that pervaded the city in these same years. A black-owned stadium served as a forum for political assertion and an arena for real political struggle for blacks in Memphis. As a social function, baseball shed a positive light on black identity. Blackball is replete with failed franchises throughout its history, yet one of the constants remained the Memphis

Introduction

Red Sox. *The Memphis Red Sox: A Negro Leagues History* seeks to shed light on this era in the city's history while filling in the gaps in the historiography of the annals of Negro leagues baseball.

Historians have primarily focused on Negro leagues teams outside of the South The documentary *Black Diamonds, Blues City* includes a myriad of interviews used to create the film that echoes this sentiment. Red Sox players repeatedly describe a lack of recognition compared to their Midwest and East Coast peers.[4] Filled with narratives examining black baseball in Chicago, Pittsburgh, Philadelphia, and Kansas City, the historiography of Negro leagues baseball has a gap in the analysis of Southern Blackball. Rob Ruck's *Sandlot* Seasons examines the roles of black athletes in Pittsburgh. William Young's *J.L. Wilkerson and His Kansas City Monarchs* focus on the life of white Negro league team owner J.L. Wilkerson. Neil Lanctot's *Fair Dealing and Clean Playing* examines the rise and fall of Ed Bolden's Hilldale Baseball Athletic Club in Philadelphia.

Other works provide biographies of Negro league players who made it to the white professional leagues. These range from Neil Lanctot's *Campy: The Two Lives of Roy Campanella* to John Klima's *Willie's Boys*. In the case of the historiography surrounding the Bluff City, few of these works incorporate the impact of sport on the city's racial past. Recent works by Preston Lauterbach—*The Chitlin' Circuit* and *Beale Street Dynasty*—have used music to develop a more nuanced understanding of life in Memphis for African Americans. *The Memphis Red Sox: A Negro Leagues History* aims to use the sport of baseball to examine life on the other side of the veil of segregation for black Memphians.

* * *

The Memphis Red Sox: A Negro Leagues History is not constructed as a fundamental historical narrative. Instead, it takes readers on a nine-inning journey to experience what it means to be a Memphis Red Sox. As a thematic approach, there are moments where these stories overlap. These quotes and descriptions help to clarify the theme of that particular inning. With the first pitch, *The Memphis Red Sox* introduces the history of black baseball in Memphis, leading to the genesis of the Red Sox organization in 1921. The second inning harkens back to baseball's classic lyric "Take me out the ballgame," as readers walk into Martin Stadium. Opened in 1923 as Lewis Park, Martin Stadium stood as a significant living monument to the black economic success of the organization. Following renovations during the Second World War, the stadium stood at the forefront of black-owned Negro league stadiums.

Introduction

This chapter attempts to recreate the fans' experience of Martin Stadium. As readers head to the top of the third inning, they are introduced more thoroughly to the black ownership group of the Red Sox. Although the team came under three ownership groups, the Martins were the longest-tenured. Under the Martin brothers, the Red Sox remained among the most respectable and financially stable Negro league teams. Other franchises struggled to stay afloat financially, and many survived through illegitimate means. Although tight-fisted with payroll, they created a robust, family-like atmosphere. Jobs in the off-season and medical care for players' families supplemented salaries.

The fourth inning chronicles the 1938 Negro American League championship season and its team members. Led by Ted "Double Duty" Radcliffe and Larry "Iron Man" Brown, the Red Sox dominated the Negro American League, claiming its only championship. The stars aligned for the Red Sox with the acquisition of Radcliffe and the return of catcher Larry Brown from the New York Black Yankees. As we move into the fifth inning of play, *The Memphis Red Sox* examines Memphis at the critical intersection of race, politics, and sport. Martin Stadium provided a safe space for black Memphians to meet as a sporting congregation and a platform for local black politicians to be seen and heard. Yet, the rigid political divide in the city led to J.B. Martin's ejection by E.H. Crump from the city.

In the sixth inning, readers experience the stories of three Memphis Red Sox players from their earliest days through their post-baseball experiences. Larry Brown, Verdell Mathis, and Joe B. Scott each experience the journey through black professional baseball. Their stories are woven together like the fabric of the Negro leagues to help readers gain personal insight.

As *The Memphis Red Sox* heads towards the seventh inning stretch, readers jump on the team bus and explore the club's chronicles as they barnstormed throughout the region and country. Players' firsthand accounts analyze players' conditions on the road in the black major leagues. In the eighth inning, we remain on the move as readers join Red Sox players seeking opportunities to play Winterball throughout Latin America. Finally, the last chapter closes the ninth inning with a look back on the final years of the franchise.

Following Jackie Robinson's breaking of the color barrier in 1947, the Red Sox continued to operate throughout the 1950s. Baseball enthusiasts can readily recall Jackie Robinson as the first African American

Introduction

The 1947 Memphis Red Sox. Back row (left to right): "Jelly" Taylor, Alex Radcliffe, Casey Jones, Red Longley, Felix Evans, Willie Davis, Riley Stewart, Neil Robinson, Fred McDaniels, Rufus Ligon (team secretary). Front row—John Huber, Leslie Green, Marlin Carter, Pierre Sharpe, Willie Wells, Jr., Bubba Hyde, Fred Bankhead, Willie Hutchinson, Verdell Mathis, and Larry Brown (J.J. Guinozzo Collection).

to reintegrate Major League Baseball. Most of these fans can place Larry Doby as the first African American to play in the American League for the Cleveland Indians in 1947. The story of the game's first African American pitcher—Dan Bankhead, a Memphis Red Sox player, whom Branch Rickey and the Brooklyn Dodgers signed in August 1947—is reinserted into the iconography. Even as black Americans followed the travails of Robinson intently and black Memphians that of Bankhead, the Martin brothers sought to continue to offer a quality product on the field.

* * *

The Memphis Red Sox remained one of the most stable franchises in Negro league history. Black ownership of the team and stadium made the franchise almost an anomaly in black baseball. Their story is often left behind the Negro Leagues' more prominent franchises: the Kansas City Monarchs, the Chicago American Giants, the Homestead Grays, the Pittsburgh Crawfords, and the Birmingham Black Barons. Branch Rickey returned to the Negro leagues to sign white baseball's first black pitcher from the Memphis Red Sox in 1947, Dan Bankhead. The nation's

Introduction

"national pastime" once played a prominent role in blacks' lives in Memphis. Historian Don Rogosin asserts, "To examine the world that Negro baseball made is to open a window on black life during segregation. Scrutiny of the life of the Negro leagues provides texture, a context necessary for grasping segregation and plumbing its irrationality." Long known as the Home of the Blues, Memphis provides a case study in the intersectionality of race and culture, a rich culture that included professional baseball only blocks away from Beale Street.

1

Early Professional Blackball in Memphis

Professional Blackball in the Bluff City dates back to one of the original professional black leagues, the Southern League of Colored Baseballists, in 1886. Newspapers in Alabama, Florida, Georgia, South Carolina, and Tennessee called for the captains of all colored baseball clubs to send their names and address to the new league offices in Jacksonville, Florida. Its 12-member board charged a $5 fee for league membership, a $1.50 fee for a subscription to the *Jacksonville Southern Leader* (the official newspaper for the league), and a guarantee of an amount to cover the visiting teams' traveling expenses.

Memphis provided two entrants to the league: the Eurekas and the Eclipse. They joined teams from Atlanta, Georgia; Savannah, Georgia; New Orleans, Louisiana; and Jacksonville, Florida.[1] A June 24 article in the *Memphis Appeal* touted the Eclipse as one of the best teams in the league after winning eight of its last twelve games.[2] The season ran through August 25. Although coverage of league play remained scant in the local newspapers, the *Commercial Appeal* proclaimed the Eurekas and the Eclipse as the champion Negro clubs of the South.

In addition, two Memphis Eclipse pitchers, William Renfroe and Robert "Tobe" Higgins, caught the local press's eye, earning regional and national recognition.[3] The *Commercial Appeal* noted that Dick Phelan, second baseman for the Memphis Reds (white Southern League), viewed Renfroe as a "wonderful pitcher." The respect Phelan displayed for Renfroe leans into the likelihood that the white Memphis Reds either would play or have played the Black Eclipse in an exhibition game. Unfortunately for the two Memphis clubs and their players, the Southern League of Colored Baseballists did not return for an 1887 season.

Renfroe pitched with Binghamton, New York, of the International League, the following year. On the 1887 Binghamton club was African

The Memphis Red Sox

American and future Hall of Famer Bud Fowler (Class of 2022). Historian Brian McKenna refers to Fowler as *"the* pioneer" [sic] in black Organized Baseball who was a stellar player in the box, behind the plate, in the field, and with a bat. The first African American in Organized Baseball had the widest-traveled career and the longest of early players by any qualification.[4] Renfroe's arrival in Binghamton designated him as the seventh colored player in Organized Baseball. Following his addition to the Binghamton roster, *The Sporting Life*, a weekly newspaper that provided national sports coverage from 1883 to 1917, queried, "How far will this mania for engaging colored players go? At the present rate of progress the international [league] might ere many moons change its title to 'Colored League.'"[5] Renfroe's Eclipse teammate, Robert Higgins, became the eighth colored player in Organized Baseball, joining the International League's Syracuse club.

Higgins, who many considered the city's most renowned player, joined the International League with the Syracuse (NY) Stars club in 1887. Higgins posted a 2.91 earned run average in 1887 while hitting .294 in 41 games during the 1887 season.[6] In Higgins's first league outing, three white Stars players fielded so poorly that the blatant attempt to throw the game made the *Toronto World's* coverage the next day: "…these players carried out their plans in the most glaring manner. Fumbles and muffs of easy fly balls were frequent occurrences, but Higgins retained control of his temper and smiled at every move of the clique. Marr, Bittman, Beard, and Jantzen played like schoolboys."[7] The white Southern players on the Syracuse club met with resistance to their coup to disparage Higgins. However, two weeks later, the club rallied around Higgins on his return to Stars Park in Syracuse with a resounding 11–4 win over Oswego.[8]

Unfortunately, Higgins found himself in the middle of racial animus when the team sat for its 1887 team portrait and two white players refused to show. The *Sporting News* deemed the story so newsworthy that it served as the lead story for its June 11 issue in an article entitled "Dug Crothers Suspended: His Offense, a Refusal to Sit Beside the Colored Pitcher."[9] As a result, the manager of the Syracuse club suspended the two white players for eight days without pay. Crothers explained his boycott of the pictures by saying, "I don't know, as people in the North can appreciate my feelings on the subject. I am a Southerner by birth, and I tell you I would have my heart cut out before I would consent to have my picture in the group."[10] Only ten years after the end of Republican Reconstruction in the South, Crothers' feelings echoed Southern sentiments towards integration in the late nineteenth century.

1. Early Professional Blackball in Memphis

A month later, at a meeting of the owners of the Independent League, Higgins and four other black players were banned from the league. Higgins was released and returned to his barbershop in Memphis.[11] Higgins's story embodies the struggles that Colored baseball players faced at the onset of Organized Baseball, and by 1908 Higgins had become a well-established barber in Memphis at 416 Beale Street. Local black historian G.P. Hamilton described him thus: "as good a barber as he was once a ball player, and that is to say, he is one of the best in the land. Mr. Higgins is the most famous player ever produced among the colored people of Memphis."[12]

Memphis political icon Lieutenant George W. Lee later echoed a similar sentiment in his book chronicling Beale Street, *Beale Street: Where the Blues Began.* In this 1934 account of the city's most famous black street, Lee describes Higgins as a man who became "nationally prominent as a baseball player and was one of the greatest pitchers of all time. He was one of the few Negroes that ever played on a big-league team."[13] Although Renfroe and Higgins had their careers cut short by the onset of the Color Line in Organized Baseball, they set a foundation proving that black baseball players from the Bluff City were big-league caliber players.

From the late 1880s through the onset of the twentieth century, scant articles remain of entries into professional baseball for local black teams in Memphis. Instead, records remain of Negro league teams barnstorming through the city to play various semi-pro Negro teams. For example, the *Nashville Globe* reported that the Nashville Standard Giants barnstormed through the city, playing an unnamed semi-pro team.[14] The Standard Giants returned from Nashville again in 1908, this time defeating the Memphis Unions handily.[15] In 1909, Memphis native Frank Leland brought his Leland Giants South on a barnstorming tour, playing a game in Memphis. Leland was a pioneering organizer, manager, and owner of Chicago's Leland Giants. He organized the club in 1907 and lured pitcher Rube Foster to Chicago to take the team's reins.[16]

Thus, Memphis's ties to organized, professional baseball in the community remained strong throughout the early period in Negro leagues baseball. John Connor, another black owner, brought his Brooklyn Royal Giants to Memphis on a Southern stint of their barnstorming tour. In 1915, C.I. Taylor brought his Indianapolis ABCs (American Brewing Company) team to play on their barnstorming tour.[17] Although the city did not develop a professional team during this period, several semi-pro teams flourished.

The Memphis Red Sox

The most prominent of these teams, the Memphis Unions, barnstormed throughout Texas in 1908, garnering the most attention in the city. During this era, other semi-pro teams included the Bluff City Baseball Club, the Memphis Giants, and the Memphis Tigers.[18] As semi-pro teams sought to solidify themselves as preeminent, branding became an essential element in success. Historian Michael Lomax has pointed out that branding is a means by which many black clubs in the early twentieth century sought to identify themselves in a crowded market. The most common team moniker, the "Giants," played off the success of the white baseball's New York Giants. Then later, the success of the Negro leagues Cuban × Giants, Philadelphia Giants, and the Leland Giants. Finally, the Chicago American Giants, by placing "American" in front of Giants, differentiated themselves as they developed a reputation as one of the best teams in black and white baseball circles.[19] Leading up through the First World War, semi-pro black teams continued to compete against each other while accepting the challenges of Northern teams barnstorming through the region. The winds of political change swept through the city when Edward Hull Crump became the city's mayor in 1910. His tenure as mayor and later political boss brought progressive change and more substantial reliance on Jim Crow. Crump's political career mirrored the city's organized black professional baseball era.

Memphis's brandishing as the murder capital of America in the early twentieth century belies the city's nuanced cultural and political constructions. Moreover, the complexities of race elicit divergent narratives that portray two towns: one black and one white. Crump set out through a series of progressive reforms to "rid the city of thieves, and thugs, break up the practices of carrying pistols, and clean up the dives which have flourished so long in this city." The police ordered blacks off the streets after midnight, and those who languished went to jail. Yet Crump's need for the black vote to maintain his slim margin of control in city politics led him to wield the hand of the benevolent father as he supported the creation of Douglass Park in black North Memphis in 1913.[20]

As E.H. Crump built his political machine, Robert Church, Jr., a prominent black businessman, set out to become the most recognizable black Republican in the country. Robert Church, Jr.'s establishment of the Lincoln League in 1916 marked the unique political dichotomy in the city. The Lincoln League sought to "regain the lost rights of a growing race and achieve political and economic emancipation" for African

1. Early Professional Blackball in Memphis

Americans. This political emancipation called for the black community to unite at the ballot under the banner of the Republican Party. Church's connection with the Republican Party and its Black and Tan faction dates back to 1912 when he served as a delegate to the Republican National Convention.[21] As World War I drew to a close, Robert Church, Jr., embarked on an ambitious plan to unify the black community politically. First, he needed E.H. Crump's support to maneuver through the muddied waters of Jim Crow politics along the Mississippi River in the Bluff City.

Church's continued push for equality for blacks and the lynching of a local black man in the city led to the opening of a local branch of the National Association for the Advancement of Colored People in Memphis in 1917. Under coercion from the local police, Ell Parsons confessed to the murder of a white girl in May 1917. A posse of white vigilantes captured Parsons, and the local press publicized the upcoming lynching. Fifteen thousand locals watched as Parsons was tied to a log, mutilated, and set on fire. Onlookers scrambled to get body parts as souvenirs before the white vigilantes wrapped his body in an American flag and threw his remains on Beale Street. The lynchers remained free as Jim Crow dictated that prosecution was not necessary.[22]

Whereas many blacks in Memphis justified their joining the Great Migration to Northern cities, Church focused his efforts on fighting for racial equality. Of the 53 race men who signed the NAACP charter in Memphis, five also became involved in the operation of the Memphis Red Sox: Josiah T. Settle, Bert M. Roddy, A.M. McCullough, E.E. Nesbitt, and J.B. Martin.[23] The racial rhetoric of self-help and racial solidarity associated with the NAACP and the Lincoln League also applied to black owners in the Negro leagues who promoted their clubs as symbols of race respectability and racial uplift.[24] Black professional baseball in Memphis modeled the racial uplift practiced by Church Jr., the Lincoln League, and the NAACP.

The 1920s marked a new sense of racial pride, including the emergence of black baseball's first organized Negro League, The Negro National League. Author Alain Locke's "New Negro" described a flowering of a new race spirit among American Negroes. The *New York Age* described this new generation of African Americans as different than their ancestors because they began to grow outside of the white man's world and to encourage pride in their achievements.[25] In Chicago, Andrew "Rube" Foster emerged as the father of modern Negro leagues baseball. One of Blackball's most prolific players at the onset of the twentieth century, Foster yearned for colored baseball players' acceptance in organized ball. Early civil rights leader Booker T. Washington's ideology called for initial segregation, allowing the black community to show its value through hard work and morality, leading to acceptance.

Similarly, Foster's goals included organizing a separate black major league to showcase the black community's ability to manage and follow specific rules and police players' conduct on and off the field. Hypothetically, after Organized Baseball saw the success of Foster's Negro National League, they would allow Foster's Negro National League admission alongside the American and National Leagues. "We are the ship; all else the sea" became the guiding principle behind Foster's league.[26]

On February 13, 1920, Foster called together all of the owners of professional black teams in the Midwest to YMCA on the Paseo in Kansas City, Missouri. The league's center was Chicago with Foster's American Giants.[27] Chicago's emergence as a central location for African American migration North, known as the Great Migration, allowed Chicago to become the focal point of the Negro National League. A growing number of sports enthusiasts developed in the city to show off new wealth and to socialize with friends from back home.[28] Rube Foster was the league leader during its early years. A product of his imagination and foresight, he ruled with an iron fist but usually with a benevolent hand.[29] Inspired by the news out of Chicago, a group of businessmen met in Atlanta, Georgia, to launch a similar league in the South. Businessmen from Atlanta, Georgia; Nashville and Knoxville, Tennessee; Birmingham and Montgomery, Alabama; Pensacola, Florida; Jacksonville, Florida; Greenville, South Carolina; and New Orleans, Louisiana, met to form the Negro Southern League.[30] Although Memphis was not in this original group of Southern cities to join organized black baseball, the foundations laid in 1920 paved the way for a Memphis franchise in the NSL the following season.

Memphis entered black professional baseball in 1921 when the A.P. Martin's Barber Boys Baseball Club became an entrant in the Negro Southern League. The club's owner and the team's namesake, A.P. Martin, was a prominent black barber in town. In 1908 he owned a shop at 87 Exchange Street. By 1920 his shop expanded to include shops at 347 Beale Street, 258 Main Street, and 78 Calhoun Street. He was also known for creating a barber college in his shops where he could teach his trade to others.[31]

1. Early Professional Blackball in Memphis

Seeking to bolster the team's attendance in its inaugural NSL season, A.P. Martin advertised its opening game in the *Commercial Appeal*. For fifty cents, fans could witness Dr. J.B. Martin throw out the season's first pitch to Mr. Buffington, owner of Buffington Tailoring Company.[32] Long the tradition in Memphis, black owners reserved seating for white patrons at Negro baseball games. A.P. Martin maintained this tradition.[33] In this way, the city's black teams showed their proficiency in America's pastime to its white sports fans.

A.P. Martin's club finished the 1921 season 17 games below .500. Montgomery and Nashville played a five-game series in Nashville, with Nashville winning four. Memphis's 52–69 record included many barnstorming games, which in the scheme of overall NSL standings, created confusion at the top of the leaderboard. The five-game NSL championship series also highlighted the need for black professional teams to play all the games in a playoff series. In contrast, a championship series in white-organized baseball was considered best-of-five.

Although the NSL served primarily as a minor league system for the stronger leagues in the North from 1920 through 1951, it opened the door for Memphis to host a team in black organized ball.[34] Memphis's proximity to Birmingham immediately provided it a natural rival. A rivalry that would survive the duration of the modern Negro leagues era. Rivalries stimulate fan interest; thus, the ballparks have more paying customers through the turnstiles, allowing the club to profit economically.

Norman "Turkey" Stearnes became the most notable player to emerge from Memphis during its time as a member of the Negro Southern League. The Red Sox signed Stearnes for the 1922 season after he spent 1920 in Nashville with the White Sox and 1921 in Montgomery with the Grey Sox.[35] His reputation as a prolific hitter and outfielder grew in the NSL, leading to his eventual signing with the Detroit Stars of the Negro National League in 1923. Stearnes credits his time in Memphis for allowing him to shine when scouts from the Negro big leagues came to see him play. "Bruce Petway (Detroit Stars) came down there to watch me. They had heard so much talk about me."[36] Stearnes' stellar playing career earned him a spot in the National Baseball Hall of Fame.

The team played its home games in South Memphis at Field's Park, located one block from the Florida streetcar line, and at Fay Avenue Park. A.P. Martin enticed Church's political lieutenant J.B. Martin, no relation, to toss out the opening pitch, which began a long relationship between professional baseball in the city and its black political

The Memphis Red Sox

organization.[37] Semi-pro baseball remained firmly entrenched in the city alongside A.P. Martin's Southern League entrance in 1921. The Memphis Unions received scant press coverage from the city's white newspapers, but they played sandlot games and barnstormed against local and regional teams.

The following year, 1922, marked the arrival of the Memphis Red Sox in the city. The Red Sox replaced A.P. Martin's Barbershop Boys Baseball Club in the Negro Southern League, and Chick Cummings managed them.[38] According to local legend, Cummings, a long-time sandlot and semi-pro manager in the city, suggested the "Red Sox" moniker.[39]

The emergence of the Memphis Red Sox as a viable entrant into the Negro Southern League and black professional baseball became part of a larger narrative of pride within the black community. However, white Memphians' views of blacks remained prejudicial. A few miles from Field's Park at Russwood Park, the Memphis Chickasaws pushed social norms by using a young black boy, Cecil, as their mascot. A May 18, 1921, article in the *Commercial Appeal* included a picture of Cecil wearing a baseball uniform and glove. The article described Cecil as "the Chickasaws' kinky-headed mascot and luck piece." White players smuggled young Cecil into the white Pullman cars on their road trips. The Chickasaw players included Cecil in their baseball superstitions, claiming that "there is a base hit and score in every kink on Cecil's shining black head."[40]

The city's white professional baseball players mirrored the cultural norms of the Jim Crow era, and the city's baseball fans' appreciation of these patterns was symbolic of the times. Over the next decade, demeaning caricatures of blacks became mainstays in the *Commercial Appeal* with the addition of J.P. Alley's caricature of *Hambone*—that the paper itself referred to as a "philosophical Southern darkey."[41] As Memphis's black community sought to gain acceptance and create a space of black expression, the Red Sox became another avenue to combat the negative tropes of Jim Crow in the city and on its playing fields.

2

"Take Me Out to the Ballgame" —Martin Stadium at Lewis Park

Martin Stadium, home to the Red Sox, provided a venue for the team to play games and a space of freedom. Owners in the Negro leagues rarely owned their stadium, allowing the Red Sox to stand out amongst its peers. It also allowed the Red Sox to schedule games at their discretion without the nuisance of being allocated less favorable dates following the release of the local white team's schedule. In addition, stadium ownership also allowed the owners to hold events while the team traveled. From sporting events to political rallies, Martin Stadium allowed the black community a space to gather outside the church, which fostered a sense of community during an era dominated by Jim Crow paternalism.

Hall of Famer John "Buck" O'Neil, a member of the 1937 Red Sox team, said he could "never forget Martin Stadium because it was a black-owned park and it was right in the middle of a black neighborhood. Everything was black."[1] Martin Stadium became an integral part of Black Memphis. From the fans that filled the stands to the players showcasing their talents on the field to the political and social icons of Black Memphis, Martin Stadium was the place to be and to be seen. Located little more than a mile from Beale Street, during the Negro leagues era in Memphis, Martin Stadium stood as a pillar of respectability.

What was best known as Martin Stadium had three iterations throughout its existence. Its first rendering opened in 1922 when owner R.S. Lewis constructed a $50,000 stadium on the corner of Iowa and Wellington in South Memphis. Thus, its name originally was Lewis Park. When the Martin brothers purchased the franchise following the 1928 season, they rebranded it as Martin Stadium at Lewis Park for the 1929 season. In 1937, the Martin brothers installed permanent lights at the stadium. Seven years earlier, the Red Sox played under the lights at

The Memphis Red Sox

Aerial view of Martin Stadium at Lewis Park before the renovations in the 1940s (John Haddock Collection).

Martin Stadium, provided by J.L. Wilkerson's traveling light standards, against his Kansas City Monarchs. In 1935, the National League's Philadelphia Phillies played under the lights at Cincinnati's Crosley Field in the first major league game played under lights in Organized Baseball.[2]

Finally, during the peak of Negro leagues baseball during World War II, the Martins invested $250,000 in renovations.[3] After its completion, Martin Stadium stood as one of the preeminent stadiums in all baseball, white or black. Unfortunately, Jackie Robinson's reintegration of Organized Baseball in 1947, only a couple of years after renovations to Martin Stadium, led to the downfall of Blackball and, in turn, the demise of the Red Sox in the Bluff City. Torn down in 1960, Martin Stadium passed into memory as part of a bygone era, a relic of a segregated past.

* * *

In the Red Sox's second season, they played games at Russwood Park as members of the Negro Southern League in 1922. Red Sox team president John W. Miller relied upon the symbiotic business relationship with the white owner of the Memphis Chicks. While the Chicks

2. "Take Me Out to the Ballgame"—Martin Stadium at Lewis Park

played games away from Russwood, Miller agreed with Thomas Watkins to lease Russwood Park. When the Chicks occupied Russwood, the Red Sox played home games at Fields Park in South Memphis on Fay Avenue.[4] The following season marked the inaugural use of a stadium owned by the club, Lewis Park. After the 1922 season, R.S. Lewis, owner of Barnett and Lewis Undertakers, became one of four majority owners of the Red Sox, moving the team to its permanent location at Iowa and Wellington (currently Danny Thomas and E.H. Crump Avenue).[5] The *Chicago Defender,* one of black America's most prominent newspapers, reported that Lewis constructed a $50,000 stadium. Equivalent to three-quarters of a million dollars in 2020, the stadium consisted of wooden bleachers stretched along the first and third baselines, with a roof overhead.[6]

Like many of its peers throughout white baseball in America, Lewis Park fit into its neighborhood, giving the stadium a unique feel. The stadium's proximity to South Lauderdale provided a short porch to right field for lefthanded hitters, while only yards behind the left field fence lie the railyards of South Memphis. Between the railyard and the stadium stood Broadway Coal and Ice Company. Directly beyond the outfield fence, Broadway Coal's mule lot awaited would be homerun ball seekers.[7] Between the railyard and Broadway Coal, the railyard workers used a crane to place three or four box cars on top of one another to see into Martin Stadium. Fans could see most of the field atop the boxcars except for left and center fields.[8] When looking out over the left field fence, fans saw the gymnasium for Booker T. Washington High School. Beyond the outfield fence in the right-centerfield stood a water tower on South Lauderdale.

Like the Polo Grounds in New York City, the symmetry of Lewis Park gave it a distinctive presence with an unusually deep centerfield.[9] When especially large crowds filled Martin Stadium, fans seated themselves on the field in the spaces in front of the pavilion down the third baseline and in front of the outfield wall.[10] A harking back to the bygone days of professional baseball where fans became the outfield fence, special occasions like these required the teams to accept any ball hit into the crowd in front of the outfield wall as a ground-rule double.

Lewis Park was a site to see and a place to be seen. The Red Sox played doubleheaders on Sundays because the black working class in Memphis worked six days a week. Sunday was their only reprieve. For African Americans in the city at the time, there were few other entertainment options on Sunday. There were only four public parks in town

The Memphis Red Sox

Catcher Larry Brown, right, "dressed to the nines" with an unidentified friend (John Haddock Collection).

2. "Take Me Out to the Ballgame"—Martin Stadium at Lewis Park

for blacks to assemble, and white policing of those parks made trips to these parks less than desirable.[11] The Sunday games led many of the city's black pastors to shorten their sermons so their congregation could get to the ballpark on time for the doubleheader. As players looked out into the stands on Sundays, they saw the stadium filled with people "dressed to the nines." Even the *Chicago Defender* noted the excitement in the Red Sox fan base: "Beale Street was out in full force (for a 1924 game against the Chicago American Giants) overalls mixing with cutaways and box back coats with Palm Beach suits."[12] The unique country cosmopolitan look of the Memphis fanbase may have been surprising to Chicagoans in attendance, but to Memphians, they looked sharp.

Architectural historian Paul Goldberger describes the relationship between the stadium and baseball as an illusion of the countryside created by a stadium in a city. The ballpark is where the dialectic between the city and the country can be experienced within a single intense, lovely piece of architecture. In this one place, the city's energy and the leisurely, relaxed pace are not mutually exclusive but mutually dependent.[13] In addition, urban migration to Memphis from the surrounding countryside meant that Lewis Park held added significance for a black populace recently arriving from surrounding agricultural communities. The daily struggle for freedom for black working-class Memphians included humiliation resulting from power relations bound in a plantation mentality.[14] Lewis Park provided a reprieve from these humiliations in a black-owned park while watching their favorite baseball players. They returned to the countryside for nine innings via the *rus in urbe* without the hassle of Jim Crow weighing them down.

Constructed out of wood, Lewis Park, like most baseball parks around the country at the onset of the twentieth century, became part of the urban fabric. It also became a part of the more prominent American urban park and cemeteries movement. Memphis's Elmwood Cemetery resembled the cemetery movement in its construction as a cultivated piece of rolling land, with clusters of trees designed to escape the city's harshness while establishing a connection to nature without physically leaving the city.[15] On the other side of the Beltline, white baseball fans witnessed their *rus in urbe* at Russwood Park. Only two and a half miles south of Russwood, Lewis Park provided this space for Memphis's black community.

Lewis' Red Sox became a rarity in Negro leagues baseball, an organization that owned its venue. The *Commercial Appeal* heralded Lewis Park as one of the country's most modern Negro amusement parks.

The Memphis Red Sox

Even as the Memphis Red Sox often outdrew the Memphis Chicks, Russwood Park remained segregated, conforming to Jim Crow norms. Segregated seating at the park was located down the third base line in the left field bleachers (J.J. Guizzano Collection).

The 3,000-seat facility, which included tennis courts, croquet grounds, and a children's playground, became the city's most spacious gathering spot for the black community. Lewis's desire to build the park included allowing black women in the city to attend baseball games without the embarrassment of Jim Crow.[16] From the beginning of professional baseball, their parks served as amusement parks in their design. Lewis Park was no different.

The St. Louis Browns, in the 1880s, played at Sportsman's Park, where team owner Chris Von der Ahe placed a beer garden in the outfield and included space for events such as cricket, handball, bowling, and shooting.[17] Esthetically, Lewis Park favored stadiums like Hilltop Park in New York City (home of the N.Y. Highlanders/Yankees) and Memphis's Russwood Park, constructed almost entirely of wood.[18] Lewis Park's grandstand extended from the first baseline around home

2. "Take Me Out to the Ballgame"—Martin Stadium at Lewis Park

plate and finished symmetrically, even with third base. Fans were allowed to bring chairs to sit down along both foul lines, creating a human wall of fans down the lines. The *Chicago Defender* noted that 8,000 fans attended a 1924 game, highlighting the park's popularity.[19]

Long a symbol of the hope of the ensuing season, Opening Day was rivaled by few other special days. It served as an opportunity to gather to support the Red Sox and demonstrate pride in their community. Symbolized by red, white, and blue bunting along the stadium's façade and down the baselines, the stadium stood at the center of the community on this day each year. On May 18, 1923, Lewis Park hosted its inaugural Opening Day ceremonies. The *Commercial Appeal* opined that Lewis Park was "one of the most modern negro amusement parks in the country."[20] With a capacity of approximately 3,000, Lewis Park surpassed the local churches and Church Park, which held 2,000 people, as the preeminent gathering space in the community.[21]

Prominent businessman Bert M. Roddy served as master of ceremonies for Lewis Park's inaugural Opening Day. Local funeral home owner Thomas H. Hayes, Sr., joined Roddy in throwing out the ceremonial first pitch. The pharmacist and future Red Sox owner J.B. Martin received the first pitch.[22] Other prominent members of the black community involved in the inaugural Opening Day ceremonies were black Republican icons Robert Church, Jr., and Lieutenant George Lee.[23] R.S. Lewis gathered a contingent of the city's most prominent black political and businessmen in a space free from white oversight.

One of Lewis Park's advantages was scheduling games with Northern Negro leagues teams following Negro Southern League competition. For example, Lewis offered a sizable sum as a guarantee to secure the Milwaukee Bears, the last-place team in Rube Foster's Negro National League, to play at Lewis Park in 1923.[24] The team's success against Milwaukee led to Lewis scheduling other Negro National League foes, Toledo, St. Louis, and Foster's Chicago American Giants. The crowds continued to pack the 3,000-seat park, and revenue from the gate and concessions allowed Lewis to seek games outside the NSL and entrench Memphis as one of the NSL's preeminent teams.

Stadium ownership placed the Red Sox in front of other fledgling Negro leagues teams looking to become the next expansion club in Rube Foster's Negro National League. Teams remained economically solvent when they controlled the best Sunday dates for league doubleheaders. Without control of the best dates, many owners suffered through scheduling issues that left them with an unbalanced schedule and a lack of

The Memphis Red Sox

home dates. The editor of the *Kansas City Call* proclaimed that "if the Negro National League [NNL] is to survive and retain the interest of fans, the schedule should be arranged so that the pennant race is a real one, with all teams playing an equal number of games with each other."[25] When more NNL teams owned their stadiums, a balanced schedule would lead to fans embracing the pennant race.

In addition to Lewis selling this point to Foster, he also signed his nineteen-year-old half-brother, Willie Foster, as a pitcher. Foster's younger brother played parts in the 1923 and 1924 seasons with the Red Sox. Willie "jumped" to Chicago with the American Giants when his older brother saw fit for the remaining parts of both seasons.[26] Lewis told Willie, "I don't have any way out. He's your brother, he's president of the league [NNL], and he's got a ball team. You gotta go."[27] Foster imposed his will upon Lewis to allow his brother to go north, while Lewis hoped that by appeasing the older Foster, the Red Sox would gain entrance into the Negro National League.

Player jumping, what modern baseball enthusiasts refer to today as unrestricted free agency, was a major stumbling block to the aggregate success of Negro leagues baseball. Black baseball's roots in semi-pro baseball fostered players jumping from one club to another for better pay. When it suited the needs of Rube Foster, he encouraged players to "jump" to his Chicago American Giants. Yet, following the 1923 creation of the Eastern Colored League (ECL), Foster reached out to Hilldale Athletic Club and ECL president Edward Bolden to discourage the ECL from tampering with players under an NNL contract.[28] Lewis combatted the practice of NNL and ECL, enticing his players to jump to their leagues for more money, while at the same time positioning himself to elevate the Red Sox from minor league to major league status. Lewis and the Red Sox would soon gain that opportunity to bring major league baseball to Lewis Park.

Hampered by the cutthroat business practices of Foster, the Red Sox ultimately gained entry into the NNL after the death of baseball mogul C.I. Taylor in Indianapolis. Following Taylor's death, Foster's grudge against his widow led to the expulsion of the Indianapolis ABCs from the NNL. The *Pittsburgh Courier* reported that the Red Sox had long-sought entry into the NNL and assumed the Indianapolis ABC's won-lost record.[29] The *Commercial Appeal* noted, "After weeks of bickering, crack Negro league team enters the league (NNL)."[30]

Owning his stadium allowed Lewis' Red Sox to complete the remainder of the ABC's 1924 NNL schedule. In addition, stadium

2. "Take Me Out to the Ballgame"—Martin Stadium at Lewis Park

ownership allowed the 1925 Red Sox to accommodate more home games, thus allowing them to maintain a balanced schedule. Only the St. Louis Stars and Chicago American Giants, teams that also controlled their venues, completed more games than the Red Sox in the NNL.[31] Professional baseball is a business, and the control of a stadium made Memphis a major league city.

Lewis, the consummate businessman, made more efficient use of Lewis Park by introducing a second Memphis franchise. Originally dubbed the Memphis Red Sox No. 2, they affectionately went by the name Memphis Cubs. The Cubs played home games while the Red Sox were on the road. The Cubs were disbanded only weeks after opening, for their poor level of play.[32] The Silas Green Minstrel Show became one of the more intriguing entertainment troupes to visit Lewis Park. Originally part of the only all-black circus in America at the onset of the twentieth century, *Professor Eph Williams and His Famous Troubadors* performed concurrently with acts like Bessie Smith. At the time, minstrel shows reinforced stereotypes and ridiculed the performers. Williams' vision for the circus challenged this system, providing an uncommon opportunity for black singers and comedians.[33] Charles Collier, a white man, and Williams' daughter took over the show when Williams died in 1921.[34]

Time magazine described the Silas Green Minstrel Show as part revue, part music comedy, part minstrel show, telling of the adventures of two Negroes, short, coal-black Silas Green and tall, tannish Lilas Bean. Crowds packed tents and stadiums throughout the South with audiences where Negroes outnumbered whites three to one.[35] Lewis continued to add music and minstrel shows throughout the team's first year in the NNL to encourage attendance at the park. In a competition for the black community's disposable income with Beale Street, Lewis continued to employ musical acts as part of the entertainment package at the stadium.

As the Red Sox's economic stability teetered on the edge of collapse in 1926, Lewis pulled the Red Sox from the Negro National League and joined the reorganized Negro Southern League.[36] The amount of money required to meet the travel schedule of the NNL, with teams in cities much farther apart than the NSL, was an issue. Although the 1926 season at Lewis Park finished below financial expectations, the park did play host to one of the game's future stars, Satchel Paige. The Red Sox hosted the NSL's Chattanooga Black Lookouts in late May.

Their rookie pitcher, Paige, received a unique welcome to Lewis

The Memphis Red Sox

Park when the team arrived. He recalls the team's bus driver dropping them off at the stadium when they rolled into town. Paige asked his manager, Alex Herman, to "have the driver drop me off at the hotel where we are staying." Herman responded, "This is where we are staying, Satch. You think we can afford staying in a hotel?"[37] Like many others, Lewis Park doubled as the hotel for the visiting team on this night.

Satchel Paige's first memories of the Bluff City included waking up the following day with what he deemed the "miseries." "My back was sore, my arms and legs ached, and my mouth was full of dust."[38] Satchel's recollection of the game the next day remains embellished in his autobiography, *Maybe I'll Pitch Forever*, as another in a long string of victories in his rookie season. However, the Memphis faithful who witnessed the game watched as the Red Sox defeated Paige's Black Lookouts 4–3.[39]

Several boarding houses near Lewis Park on Fourth Street and Linden Avenue provided accommodations if visiting teams could afford it. Visiting teams staying at these homes opened up opportunities for kids like Verdell Mathis to find another avenue into the stadium. First, Mathis waited to hear from the public announcer who the next opponent would be. Then he ran down to the boarding houses on Fourth and Linden, sat on the front steps, and waited for the next opponent to arrive. Once they arrived, Mathis secured the team's batboy position for the series.[40] Mathis also knew where the cracks in the fence were at the stadium if that did not work. He would bring a pocket knife, find a favorite crack in the fence, and dig out a hole big enough for them to see the game and watch the next nine innings.[41]

Mathis and his Booker T. Washington High classmates were only a stone's throw from Lewis Park when school let out. Head south on Lauderdale, across the railroad tracks, and in less than a block the sidewalk met the right field wall of Lewis Park. Today a walking bridge takes one up and over the railroad tracks that dissect South Lauderdale Street, but during the era that Lewis Park and Martin Stadium existed, you carefully walked across the rows of tracks to get to the field.

Rufus Thomas, who later became a well-known musician on Beale Street, preferred catching a foul ball outside the stadium to gain admission into the game. When kids returned a ball at the front gate, they gained free entry to the rest of the game. The kids got in for free, and the Red Sox saved money on baseballs. Like Thomas, many of the kids in the neighborhood waited on the Lauderdale side of the fence for balls. The cost of baseballs for sandlot games was prohibitive. Instead of buying

2. "Take Me Out to the Ballgame"—Martin Stadium at Lewis Park

balls from local sporting goods stores, they waited outside Martin Stadium for a foul ball or home run ball to clear the fence and provide them with a new ball.[42] Another option for young fans was to wait for the seventh inning when the gates opened and allowed admission for the remainder of the game.[43]

The revival of the Negro Southern League in 1926 brought renewed vigor to the Memphis fanbase. League teams provided a much more regional flare, and local rivalries emerged. Most of the league's teams shared stadiums with teams in the white Southern Association. Red Sox ownership of Lewis Park placed them in the front of the league regarding scheduling. The city's white newspaper, the *Commercial Appeal*, joined the excitement throughout the summer posting the batting averages for the NSL, a rarity among Negro leagues historical records. This

Martin Stadium (shown from left field line) overflowed with fans on Easter Sunday and again on the Fourth of July when doubleheaders brought the fans to the park. Allowing as many fans in as possible meant having overflow fans sitting down the baselines in foul territory and in front of the outfield wall. Any hit to where fans sat in the outfield resulted in a ground-rule double (Withers Family Collection).

extended press coverage points to the prominence of the Red Sox organization in the NSL and the respect they received from white Memphians. In their desire to mimic Organized Baseball, black news outlets like the *Chicago Defender* became frustrated when box scores came in sporadically. Although the local *Commercial Appeal* received box scores regularly, the *Chicago Defender* accused the Red Sox of sending in box scores in four or five sets without dates.[44] The inability of the black press to coordinate with Negro leagues teams reiterates the difficulties Blackball experienced in being recognized as legitimate by Organized Baseball.

Along with Opening Day festivities and the annual Fourth of July doubleheaders that became Negro leagues mainstays, Lewis attempted to use Lewis Park as a venue for multiple sports. Using the lawn on the Iowa Avenue side of the stadium, the Red Sox secretary, Samuel R. Brown, organized a tennis tournament. Lewis identified the side lawn as the Unique Club, as Lewis Park held its inaugural and only tennis tournament.[45] Although this late July lawn tennis tournament did not draw enough to continue in the following years, the *Commercial Appeal* described the tournament as relatively successful.[46]

As opening days grew in popularity and the team became more entwined in the community's social fabric, R.S. Lewis expanded ceremonies to include a parade. In 1928, the Red Sox and their opponent, the Kansas City Monarchs, paraded from Lewis Park to Beale Street. Admission to Lewis Park for games in 1928 stood at 55¢ for children, 60¢ for general admission, and 75¢ for box seats.[47] Lewis aimed to keep prices down for the 1928 season following flooding the previous winter. In 1927 the Mississippi Valley suffered some of the worst floodings in the region's history. The economic impact on the black community in the Bluff City was devastating.

The failure of black banks, including the most prominent, the Fraternal and Solvent Bank and Trust Company, led 28,000 Blacks in Memphis to suffer near financial ruin, including black business owners. For many in the community, their lifetime savings disappeared overnight. Thousands of blacks lingered around the Fraternal and Solvent Trust Company building on Third and Beale, awaiting a financial reprieve that never came.[48] The heavy spring rains spelled disaster at the turnstiles for the Red Sox. In their opening series with the Kansas City Monarchs, the Red Sox won only two of five games.

Yet, the fans filled the stands at Lewis Park the entire weekend, and even the white *Commercial Appeal* noted the overflowing crowd at

2. "Take Me Out to the Ballgame"—Martin Stadium at Lewis Park

Sunday's doubleheader labeling it "the largest crowd in Red Sox history."[49] Lewis Park became a symbol of the resiliency of the black community to withstand the imminent economic collapse facing the city and the country. As black-run businesses continued to fail throughout the 1928 season, Lewis Park remained open as a symbol of pride.

As Lewis had the previous season, he scheduled local semi-pro teams at Lewis Park. Lewis and the Red Sox ownership group bankrolled a local semi-pro team in 1928, the Memphis Giants. The Giants used Lewis Park for games when the Red Sox were out of town, keeping the turnstiles turning at the park. As a member of the Negro National League, Lewis kept in contact with the Negro Southern League by scheduling barnstorming games against Southern League member the Nashville Elite Giants with his Memphis Giants. Lewis's use of the moniker Giants for his semi-pro term reflected the business strategy of Negro league owners throughout the country. Branding is a means to achieve product differentiation. As historian Michael Lomax has noted, many clubs in the Negro leagues era used the nickname Giants to identify their team. Lewis was no different as he understood name recognition and its economic value and applied it to his local semi-pro team, hoping to profit off the next great "Giants" team.[50]

The spring of 1929 brought changes to Lewis Park with the transfer of ownership from Lewis to the Martin brothers and local doctors. They immediately sought to impact the local and national view of the franchise by making improvements to the park's physical plant and turning the stadium into one of the most modern in the country.[51] Although the park remained Lewis Park, in honor of R.S. Lewis' role with the franchise, the stadium became Martin Stadium.

The Martins continued booking semi-pro games during the 1929 season at Martin Stadium. Along with these, they added several games between local schools. Booker T. Washington High, located only a few hundred yards from Martin Stadium, squared off against LeMoyne College's nine in late May.[52] Both schools sat as symbols of racial pride. The Martins endeared themselves and the club to the community by bringing other baseball teams to Martin Stadium. Sports at historically black colleges and universities highlighted student culture's vitality on campuses.

Prep school and collegiate athletics offered a limited means through which historically black schools could become assimilated, on their terms, into the national collegiate culture.[53] Other clubs, like the Atlanta Black Crackers, regularly picked up players from local colleges.

The Memphis Red Sox

The Black Crackers played against Clark Atlanta, Morehouse, and Morris Brown universities in their early years.[54] Following these games, they signed players to improve their rosters. In Memphis, games between LeMoyne College and Booker T. Washington High provided a window into the local talent available to the Red Sox.

During the 1920s and 1930s, Memphis's boxing scene began to gain credibility. Seizing an opportunity to occupy the stadium, the Martins hosted boxing matches. Lewis Park hosted a night of pugilism at the park as part of the Missouri-Pacific RR Colored Booster Club's fisticuffs series. With three fights on the card, local fighters took precedence. Kid Roux knocked out another local, Memphis Spark Plug, in the lightweight class in the third round. In another lightweight match, Chicago native Battling Grimm lost to another local, Young Jack Johnson. Although no records remain from the turnstiles, the *Commercial Appeal* reported a large crowd at the event.[55] The following week, the stadium again hosted the open-air arena matches for the Missouri-Pacific RR Colored Booster Club, with Young Jack Johnson highlighting the card.[56] Martin Stadium became a prominent gathering space for the city's black sporting community.

During the 1930 season, the city witnessed the Martins welcoming baseball into a new age: games under lights. J.L. Wilkerson, the Kansas City Monarchs' white owner, looked to profit from using lights to play baseball at night. A keen observer of the sports scene, Wilkerson took his Monarchs to Lawrence, Kansas, in 1929 to practice under the lights at Haskell Institute for Indians.[57] That same year Wilkerson commissioned the Giant Manufacturing Company of Council Bluffs, Iowa, to manufacture a portable lighting system. The equipment consisted of four telescoping poles designed to elevate lights forty-five feet above the playing field. Each pole was fastened to a truck on a pivot and raised into position by a winch. When deployed, each pole supported six floodlights measuring four feet across. Wilkerson first employed his new lighting system on April 28, 1930, against the Phillips University baseball team in Enid, Oklahoma.[58] Two weeks later, Wilkerson introduced his lights to the Negro National League when the Red Sox hosted the Monarchs under Wilkerson's new lighting system at Martin Stadium. The game became the first baseball game played under lights in Tennessee.[59]

In anticipation of the overflowing crowd at Martin Stadium, they added 2,000 extra seats to increase the stadium's capacity to 5,000. Night baseball's excitement permeated the city as white and black fans headed to Martin Stadium to see Wilkerson's contraption. Per Jim Crow

2. "Take Me Out to the Ballgame"—Martin Stadium at Lewis Park

segregation, the stadium and entryways became segregated for the night game. Whites entered on the east side of the stadium.[60] The Red Sox added to the excitement when they defeated the Monarchs in two of the three games they played before the first night game in Negro National League history. Only two weeks into Wilkerson's experiment, the Monarchs were now in the habit of playing three games daily, two under the light of day and one under the lights.

The Monarchs' players complained about playing three games daily and returning to the hotel "dog tired."[61] Yet, the Monarchs held the advantage in night games as one of the few teams who played nearly every day under lights. The generators dimmed lights during the game, and the outfielders were barely visible from home plate. The pitchers struggled to see the catcher's signs, leading to catchers developing new ways to signal pitches to their battery

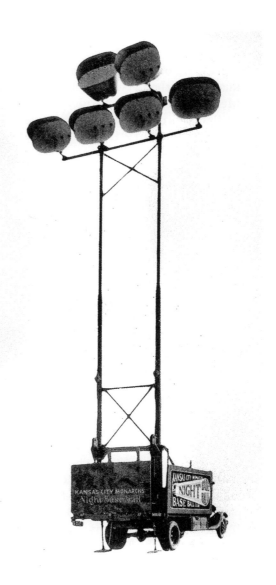

The Kansas City Monarchs used their lighting system at Martin Stadium on May 1930 against the Memphis Red Sox. It became the first baseball game under lights in Memphis (John Haddock Collection).

The Memphis Red Sox

mate on the mound.[62] These advantages led to the Monarchs defeating the Red Sox 8 to 4 in the first night game in NNL and Memphis history.[63]

The Red Sox's role in ushering in this new era placed Martin Stadium ahead of the curve and provided another moment of racial pride for Memphis's black community. Negro leagues baseball playing games under lights foreshadowed where professional baseball was heading in the twentieth century. It also illuminated the need for Negro leagues teams to get in as many games in a day as possible to keep the turnstiles moving. The *Commercial Appeal* and the *Press-Scimitar* sang the praises of the lights and their importance to baseball moving forward. The highlight of the 1930 season would remain the first game played under lights in the history of the Negro National League. Unfortunately, the Red Sox struggled through the remainder of the schedule, leading the Martin brothers to drop their membership in the NNL and return to the Negro Southern League.

The 1931 season saw the return of celebrated catcher Larry Brown to Martin Stadium as player/manager for the Red Sox. His success in Memphis led to appearances with the Chicago American Giants, Detroit Stars, the New York Lincoln Giants, the Harlem Stars, the New York Black Yankees, and the Philadelphia Stars. *The Press-Scimitar* described him as "one of the highest-paid negro players," and the *Commercial Appeal* referred to him as "one of the greatest negro ballplayers in the country."[64] The Red Sox held a drawing card of their own for the first time: a catcher among the game's best. Brown's return to the Red Sox sparked the team to dominate the first half of their Negro Southern League schedule, holding claim as the league's first-half champion.[65]

Representative of the scheduling problems in the Negro Southern League in 1931, the Chattanooga Black Lookouts failed to attend a weekend series in late July. The Martins, leery of losing the gate from an empty weekend, scheduled the Red Sox in a series of exhibition games against local semi-pro teams and only charged 50¢ admission.[66] The following weekend, Martin Stadium welcomed the Cuban House of David to town to fill another empty slot in their schedule. Formed in 1903 in Benton Harbor, Michigan, the House of David team represented the religious colony of the same name. The long beards of their players distinguished them from other teams. By 1931, the House of David team spent more time capitalizing financially on the gimmick of their beards than on sharing the gospel. In the 1930s, they broke into numerous iterations, including the Cuban House of David, which visited Memphis to

2. "Take Me Out to the Ballgame"—Martin Stadium at Lewis Park

capitalize on their financial success.⁶⁷ The Martins hoped their exoticism lent itself to a strong enough curiosity to bring fans to the stadium.

Both local white newspapers commented on the unique brand of shadow ball displayed by the House of David before the game. Shadow ball is best known as a warmup routine used to entertain. The players take their positions on the field and then take infield practice without the ball. Each player mimics the motions associated with routine drills, only without a ball. The House of David's familiarity with this routine dates back to their numerous barnstorming engagements with professional Blackball teams. Both white and black fans flocked to Martin Stadium to watch as the Red Sox won two of three games from this unique brand of ballplayers from the Midwest.⁶⁸

That same weekend the Red Sox welcomed home one of Memphis's own, W.C. Handy. The son of formerly enslaved people, Handy earned the title Father of the Blues following the 1912 publication of his song "Memphis Blues." Handy's songs helped create an entire Blues industry, which in 1925 allowed him to live comfortably in New York City's affluent suburb of Yonkers.⁶⁹ Later that same year, following the urging of Lieutenant George Lee, Boss Crump dedicated a park to the famous Memphian. Twenty thousand people attended the park's dedication ceremony on Beale Street, including Crump, Lee, Robert Church, Jr., and W.C. Handy.⁷⁰

Although the Martins competed with Beale Street for the limited disposable income of the city's black populace, they also understood the importance of music to the city and of W.C. Handy to that legacy. Martin Stadium stood as a bastion of political expression and a space where Handy could return, feeling welcome and safe in a space only blocks away from Beale Street. The bond between the city and baseball continued to grow. The Martins hoped this bond would be as strong as its bond with the blues.

With momentum building, the Red Sox looked to be on their way to claiming the Negro Southern League pennant. The Achilles heel of the Martin ownership group would always be its tight-fisted rein on salaries. Although the Martins never missed a payday, they rarely paid players equitably compared to other teams in Negro leagues baseball. The Red Sox manager and star player, Larry Brown, became disgruntled over salaries—not his salary but that of his players. When J.B. Martin refused to budge, Brown jumped ship midseason in 1930, leaving the Red Sox without their main attraction and a manager whose experience would include managing in the prestigious East-West All-Star game.

The Memphis Red Sox

In 1925, Boss Crump dedicated a park in Memphis to W.C. Handy, honoring his 1912 Blues classic "The Memphis Blues." Martin Stadium's proximity to Beale Street connected the club to the city's rich musical tradition and nightlife (Memphis Public Library).

The Red Sox limped through the remainder of the season, claiming they were first-half champions. With limited media coverage in NSL cities and the league offices unwilling to adjudicate disputes, the Nashville Elite Giants also claimed the first-half pennant. The Elite Giants played the pennant winners from the Negro Texas–Louisiana League in a seven-game series.[71] Back in Memphis, the Red Sox prepared for their NSL championship with the second-half winner of the NSL, the Montgomery Gray Sox. Following the split of a weekend series with the Gray Sox in mid–September at Martin Stadium, reporting in both cities ceased. The series remained knotted at three games apiece. No winner on the field existed, leaving the fans in Memphis wondering if their Red Sox were the 1931 Negro Southern League Champions.[72]

Rube Foster's death in 1930 and the imminent collapse of the Negro National League in the fall of 1931 meant the Negro Southern

2. "Take Me Out to the Ballgame"—Martin Stadium at Lewis Park

League became the preeminent professional black baseball league for the 1932 season.[73] Capitalizing on their new role as members of the lone major league in professional black baseball, the Martins added depth to their 1932 roster and physical improvements to Martin Stadium.[74] Unfortunately, the new playing surface at Martin Stadium never lived up to today's standards for ballparks. Across town, Russwood's infield included a turtleback infield where the water drained off following a storm.[75] Martin Stadium lagged in design, but the Martins invested in red clay from Birmingham, Alabama, to improve drainage.

Unfortunately, they did not invest in tarps to cover the infield. Instead, if it rained, the grounds crew, a small group of two or three, ordered gallons and gallons of gasoline. They poured the gas over the field and burned the excess water from the infield dirt. The players often joined with the grounds crew spreading the gasoline and lighting the infield on fire. The outfield also provided a unique twist in the off-season when Dr. W.S. Martin brought his forty head of cattle from his farm in

The Red Sox played at Russwood Park in 1922 and again in the 1940s while the Martins renovated Martin Stadium. The Claybrook Tigers, an NSL rival of the Red Sox, also used Russwood as its home park in 1937 (J.J. Guizzano Collection).

The Memphis Red Sox

Mississippi to graze in the outfield.[76] Despite these deficiencies, Martin Stadium remained a source of pride as one of the few black-owned stadiums in Blackball.

The Martins also set out to claim the Silver Trophy, presented to the franchise with the highest attendance for Opening Day in the Negro Southern League. On Opening Day, the Martins lowered student ticket prices to 15¢ for all Memphis area black schools. The Red Sox encouraged fans to join the two-mile parade route from Beale Street and Third Avenue to Martin Stadium at Lewis Park. A Hooks Brothers Photographer commemorated the Silver Trophy's capture with a picture published in the *Memphis World* to acknowledge the accomplishment.[77]

Dropping the home opener to the Birmingham Black Barons symbolized the troubled season ahead for the Red Sox and the NSL. Throughout the season, the Great Depression forced NSL teams to fold. The Atlanta Black Crackers left the league, followed by the Little Rock Grays, and finally the Louisville Black Caps left league play. As a result, Martin Stadium went five weeks without holding an NSL league series.[78] Black professional baseball's position economically remained tenuous. The Red Sox's ability to maintain its travel schedule provided economic stability amid the financial woes of the Great Depression.

The Red Sox's financial stability in 1932 mirrored that of the Monroe Monarchs. After years in the Louisiana-Texas League, the Monarchs jumped to the NSL in 1932. The owner of the Monarchs, a white man named J.C. Stovall, made his money in oil drilling in the Gulf. Stovall's ballpark included a swimming pool and a dance pavilion. The Monarchs' success made Stovall a rich man, and in return, he felt that it was only fitting for him to offer the black community in Monroe recreational opportunities.[79] Like Stovall, the Martins continued reinventing ways to bring fans to the ballpark and keep black baseball alive.

Martin Stadium opened the 1933 exhibition season with a two-game set against Gus Greenlee's Pittsburgh Crawfords. Billed as one of the greatest teams to ever perform at Lewis Park by the *Commercial Appeal*, Greenlee's Crawfords brought crowds to stadiums wherever they played. Greenlee, a purveyor of the numbers racketeer in Pittsburgh, set out two years earlier in 1930 to assemble the best team money could buy. By 1933, Greenlee's Crawfords lured Cool Papa Bell from the Detroit Stars, Walter Cannady and Judy Johnson from the Hilldale Athletic Club, and Oscar Charleston, Josh Gibson, and Ted "Double Duty" Radcliffe from the Homestead Grays with larger contracts.[80]

Then Greenlee added pitcher Satchel Paige in 1932. As a result, the

2. "Take Me Out to the Ballgame"—Martin Stadium at Lewis Park

Crawfords' lineup included the game's top two stars in Negro leagues baseball, Paige and Gibson, and four other future Hall of Famers. The Crawfords cruised to a 20 to 2 victory over the Red Sox in the first game. The following day the Red Sox held the lead for most of the game before dropping the contest 11–9 on a two-run home run by Starkville, Mississippi, native "Cool Papa" Bell.[81] Once again, Martin Stadium hosted the game's best players, proclaiming Memphis's major league status.

The financial rollercoaster of the 1930s saw the Red Sox watch the NSL disintegrate in the middle of the 1933 and 1934 seasons. Constantly looking for new angles, J.B. Martin visited Chicago to meet with Gus Greenlee to create a North-South All-Star game. He offered Memphis as the host site for the inaugural event in 1934. Martin's plan included mimicking Greenlee's concept used in Chicago for the East-West All-Star Game. A North-South game would expose the game's best black players to Southern audiences. The East-West All-Star Game evolved into a superior money-making proposition for league teams and a showcase of black talent for white America, demonstrating the game's financial feasibility.[82]

If Martin could recreate a similar atmosphere in Memphis, then his Red Sox organization stood to profit. Martin contacted Thomas Watkins at Russwood Park to play the North-South All-Star Game at Russwood Park because of Russwood's ability to handle larger crowds.[83] Like the East-West game, the *Chicago Defender* and other newspapers would hold the balloting just like the East-West game. The format and venues for the original North-South game repeatedly changed throughout September. Playing a three-game set in October in Nashville at Sulphur Dell Park, the North-South game started inconspicuously outside Memphis.[84] Martin's work in 1934 laid the groundwork for later North-South All-Star games in Memphis.

Over the next two years, the Red Sox experienced a low point in Memphis when the rival Claybrook Tigers nearly gained control of the Memphis fanbase. John C. Claybrook, a Memphis native, made his fortune by selling plots of land to black farmers in Mississippi, amassing a small fortune. Later, he purchased a farm in Arkansas and began making money in the timber industry. Like the Martins and R.S. Lewis, Claybrook's financial means allowed him to confront Jim Crow head-on periodically.

On one occasion, Claybrook, who was wearing overalls, walked into a local Cadillac dealership to purchase their latest model. The white salesman refused to sell a car to him because of his appearance. Claybrook

The Memphis Red Sox

left the dealership and returned shortly with cash in hand to purchase the vehicle. As a result, the white salesman lost his job.[85] Stories of Claybrook's resistance uplifted the black community as he became a model for black success throughout the region.

Across the river, his farm became known as Claybrook, Arkansas, and became the home to a new team, the Tigers. He stocked his team with quality players as his club grew from a local semi-pro club to a full-fledged member of the NSL in 1935.[86] With the increased competition for fans, the Martins repaired the wooden seats at Martin Stadium, improved the screening behind home plate, and installed new speakers at the park.[87]

Tensions peaked when the *Commercial Appeal* announced to the city that both clubs agreed to a winner-take-all, from a series of home and away gate receipts, between the two.[88] The Red Sox defeated the Tigers in the first game at Martin Stadium but lost a doubleheader two weeks later. Claybrook cleared the gate receipts for close to 5,000 fans for the two dates and earned the respect of the fans and the local press.[89] In July, the Red Sox vindicated themselves on the field when they swept the Claybrook Tigers in a two-game set at Martin Stadium to claim the Negro Southern League's first-half pennant.[90]

Although the Red Sox reclaimed their pride for the moment, the rivalry continued as the two clubs met again for the Negro Southern League championship in September. The Tigers prevailed in this best-of-seven series, leaving the Red Sox as bridesmaids in their city.[91] The 1935 season saw the Tigers draw an average of 6,000 fans per game, while the turnstiles at Martin Stadium cleared only 2,000 per game. The Tigers were winning the Red Sox fan base over.

Following their 1935 pennant-winning season, the Claybrook Tigers rented Russwood Park from the Memphis Chicks for home games. Russwood's 10,000-seat capacity and the Tigers' growing fan-base left Martin Stadium as a second-tier venue. Then the Tigers signed one of Blackball's best drawing cards, Ted "Double Duty" Radcliffe. The Tigers regularly sold out Russwood Park. As the Claybrook Tigers continued to dominate their crosstown rivals, players from the Red Sox began to jump to the Tigers. In June, infielder Jimmy Ford, enticed by the opportunity to make more money and play in front of larger crowds at Russwood, joined the Tigers.[92] The Tigers again reigned supreme in the Negro Southern League, claiming the league championship for the second year.

Confronted with a dwindling fan base from a budding rivalry, the

2. "Take Me Out to the Ballgame"—Martin Stadium at Lewis Park

Martins accepted an opportunity to become part of Blackball's newest major league, the Negro American League. The NAL looked strikingly similar to Rube Foster's Negro National League and offered franchises, like the Memphis Red Sox, an opportunity to gain national exposure. The NAL, designed to rival the East Coast's Negro National League circuit, began under the guidance of veteran Blackballer Major Robert Jackson. Jackson's experience as a veteran of the Spanish-American War and official with the Leland Giants and the Chicago American Giants gave the league the expertise the nascent league needed to succeed.[93] In addition, Jackson's affiliation with the Republican Party in Chicago expanded the Martins' national influence in the Republican Party.

The creation of the NAL appeared serendipitously for the Red Sox organization, granting the club an opportunity to be in the major leagues again and to outshine the surging Claybrook Tigers. Major league talent from the NAL allowed Martin Stadium to host more big-name players than the Claybrook Tigers and the Negro Southern League brought to Russwood Park.

For their inaugural Negro American League season in 1937, Martin Stadium added light standards to draw more Memphis's black working-class to weeknight games.[94] Lights allowed the team to market games at the stadium in new ways. For example, the team advertised a Tuesday doubleheader, with the Kansas City Monarchs and the Chicago American Giants playing the opener and the winner facing the Red Sox. This approach was so successful in May that the team used this approach again in July and August. This marketing ploy, aided by the ability to play doubleheaders on weeknights, allowed the Red Sox to bring multiple teams to Martin Stadium in 1937, including the Nashville Elite Giants, Cincinnati Tigers, New York Black Yankees, and the Indianapolis ABCs.[95]

The lights also brought the North-South All-Star game to Memphis. Martin Stadium hosted over 4,000 fans for the August game, pitting the best players from the NAL split into Northern and Southern teams, including Willie Foster, Turkey Stearnes, and "Double Duty" Radcliffe.[96] As a result, Martin Stadium was once again the central gathering space for Memphis's black sporting community.

Just as quickly as the Claybrook Tigers nearly brought the Red Sox to extinction, the Red Sox's inclusion in the Negro American League opened the opportunity for the city's only major league pennant in 1938, chronicled later in Chapter 4. Falling back into sub-par baseball, Martin Stadium's joy in 1939 existed in the exploits of Red Sox slugger Neil

The Memphis Red Sox

"Shadow" Robinson. By July, he totaled 35 home runs; by the end of the season, he parlayed 59.[97] These numbers were in a park so deep that it was best known as a park where "fly balls went to die." In honor of Robinson's heroics, the Martins honored Red Sox fans by offering free admission on August 3.[98] "Shadow" won back-to-back home run titles as a Red Sox during the 1938 and 1939 seasons.[99] His frequent trips to the East-West All-Star game validate his talent, yet playing in Memphis, away from the nation's most prominent black periodicals, he never received the accolades of a slugger like Josh Gibson.

As the world sat on the edge of world war, Martin Stadium continued to bring the city's black sporting community together in new and exciting ways. On the field, the Red Sox welcomed rookie sensation Verdell "Lefty" Mathis to its battery. In addition, local bathing beauty Pearline McIntyre took home the team's annual beauty contest.[100] Later in the season, Martin Stadium hosted American Olympic track star Jesse Owens. Owens, the hero of the 1936 Summer Games in Berlin, raced a motorcycle around Martin Stadium. Red Sox speedster Bubba Hyde claimed he challenged Owens to a race around the base paths and defeated him both times.[101]

The most crucial development was the reincarnation of the

Jesse Owens came to Martin Stadium on numerous occasions to run exhibition races against the fastest players in the Negro leagues. Front row, left to right: Cornelius Robinson, Jesse Owens, and an unknown Homestead Gray (John Haddock Collection).

2. "Take Me Out to the Ballgame"—Martin Stadium at Lewis Park

The Martins held Bathing Beauty contests once a year to increase attendance at games, and the winner earned an excursion to the East-West ASG in Chicago (John Haddock Collection).

Birmingham Black Barons under the ownership of Memphis's Thomas Hayes, Jr., whose resurrection of the Black Barons rekindled the rivalry between the two cities. His position as a member of one of Memphis's more prominent African American middle-class families elevated the rivalry. The T.H. Hayes and Son Funeral Home on South Lauderdale stood as a pillar of black economic success in the city, forging one of the few paths to prosperity shared among African Americans in the pre-civil rights South.[102] Hayes' position within the black bourgeoisie of Memphis mirrored that of the Martin brothers and created a rivalry within the rivalry.

Throughout the 1940 season, the Martins continued to offer special days at the park to attract fans to Martin Stadium. A "Men's Day" offered men free admission for a Thursday night game in July, followed by Fan Appreciation Day in August, where all fans were admitted free of charge for the Friday night game against the St. Louis Stars.[103] Both

The Memphis Red Sox

of these marketing ploys speak to the success of the Red Sox at the turnstiles since joining the Negro American League only three years earlier. The 1941 Red Sox battery included pitching sensation Verdell Mathis, veteran catcher Larry Brown, the Negro baseball's homerun leader Neil "Shadow" Robinson, and Ted "Double Duty" Radcliffe. After Reuben Jones's one-year stint at the helm, Radcliffe returned to manage the Red Sox.[104]

The Red Sox remained one of the top entertainment choices in town. In support of the National Negro Business League's 1941 Convention in Memphis, the Martins paired with Thomas Hayes, Jr., to host a fundraiser. In addition, Martin Stadium hosted black-owned organizations and supported black-owned businesses through charity events.[105] Although the team did not secure the NAL pennant on the field, they battled with Birmingham for a second-place finish before succumbing late in the season to finish third.

The onset of World War II for the Negro leagues meant that many teams lost players to the draft. After the Japanese attack on Pearl

Memphis Red Sox catcher and manager Larry Brown arrives safely at third against the K.C. Monarchs at Municipal Stadium in Kansas City (during World War II—V on left sleeve) (John Haddock Collection).

2. "Take Me Out to the Ballgame"—Martin Stadium at Lewis Park

Harbor, Red Sox first baseman Olan "Jelly" Taylor was among the first players from the Negro leagues to be inducted into the Army. Drafted a few weeks into the 1942 season, he spent the next three seasons in the military before returning to the Red Sox in 1945.[106] Later, second baseman Marlin Carter served with the United States Coast Guard for three seasons. He witnessed firsthand the damage done by the atomic bomb at Hiroshima and Nagasaki before returning to Martin Stadium in 1946 with the Red Sox.[107]

Fortunately for the Red Sox, they lost only two men to the war effort when major league rosters were devastated by the draft. The *Pittsburgh Courier's* "Double V for Victory" campaign sought victory from fascism in Europe and at home. Blacks nationwide poured into ballparks to watch baseball as a source of pride.[108] The Red Sox home uniforms during World War II included a large red "V" on the sleeve, and away-game jerseys displayed a patch in the form of a red, white, and blue shield on the left sleeve to honor American servicemen.[109] They also rewarded the Red Sox faithful during the annual Fourth of July doubleheader with free food served in the concessions stands against the first-place Kansas City Monarchs, drawing close to 4,500 attendance.[110] The Red Sox finished the Negro American League season one game under .500 and in fourth place. Yet, the club's popularity remained at an all-time high.[111]

Martin Stadium and the Red Sox welcomed "Jelly" Taylor for their Opening Day game in 1943 while he was on leave from the Jefferson Barracks in Missouri.[112] The wartime surge in attendance exposed the

Memphis Red Sox 1943 team picture at home plate of Martin Stadium. Managed by Larry Brown (kneeling third from right), the Red Sox finished 44–55–4 overall and 34–51–4 in the Negro American League (*Tri-State Defender*).

The Memphis Red Sox

aging physical body of the stadium. It became apparent that the original wooden bleachers erected by R.S. Lewis in 1922 and improved upon by the Martins in 1929 and 1932 were insufficient. Sunday doubleheaders and the North-South All-Star game were all moved to Russwood Park in 1943 because of the decaying conditions of Martin Stadium, and the next three seasons saw the Red Sox move all their games to Russwood Park.

Although the team had no choice but to schedule their Negro American League games around the Chicks' Southern Association home schedule, the Martins continued to prosper from the wartime enthusiasm in the community for the Red Sox. Keeping within the norms of Jim Crow segregation, they specifically noted the availability of segregated seating at Russwood Park for white fans wanting to remain segregated.[113] World War II provided substantial financial growth for the team—which, in turn, allowed the Martin brothers to renovate Martin Stadium.

In 1944 the Martin brothers began the renovation process of the stadium. With attendance at an all-time high, the Martin brothers looked to capitalize by refurbishing their stadium. Red Sox pitcher Frank "Wahoo" Pearson, a Memphis native, recalled that they drew larger crowds when they played at Russwood than the Chicks did for their home games.[114] Close to 7,000 saw Verdell Mathis pitch his way past the Cleveland Buckeyes in a March 31, 1946, exhibition game, followed by Pearson's own 3–1 victory over the Cincinnati Clowns in the season-opener in front of 8,346 at Russwood Park.[115]

The 1946 season saw the Red Sox play in front of larger crowds, including many white Memphians.[116] Most whites were unfamiliar with the organization. The city's stringent segregation laws dictated that white Memphians lived in a separate world from its black citizens. From 1944 through 1947, baseball became a way for Memphians to assemble in one space and cheer for the common goal, a Red Sox win.

A game between the Chicks and the Red Sox remained out of the question in Jim Crow Memphis, even after Jackie Robinson broke the MLB color barrier in 1947. Russwood Park allowed the Red Sox to play at their facility and let blacks and whites watch games, but they would not break the color barrier on the field. The manager and part-owner of the Chicks in 1946 and 1947 was a local man, Thomas "Doc" Prothro. A graduate of the University of Tennessee at Memphis Dentistry School, Prothro began his professional baseball career later than most after impressing scouts in a semi-pro game in Dyersburg, Tennessee (about 45 minutes north of Memphis). The Chicago Cubs drafted him in 1927.

2. "Take Me Out to the Ballgame"—Martin Stadium at Lewis Park

After his playing career, Prothro spent three seasons as the manager of the Philadelphia Phillies from 1939 to 1941. Back in Memphis in 1942, Prothro took ownership of the Chicks and managed the team through the 1947 season.[117] A lifelong Tennessean, Prothro understood the unwritten segregation rules in the city. A lifelong baseball man, he likely barnstormed against the Red Sox as a semi-pro player, but for professional white baseball to play the Red Sox was out of bounds. Frank "Wahoo" Pearson recalled that they offered to play the Chicks to no avail during the two years the Red Sox played at Russwood Park.[118]

The renovated Martin Stadium opened for the 1948 season with state-of-the-art amenities. Along the stadium's third baseline ran a section of apartments where up to twenty people could live.[119] Each apartment included a shower, a bedroom, and a small kitchen. Players for the Red Sox from out of town lived in these apartments. In addition, the Martin brothers often offered out-of-town players jobs in the winter and allowed the players to live in these same apartments in the off-season.[120] The modernized concession stands served Memphis-style pork BBQ in between innings, roasted over the stadium's barbecue pit. Fans could grab a variety of local beers. Also available was the Southern delicacy, chitterlings (chit-lənz).[121] As a kid, Rufus Thomas remembered the smell of popcorn, Coca-Cola, hot dogs with slaw on them, and that distinct smell of chitterlings that filled the air on game days.[122]

A dirt parking lot south of the stadium welcomed fans as they approached the ticket booth to purchase tickets. The concrete façade provided the foundation for a four-story structure. A metal roof, supported by steel beams, arched around the infield. Once inside the stadium, fans entered the grandstands through two concrete portals. Four rows of box seating gave fans an up-close view of the game. Seating for white fans was in the box seats down the first baseline.[123] Also, down the first baseline, a 12-foot wall kept the fans outside the stadium from catching any action. Dr. W.S. Martin also put up a sheet to prevent residents across Lauderdale from seeing into the game from their second-floor apartment balconies. However, the terraces were high enough to see over, and the fans found ways to take the sheet down if it was too high.[124]

A pavilion on the third baseline ran from the edge of the grandstand to the outfield wall. Box seating was available in the front four rows down the third baseline, and grandstand-style seating for another ten rows behind the box seats under the pavilion's roof. The extended seating down the third baseline created a sightline issue for fans on the third baseline

The Memphis Red Sox

side of the renovated grandstand. The overhang for the pavilion became an obstacle for fans halfway up the grandstand as they attempted to see the action in left field. Steel girders in the grandstand used to support the steel overhang above the grandstand from the first base to the third base lines created minor sightline issues common to baseball stadiums of the era. Yet, despite these minor flaws, the renovated Martin Stadium provided Red Sox fans with a stadium unequaled in Blackball.

Behind the right field wall on the Iowa Avenue side of the stadium sat the Harlem House restaurant. Players ate there during spring training and after many ball games.[125] Former Red Sox pitcher Charley Pride, who lived in the apartments down the third baseline at Martin Stadium, fondly remembered the Harlem House. For 50¢, a customer would get two hot dogs and a basket of fries.[126] The updated press box accommodated reporters from the *Commercial Appeal, Memphis World, Press-Scimitar,* and local radio stations wanting to broadcast games. The renovations that began in 1946 would cost the Martins $250,000, or approximately $3 million in 2020.[127] Black baseball was at its peak when soldiers returned home from World War II, and the Martins positioned themselves to profit from the postwar boom.

* * *

The return of soldiers from the war ushered in a new era of prosperity for Americans and a new sense of urgency to break down the walls of inequality cast by segregation. The *Pittsburgh Courier's* "Double V For Victory" campaign urged Americans to confront fascism at home as readily as it had in Nazi-controlled Europe. Jackie Robinson and Larry Doby's integration of Organized Baseball in 1947 became a symbolic spearhead for what became known as the civil rights movement of the 1950s and 1960s. The paradigm of Jim Crow that necessitated Negro leagues baseball began to disintegrate. The Red Sox organization's downfall left Martin Stadium as a memorial to a bygone era. Martin Stadium stood at its height as a pillar of Memphis's black community—a space where black kids dreamed of becoming major leaguers, and a place where the black working and middle class gathered to catch a glimpse of the game's greatest players. It offered a refuge from Jim Crow's realities in Boss Crump's Memphis. Martin Stadium served as a social, economic, and political focal point for black Memphians.

3

Black Owned and Operated

The black owners of the Memphis Red Sox brought respectability and pride to the Bluff City's Negro leagues franchise. They stood out as one of the few black-owned and operated clubs that owned their stadium during the Negro leagues era. However, ownership stood out as a point of contention with white major league baseball. White owners viewed owners in the Negro leagues as nothing more than glorified booking agents, placing them under heavy scrutiny from their white counterparts. In addition, white owners of Negro leagues teams faced scrutiny from the black community as men profited from black players' labor. Successful black owners like Rube Foster in Chicago (American Giants) and Edward Bolden in Philadelphia (Hilldale) remained an anomaly with the odds stacked against black ownership. Neither Foster nor Bolden held ownership of the stadium where their clubs played. Historian Neil Lanctot concluded that most observers of Blackball believed that black professional teams would never genuinely operate on a scale comparable to white minor and major league baseball unless all franchises owned and controlled their parks.[1] R.S. Lewis and the Martin brothers brought to Memphis and Negro leagues baseball a formula for success in a Southern market firmly rooted in black economic nationalism. The legal axiom that drove Jim Crow throughout the South remained separate but equal, yet one of black baseball's most financially secure and longest-lasting franchises endured within this framework.

Black men owned and operated the Red Sox from the team's inception in 1921. In a city strictly defined by the Jim Crow social and economic realities, the Memphis Red Sox ownership symbolized racial pride. R.S. Lewis' ownership of the franchise from the 1922 season through the onset of the 1929 season laid the foundation for black control of the club. Following the spring floods of 1927 along the Mississippi River Valley, many within the black business community fell on hard times, including Red Sox owner R.S. Lewis. He then incorporated

The Memphis Red Sox

R.S. Lewis (located on the far left of the picture) bought the team in 1922 and built the club into a respectable organization before selling the team to the Martins in 1928 (George W. Lee Collection, Memphis Public Library).

the franchise and the stadium with several local black businessmen to save the financially faltering club.[2]

However, just as Lewis looked to consolidate his debt and maintain control of the Red Sox organization, the Martin brothers called in several of Lewis's loans held by the Martin family. Lewis had used the team's stadium as collateral for the loans. Following the 1928 season, Lewis could no longer fulfill these financial obligations to the Martins, leading to the Martins foreclosing on Lewis Stadium.[3] Local legend posits the possibility of Lewis losing the franchise to J.B. Martin through a gambling debt. Documentable evidence points to the financial crises that followed the 1927 floods as the legitimate cause for Lewis turning ownership of the club over to the Martins.

The Martin brothers controlled the franchise from 1929 through the franchise's demise in 1960. They provided Memphis with an ownership group from the city's black bourgeoisie. The four Martin brothers—

3. Black Owned and Operated

W.S. Martin, physician; J.B. Martin, pharmacist; A.T. Martin, physician; and B.B. Martin, dentist—were prominent actors socially and politically in the city. W.S. Martin was the Collins Chapel Hospital superintendent, the Bluff City Medical Society president, a Shriner, and a Mason. J.B. Martin's drugstore on Florida Street served as a central gathering place for the city's black community. They had the financial wherewithal to rescue the Red Sox from financial ruin following the 1927 flood. Ownership of the Red Sox allowed the Martins a platform for their social, economic, and political agendas, allowing them to increase their financial stability.

Red Sox owner W.S. Martin delivers an Opening-Day message at Martin Stadium (T.H. Hayes Collection, Memphis Public Library).

* * *

During the Negro Southern League's inaugural season in 1922, two black men owned the Red Sox: Larry W. Miller and Moses Dandridge. Both held ties to the Memphis underworld. Dandridge's underworld

The Memphis Red Sox

ties in the city linked him directly with Amos McCullough, the infamous owner of the Panama Club. A fixture on Beale Street, the Panama Club was a three-story red-brick building at Beale Street and Fourth Avenue. Lieutenant George Lee claimed, "McCullough came closer to controlling Beale Street than any other colored man."[4] McCullough strengthened his position on Beale Street as part of the Crump machine's desire to collect poll-tax receipts and registrations. As a part of saloons friendly to the Crump machine, McCullough avoided police intimidation and retribution.[5] Later, after selling the Red Sox, Dandridge and McCullough lost their lives in gunfire at the Panama Club.[6]

Following the tumultuous 1922 season in the Negro Southern League, Miller and Dandridge sold the club to R.S. Lewis. Lewis, the black owner of Barnett and Lewis Family Funeral Home, later R.S. Lewis and Sons Funeral Home, purchased the club and built a state-of-the-art ballpark at the intersection of Iowa Street and Lauderdale Avenue.[7] With Lewis as the franchise owner, the club elevated itself to newfound respectability. Historian David Tucker posits that in urban Southern cities like Memphis, black capitalists provided aggressive political leadership, business acumen, and a sense of racial pride second only to the black church.[8] Moreover, Lewis' new position as the majority owner of the Red Sox brought him into a group of respected black middle-class businessmen, including W.S. Martin and Robert Church Junior.

The early 1920s saw black Memphis businesses blossoming on Beale Street, only blocks away from Lewis Park. Local black investors deposited more than $1,000,000 in the Solvent Savings Bank, $500,000 in the Fraternal Savings Bank, and multiple investments in local businesses on Beale Street. Bert Roddy capitalized on the postwar economic boom of the 1920s in Memphis to incorporate Citizen's Cooperative Stores when he opened fifteen black-owned grocery stores. Wayman Wilkerson launched the black-owned Tri-State Casket and Coffin Company. When Mississippi Life moved to Memphis in 1919, the city acquired its largest black-owned business, a company qualified to underwrite various insurance from industrial to endowment policy.[9] Memphis was on its way to becoming the center of Negro business in the South. Lewis' ownership of the Red Sox added another valuable piece to the growing financial community in the city.

Robert Stevenson Lewis, the son of Oscar and Ella Lewis, was born in Memphis in 1873 and remained a lifelong figure in the Memphis business community. After graduating from Fisk College, he

3. Black Owned and Operated

became a cotton sampler with the Planters Press Company before joining his father's funeral business. Oscar Lewis opened Lewis and Barnett Funeral Home in 1914 on Fourth and Beale Streets in the heart of Black Memphis. On September 29, 1915, R.S. Lewis married Lillia Eugenia McDonald of Holly Springs, Mississippi. While working under his father at the funeral home, Lewis teamed with Bert Roddy to operate the Iroquois Café on Beale Street.[10] Lewis's business acumen allowed him to team with other prominent black businessmen in the city early in his career. His business acumen and solid family name created an opportunity in 1923 to become the majority owner of the fledgling Red Sox. His growing position in the city solidified his opportunity to own a professional sports franchise.

Joining R.S. Lewis in the ownership group of the Red Sox was J.T. Settle, a prominent businessman on Beale Street. Settle partnered with Bert Roddy, T.H. Hayes, M.L. Clay, and Robert Church, Jr., to establish the Solvent Bank and Trust Company on Beale Street.[11] Teaming with Settle provided R.S. Lewis's financial stability to steady the young Negro Southern League franchise. When the NSL met in Birmingham on April 2, 1923, Settle, representing the Memphis club, was elected president.[12] The city's black team began ascending to stability and prominence within Blackball. However, the team needed a permanent home for its games. Lewis forged ahead, building a permanent stadium on Iowa and Wellington Streets. Aptly named Lewis Park, it opened to rave reviews. Lewis later told reporters that one of the major impetuses for building the park was to "fill a need for a Baseball Park [sic] for our people where our women could attend baseball games without the usual embarrassment that accompanies jim crow [sic] conditions."[13] The strictures of Jim Crow also led Lewis to allow opposing teams to use his family's funeral home as lodging to avoid racially segregated hotel accommodations in the city.[14]

The Red Sox's early success in the 1923 season led Lewis and the ownership group to abandon the Negro Southern League in the second half of the season and seek membership in the Negro National League (NNL).[15] The city showed every sign of being on its way to becoming a major league city within Blackball. Lewis sent Settle to Chicago to negotiate with Rube Foster. Word out of Chicago pointed to the two Southern clubs, Birmingham and Memphis, becoming conditional members based on attendance numbers desired by the Negro National League.[16]

Lewis' goals remained upwardly mobile for himself and the club

The Memphis Red Sox

heading into the 1924 season. In 1924, the Red Sox fully transitioned from the NSL to the NNL. Without the Birmingham Black Barons and the Red Sox, the NSL became a loose association of independent ball teams. Without its two most dominant members, the fledgling league struggled. For the Red Sox and the Black Barons, the elevated level of play in the NNL kept both teams under .500. In addition, the extended travel of teams in the more expansive NNL meant going to Northern cities, including Chicago, Kansas City, and St. Louis. Lewis felt the pinch of the expanded travel schedules. After two financially strenuous seasons, the Red Sox returned to the NSL for the 1926 season.[17] Facing the same dilemmas, the Birmingham Black Barons joined the Red Sox in returning to the NSL.

As the 1926 season approached, R.S. Lewis called a meeting of prospective owners to revive the Negro Southern League. This two-day meeting in Memphis led to the election of black Memphis businessman Bert T. Roddy as league president. Dr. J.B. Martin joined Lewis and Roddy at the 1926 NSL organizational meeting, signaling his early interest in the club as part of the club's ownership group.[18] Roddy opened the first black-owned grocery store in the city, along with his involvement with Lewis in operating the Iroquois Café. His influence in the city extended outside of business and included political ties. In 1914, Roddy penned a letter to the national president of the NAACP requesting a chapter in Memphis. Two years later, Roddy became a charter member of the Lincoln League, a Republican political organization established in the city by Robert Church, Jr.[19]

Church stood at the center of nearly every black political movement during the first half of the twentieth century. At the height of his career, he possessed as much power and influence as many of his contemporaries. Presidents, members of Congress, businessmen, entertainers, and intellectuals all corresponded with Church and sought his advice about uplifting the race.[20] The Red Sox ownership group belonged to a prominent group of African American men who set out to uplift the race through politics, business, and baseball.

Within the Negro Southern League, Roddy's role as president grew, placing Memphis as a significant player in black professional baseball. This newfound position elicited an internal dispute within the league. Before Opening Day in 1926, Roddy mediated a dispute in Birmingham over the ownership of the Black Barons. A white man from Birmingham, W.N. Kritzky, claimed that Rube Foster and the Negro National League acknowledged his position as the owner of the Black Barons

3. Black Owned and Operated

over Joe Rush, a black man who held ownership of the Black Barons over the previous three seasons.

Although credited with founding modern professional Blackball, Rube Foster was also known for his iron-fisted control over all aspects of the game. He viewed the NSL as "minor league" and a pawn in his more extensive control of Blackball. By intervening in an NSL issue, Foster looked to assert his dominance. Instead, Roddy personally drove from Memphis to Birmingham to mediate the dispute. Following Roddy's intervention, Rush retained his position as the club owner, followed by Kritzky and Foster relinquishing their claim to the club.[21] Roddy's position as NSL president precipitated a bold move to unify the smaller NSL and secure the rights of one of its black owners. Roddy strengthened Memphis's position in Blackball's power structure by repelling Foster's attempt to seize control of the NSL.

Arguably the most influential black Republican in America at the onset of the twentieth century, Robert Church, Jr., remained close with Red Sox owner J.B. Martin (Memphis Public Library).

By midway through the 1926 season, Roddy needed to step in again and settle another dispute. This time on the field of play. The *Chicago Defender* questioned Roddy's and the league office's initial delay in designating a first-half pennant winner. The *Chicago Defender* claimed that if Albany, Georgia, won the pennant from a small market, the league would lose money in a fall playoff between the winners of the two halves.[22] One week later, the *Pittsburgh Courier* reported that Roddy stated, "Due to the fact that there are multiple claimants to the first half pennant, the pennant will be decided on the diamond, not in a meeting."[23] Roddy's savvy allowed the NSL to secure respectability with fans while maintaining financial solvency off the field. In addition, Roddy's role as president of the NSL placed a prominent black Memphis businessman at the forefront of Negro leagues baseball in the eye of the national media.

As Roddy elevated the city's and its team's status, Blackball stood at a significant crossroads. Institutionalized following a mental breakdown, Foster remained in a mental facility in Kankakee, Illinois, beginning in the middle of the 1926 season until he died in December 1931.[24] During Foster's thirty years as a player, owner, and administrator, black professional baseball developed into a legitimate business with corresponding increases in attendance, salaries, and press coverage.[25] The Negro National League elected Judge William C. Hueston, an attorney practicing in Gary, Indiana, as its next president to replace Foster. With Hueston guiding the ship, the Red Sox returned to the NNL for the 1927 season. The Birmingham Black Barons joined the Red Sox in returning to the NNL.[26] Although the NNL faced a downward trajectory following Foster's passing, the Red Sox once again elevated themselves to the major league level.

Although no longer a member of the Negro Southern League in 1927, Bert Roddy remained president, further entrenching Memphis as a significant player in Blackball. R.S. Lewis kept a franchise in the NSL. He entered the Memphis Cubs, a pseudo-farm team for the parent Red Sox club. Lewis maintained a farm team by mimicking a scheme employed by Foster in years past. The Cubs played at Lewis Park when the Red Sox were on the road.[27] According to the *Commercial Appeal*, Lewis aided in organizing the Memphis Giants, another black professional team, to fill empty dates at Lewis Park.[28] Lewis's ability to control so much of the black baseball talent in the city further entrenched his position as the city's leading baseball man. Lewis needed to keep fans coming through the turnstiles at the park. As the team's mediocre performance on the field drew fewer fans, Lewis explored other options to maintain the Red Sox financially.

Over the winter, ownership of the Red Sox expanded as Lewis' financial portfolio weakened with the demise of the city's two most prominent banks. The Solvent Savings Bank and Trust Company merged with the Fraternal and Solvent Bank Company in 1927 to form the Fraternal and Solvent Bank and Trust Company, referred to as the Fraternal and Solvent Bank. The economic despair that became known as the Great Depression had its grip firmly established in black Memphis in 1927. No longer able to support the club financially on his own,

3. Black Owned and Operated

R.S. Lewis incorporated the franchise. Joining Lewis on the newly formed board of directors were A.M. McCullough, M.B. Burnett, C.B. King, W.H. Cole, and Dr. E.E. Nesbit.[29]

Amos "Mack" McCullough ran several dives in the Shinertown neighborhood in the city, connecting the Red Sox with the city's underworld.[30] Marshall B. Burnett was the American Home Investment Company's secretary and a cashier at the Fraternal and Solvent Bank. Charles B. King was the agency director for the local branch of the National Benefit Life Insurance Company. The sixth member joining the board was Wheeler H. Cole, whom the *Memphis City Directory* labeled a "timber contractor."[31]

Lewis's incorporation of the Red Sox mimicked prominent Negro leagues team owner J.L. Wilkinson's 1920 incorporation of the Kansas City Monarchs. The *Commercial Appeal* reported a charter for $50,000, and a considerable amount of cash was made available to the club.[32] The *Chicago Defender* proclaimed the Red Sox's financial rating as among the best in Negro National League with this type of backing.[33] But, amid the impending economic disparity, outward appearances disguised inner financial troubles.

In the middle of the 1928 season, the ownership group took a financial hit when news broke that three significant Fraternal and Solvent Bank figures were tried and convicted of theft of funds.[34] Although none of the three men indicted were a part of the Red Sox ownership board, the club's financial stability weakened. Like many Negro leagues teams, the Red Sox teetered on the edge of financial ruin during the 1928 season. Unable to steady the franchise through incorporation, R.S. Lewis looked to sell the club during the off-season. Historian Phil S. Dixon claims that after a series of rainouts during the 1928 season, J.B. Martin and W.S. Martin forced Lewis' hand when they foreclosed on loans made to the Red Sox corporation and Lewis.[35]

The *Commercial Appeal* announced in its March 17, 1929, issue that "the Martin brothers have purchased the rights to Lewis Park and will be associated in the club's direction."[36] The Martins vowed to update Lewis Park to match it with other league members, and they maintained the services of Dr. E.E. Nesbitt as the team's president for the 1929 season.[37] The Martin brothers sought to steady the Red Sox financially. They immediately took a trip to Chicago to maintain their position in the Negro National League.[38]

The Martin family, arguably one of the most notable black families in the city's history, left their mark on Memphis as medical practitioners, political brokers, and the owners of the Red Sox. The Martin family originated in Senatobia, Mississippi, before their father, Lee Martin, migrated to Memphis. The light-skinned complexion of each of the brothers traces back to their white paternal grandfather.[39] The family included four brothers and a sister, Hattie. Each of the brothers attended LeMoyne Normal Institute before matriculating at Meharry Medical School on Tennessee Normal Institute's campus (Tennessee State University).[40]

William S. Martin was the oldest of the four brothers, born in 1879, followed by J.B. Martin in 1885, A.T. Martin in 1886, and then B.B. Martin in 1889. Two conflicting versions of how each brother paid for medical school exist. The first claims that William earned his way through college and then paid for J.B.'s school, J.B. paid for A.T., and finally, A.T. paid for B.B.'s schooling. Lieutenant George Lee, a close family friend, posited the first version. However, W.S. Martin's longtime confidant and common-law wife, Eva Cartman, claims that W.S. bankrolled all of his younger siblings' education after returning to Memphis.[41] Regardless of the version of events, the bond between the brothers remained strong, and their education elevated them as a group into one of the city's most respectable families.

William S. Martin worked numerous odd jobs as a young man, including time as a Pullman porter, to pay for his studies at LeMoyne Normal College in Memphis and Meharry Medical School.[42] While at Meharry, he completed an internship at Bellevue Medical Hospital in Manhattan, New York. Considered by many as New York City's preeminent medical facility, Bellevue Hospital provided free medical hospital care to the indigent as a right, not a privilege.[43]

This NYC internship set the stage for William's successful medical career. He joined the likes of Dr. Audrey Maynard and Dr. Roscoe Conkling Giles. Maynard, a black thoracic surgeon, is best known for operating on Dr. Martin Luther King, Jr., in 1956 following an attack by a deranged woman during a book signing. Giles became the first African American doctor to obtain the American Board of Surgery certification.[44] William S. Martin's internship at Bellevue placed him among the country's prominent black doctors.

After graduating from Meharry, William returned to Memphis and opened a practice on the corner of Florida and Broadway streets in 1907. African American Dr. Miles V. Lynk moved the all-black University of West Tennessee to Memphis that same year. The school aimed to provide medicine, dentistry, and nursing education to the region's

3. Black Owned and Operated

black community. William Martin's relationship with Dr. Lynk led to his life-long association with the Bluff City Medical Association.[45] As a member of Collins Chapel Christian Methodist Episcopal Church in 1910, he joined in helping establish the Collins Chapel Connectional Hospital at 416–418 Ashland Street. Collins Chapel Hospital opened as a 75-bed regional hospital for Memphis's black community, including operating and maternity wards.[46]

Martin's medical practitioner and surgeon skills earned him a promotion to superintendent at Collins Chapel Hospital in 1920.[47] Committed to the success of Collins Chapel, William made 418 Ashland Street his home. As a climbing member of the black bourgeoisie of Memphis, W.S. began purchasing apartments throughout black Memphis.[48] As the oldest brother, many perceived William as the level-headed, conservative head of the family. William remained an assimilationist politically, working within the system of Jim Crow. His ability to maneuver through the rigid racial structure of Jim Crow Memphis during the Crump years allowed Collins Chapel Hospital to become the preeminent black hospital in the city, funded under the watchful eye of Boss Crump.

The second Martin brother, John B. Martin, remains one of the city's most prominent and controversial black figures. J.B. Martin's inner political drive began early as a paperboy for the *Evening Striker*, a local black newspaper, in the late 1890s.[49] Like the *Evening Striker* and the *Chicago Defender*, black newspapers of the era espoused the American values of self-reliance and capitalist success, along with the constitutional gospel of freedom of speech and legal equality for black Americans.[50] Although medicine was the family business, J.B.'s interest in politics began by reading articles in the *Evening Striker*. He attended Meharry Medical College in 1910, like his brother William before him. Following graduation, he borrowed $250 from his older brother and opened his drugstore, the South Memphis Drugstore, which would grow to be the most respected in the black community and, by 1930, filled more prescriptions than any other drugstore in Memphis. His business acumen led to his purchasing several other drugstores in town. As he accumulated wealth, he became one of Memphis's most prosperous black businessmen.[51]

Traced back to his involvement with the Lincoln League, J.B. Martin's political footprint remains one of the most substantial of this era. He attended every Republican national convention starting in 1916. His political stature grew with leadership positions in the Lincoln League and the West Tennessee Civic and Political League.[52] As a member of

The Memphis Red Sox

Owners of the Red Sox in front of the South Florida Street drugstore. Many of the Negro Southern League's annual meetings occurred at the South Memphis drugstore owned by J.B. Martin. This drugstore also served as a post office and held the only malt shop on the black side of town (Memphis Public Library).

the Lincoln League, J.B. Martin was part of a core group that mobilized the black community starting in the 1920s. The Lincoln League organized political rallies, gave speeches, held large weekly meetings in Church Auditorium, collected donations to pay poll taxes, and eventually registered over 10,000 voters. According to Robert Church, Jr., the Lincoln League's purpose was "for the race's second emancipation, when it would free itself from lynching and Jim Crowism by using the ballot box."[53]

J.B. Martin also was one of the original members of the National Association for the Advancement of Colored People branch in Memphis, joining Church and other prominent blacks in the city in chartering the city's first local branch. In addition, Martin helped Church guide his political machine within the black community. This relationship led to political patronage and a sub–post office in his South Memphis Drug Store, a source of pride for the city's black community.[54] J.B. Martin remained the most politically active of his brothers throughout his life. Unfortunately, his political activism came with a price when Boss Crump and his cronies ran him out of town.

3. Black Owned and Operated

Although J.B. Martin remained the most prominent of the brothers in Negro leagues baseball, the roles of the remaining brothers with the Red Sox remained vital in understanding the city's complex racial and political relationships. Like W.S. and J.B. Martin, both A.T. and B.B. Martin received medical degrees from Meharry Medical School in Nashville. B.B.'s role with the Red Sox varied over the brothers' years of ownership, from team statistician to general manager. Capable of relating to the younger players better than W.S. and J.B., B.B. maintained a lifestyle comparable to many players: a divorcé, B.B. Martin lived next door to brother A.T. and his wife, Valerie, on South Parkway.

A.T. Martin chose to distance himself the most from the club when he elected to pay his own way into games in lieu of entering on a pass and then later be called upon to pay his share of the team's deficits at the end of the season.[55] A.T. and B.B. worked in the Martin Medical Building on South Third and Beale streets. The Martin Medical building offered a restaurant, a barbershop, and medical offices for W.S. and A.T.

Red Sox owner and Republican political icon J.B. Martin meets with Republican President Dwight D. Eisenhower (John Haddock Collection).

The Memphis Red Sox

Martin and dental office space for B.B. As a Top Hat and Tails Social Club member, B.B. remained inclined to enjoy a vibrant social life on Beale Street.[56] Lt. George Lee described B.B. Martin as "a tall brown Adonis who has his way with the ladies. Beale Street's answer to the maiden's prayer."[57]

B.B., who turned 43 shortly after the 1932 spring NSL meeting, remained comfortable around the Red Sox players. Whereas many players remained cautious around W.S. Martin or J.B. Martin, the players relaxed around B.B. and could talk freely without offending the older brothers. Marlin Carter, known for letting his true feelings be known, knew that W.S. Martin expected his players to refrain from vulgarity when speaking with him. Therefore, he made a concerted effort to do most of his business with the younger B.B. Martin.[58]

Purchasing the team in 1928 at the onset of the Great Depression posed economic hurdles for the Martin brothers. Coupled with the growing political power of Boss Crump since the election of Democratic president Franklin Delano Roosevelt to the White House, the social climate in the city grew tense. As jobs in Northern cities began to decline, the number of African Americans leaving the city fell. At the same time, the number of black migrants moving to Memphis from Mississippi increased. The city's black population grew exponentially as the city's black economic infrastructure collapsed. Upon arriving in town, strict segregationist policies met these new residents. The Red Sox became one of the few vestiges of hope for the black community. The Martin brothers' financial stability allowed the Red Sox to remain solvent.

The Martins returned the Red Sox to the Negro Southern League following the 1930 season after facing similar financial constraints to those that forced R.S. Lewis to return the Red Sox to the NSL in 1926. The turnstiles slowed considerably in 1930 when the team finished twenty games below .500. Traveling expenses to Detroit, St. Louis, Chicago, Kansas City, Louisville, Nashville, and Birmingham became too much for the club to stay financially solvent.[59] The economic woes of the Great Depression and the extended travel schedule forced the Nashville Elite Giants and the Birmingham Black Barons to rejoin the NSL.

The passing of Rube Foster in December 1930 marked the end of an era in Blackball.[60] The imminent demise of the Negro National League caused by the power vacuum following Foster's absence and the burgeoning economic crisis placed black professional baseball in a tenuous position. As a result, Blackball's center moved from the Midwest to the

3. Black Owned and Operated

East in the 1930s. The emergence of Cumberland Posey and Gus Greenlee in Pittsburgh shifted the center of power eastward. Yet, the Martin brothers and the Red Sox continued to survive, keeping Memphis on the map as a major league city.

The 1932 Negro Southern League season may have been the league's most successful season, but it spoke to the utter chaos Blackball faced during the early years of the Great Depression. The Negro National League did not operate in 1932. The Eastern Colored League was defunct, and its successor, the American Negro League, played only one season in 1929. The 1932 NSL became an amalgamation of teams from the Negro National League, the Eastern Colored League, and the Negro Southern League. To the delight of the Martin brothers and Memphis fans, the Red Sox returned to prominence. They celebrated the onset of the 1932 season by bringing local black political icon Robert Church, Jr., to Martin Stadium to throw out the season's first pitch. Church threw the first pitch out to the owner of the Birmingham Black Barons, Memphian Tom Hayes, Jr.[61]

T.H. Hayes, Jr., was from a prominent black family in Memphis, and his connection with the Martin brothers, specifically B.B. Martin, led to his purchase of the Birmingham Black Barons. Left to right: Thomas H. Hayes, Jr., Mrs. T.H. Hayes, Sr., Thomas H. Hayes, Sr., and Taylor Hayes (T.H. Hayes Collection, Memphis Public Library).

The Memphis Red Sox

When the 1932 Negro Southern League's spring meetings convened, B.B. Martin, the youngest Martin brother, represented the Red Sox. The Martin brothers had recently welcomed Dr. Audrey Carter to their ownership group. The office of Carter, who was a dentist like B.B., was located directly above J.B. Martin's South Memphis Drug Store on 907 Florida Ave.[62] B.B. Martin's role increased steadily during the 1930s. Throughout the Great Depression, the Martin brothers kept the Red Sox solvent while teams around the country folded.

Nevertheless, the team remained an integral piece in keeping the Negro Southern League viable. The year 1933 marked J.B. Martin's ascension to the position of league president.[63] This signaled his welcome into the power structure of Blackball on a national level. Although J.B. Martin did his best to hold the NSL together, the reality of the economic plight of African Americans in 1934 led to the demise of most league teams. Memphis's own Beale Street lay scattered with failed businesses. Beale Street became the burial ground for the ambitions of black folks, lured to the city with high hopes.[64] Yet, a few blocks away on Iowa and Wellington, Martin Stadium remained one of the city's few thriving enterprises.

J.B. Martin focused on keeping the Red Sox solvent while the Negro Southern League failed to complete an entire season. Teams like the Red Sox, which remained financially stable, barnstormed during the second half of the summer. The *Commercial Appeal* hailed the Red Sox as the 1933 Negro Southern League champions. Likewise, The *Times-Picayune* (hometown paper for the New Orleans Crescent Stars) proclaimed the Crescent Stars as NSL champions for 1933.[65] Unable to validate league standings with box scores from league games, the NSL had no way to determine its champion. As teams folded during the season, league schedules became unbalanced, leaving teams playing a different number of games. Thus, local newspapers, like the *Commercial Appeal* or *Times-Picayune*, declared their local nine as league champions. As the NSL disintegrated throughout the season, the NSL transformed into a loose coalition.

J.B. Martin retained his position as president of the Negro Southern League for the 1934 season. Dr. A.B. Carter relinquished his role as general manager, allowing B.B. Martin to take on that position.[66] The *Pittsburgh Courier* referred to the inaugural 1934 NSL meetings as "the largest gathering of Southern League Moguls."[67] When the NSL held its 1934 meetings in the offices above his South Memphis Drug Store, J.B. Martin solidified his position as a Southern Blackball mogul. Joining J.B.

3. Black Owned and Operated

Martin at this inaugural 1934 NSL meeting were J.L. Wilkinson, Kansas City; Al Monroe, sports editor of the *Chicago Defender;* Thomas Wilson, Nashville; C.M. Carter, Chattanooga; J.A. Nance, Knoxville; Frank Johnson, Monroe (Louisiana); and W.H. Lanoy, Little Rock. In addition, J.L. Wilkerson from the Monarchs and journalist Al Monroe from the *Chicago Defender* gave the NSL and Martin national credibility.

J.B. Martin consolidated the league from its 1933 construction to one more regional for the 1934 season. Located closer together, teams now took shorter road trips. In addition, the league's teams were located in cities with larger populations to support professional baseball. Finally, Martin instituted a salary cap to enable each club to finish with a cash surplus at the end of the season.[68] Then, in a savvy move to prevent Northern Negro leagues franchises from raiding NSL rosters, J.B. Martin announced that he affiliated the Negro Southern League with the Negro National League. In these negotiations with NNL president Gus Greenlee, Martin secured spring training facilities in NSL cities for the Chicago American Giants, Cleveland Stars, and the Pittsburgh Crawfords in exchange for protecting players on NSL rosters.[69]

As the 1934 season unfolded, J.B. Martin remained optimistic about the state of black baseball in the South. Although only four teams arrived for the midseason meeting in Memphis, Martin took this opportunity to announce the creation of a North-South All-Star Game to mimic Gus Greenlee's East-West All-Star Game.[70] The best players from the Negro Southern League matched up against the best players from the Negro National League in an All-Star game. J.B. Martin secured Memphis's Russwood Park for the inaugural game. After that, his plan called for the game to shift annually to another Southern city with a large African American population.[71]

Martin's introduction of an all-star game in the South places him at the forefront of innovation in Blackball in the mid–1930s. Within the constricts of codified Jim Crow, Martin duplicated Greenlee's all-star game concept for black baseball fans in the South who could not afford to get to the game in Chicago. Although the East-West All-Star games remained the standard, Martin's courage to seek equitable opportunities in the South for black players deserves greater recognition.

With the onset of the 1935 season, J.B. Martin continued his ascendancy as one of the game's elite owners, and young B.B. Martin continued as the club's general manager while adding on the responsibilities of the team's statistician. Naysayers of black professional baseball contended that the leagues remained poorly organized and resembled loose associations, not leagues. The lack of accurate statistics led to sportswriter Dan Burley's calling Negro leagues baseball "a makeshift affair in which team owners pocket large amounts of money while telling fans of some kind of half or pennant."[72] Reporters of the era struggled to put together statistics from individual games, series, and seasons.

Black owners were well aware of this opinion by many white sportswriters and baseball officials. Yet, by withholding statistics, men like B.B. Martin understood that their best players would be less likely to seek raises or jump ship to join another franchise. B.B. Martin continued to act as the team's statistician through the 1940s. Throughout his time as team statistician, players understood the Martin brothers' underlying reasons for not reporting statistics: keeping salaries low.

J.B. Martin set in motion a series of moves in the spring of 1937 that catapulted him and the Red Sox further along the echelon of elite black owners and teams. The power structure in Negro leagues baseball in the early 1930s centered around Pittsburgh's Gus Greenlee and his Crawford club. Following the demise of Rube Foster in the late 1920s and his Chicago American Giants, J.L. Wilkinson stood as the most formidable power broker in the Midwest. Wilkinson's Kansas City Monarchs became the heir apparent to the American Giants on the field and in the boardroom. Wilkinson's knowledge of the barnstorming routes throughout the Midwest made the Monarchs one of the most financially successful Negro leagues teams in the 1930s. Thus, J.B. Martin positioned himself to gain considerably by attaching himself and the Red Sox to the new Negro American League.

Created out of the perennially important baseball towns of Detroit, St. Louis, Chicago, Kansas City, Memphis, Atlanta, and Birmingham, the Negro American League, according to historian Donn Rogosin, was a reflection of growing Southern urbanization and a strengthening of North-South black community relationships.[73] As a white man, Wilkinson understood the racial dynamics in Negro leagues baseball. So, he allowed J.B. Martin an insider's position in the new organization to deflect attention away from himself.

First, Wilkinson hand-selected Horace G. Hull, a Chicagoan who purchased the Chicago American Giants from Robert Cole, as the league's president. Then, Wilkinson strong-armed the nomination of Major R.R. Jackson, then in his eighties, as the commissioner. J.L. Wilkinson remained in the background as the NAL's vice president. According to historian Mark Ribowsky, Hull worked as an assistant to J.B. Martin.[74] Thus J.B. Martin maneuvered his way into the inner

3. Black Owned and Operated

circles of one of Blackball's boardrooms. No longer seen as the president of a second-tier league from the South, J.B. Martin became a fixture in the Negro American League from 1937 through its demise in the 1950s.

In a surprising move, the Martin brothers set out to radically improve their on-field performance for the 1938 season when they purchased the Cincinnati Tigers organization. Former Olympic sprinter and gold medalist William DeHart Hubbard owned the club and, in 1937, joined the Martin brothers as a founding member of the Negro American League. Hubbard was the first African American to win a gold medal at the Olympics as an individual, placing first in the running long jump at the 1924 Paris Olympiad. Hubbard was a Cincinnati native and attended Walnut Hills High School.[75] Like many other black athletes returning from Olympic success, Hubbard looked to parlay that success on the field as an owner in Negro leagues baseball. Hubbard's connection to baseball in Cincinnati began with an amateur club called the Excelsiors. He added veteran Negro leaguers Josh Johnson, Marlin Carter, and Neil Robinson to create the first Tigers roster.

After three years of successful independent play, the Tigers legitimized themselves by joining the NAL as a founding member in 1937. Hubbard signed the eccentric Ted "Double Duty" Radcliffe as player-manager to draw fans to Crosley Field.[76] The Cincinnati Reds of the National League donated their previous year's road uniforms to the Tigers to help defray costs for Hubbard.[77] The Reds also allowed the Tigers to use Crosley Field when the Reds were out of town. The Tigers averaged between 5,000 and 10,000 fans per game at Crosley Field, where the Reds averaged little more than 5,700 per game. When the Homestead Grays or Pittsburgh Crawfords arrived in Cincinnati, the Tigers drew up to 15,000 fans.[78] Cincinnati baseball historian Lonnie Wheeler described the Tigers as a low-budget team that traveled in a Studebaker bus handed down from a musical group called McKinney's Cotton Pickers.[79] Even with the sizable crowds and favorable terms for using Crosley Field, Hubbard struggled to stay afloat financially.

Even though the Tigers finished a respectable 44–25, good enough for a second-place finish in the Negro American League, Hubbard disbanded the club after the 1937 season.[80] Like many other professional black baseball owners during the Depression, Hubbard determined he could no longer afford to maintain the club's expenditures. The Martin brothers' ability to purchase Hubbard's defunct franchise to rebuild the Red Sox roster speaks to their financial stability as owners in the Negro leagues. Still acting as owner and general manager, J.B. Martin

The Memphis Red Sox

understood the value of Tigers manager Radcliffe after watching his success across town with the Claybrook Tigers in 1936. Radcliffe's success with the Claybrook Tigers, who played at Russwood Stadium in 1936, cost the Martin's dearly at the gate.

Now in a position to acquire the Tiger's roster, the Martins secured the entire 1937 Cincinnati Tigers roster by purchasing the franchise as a whole from Hubbard. J.B. Martin's role as president of the Negro Southern League in 1936 placed him in a precipitous position with Hubbard, whose Tigers were members of the NSL in 1936 before joining the NAL. J.B. Martin's coup also included the Red Sox re-signing local fan favorite Larry Brown away from the Philadelphia Stars. Brown's return to the Bluff City, coupled with a line-up bolstered by the best players from the Cincinnati Tigers, led to the club's only championship season in 1938.

Following the 1938 baseball campaign, J.B. Martin pivoted his focus from his role as owner of the Red Sox to political chief. As a member of the city's Black and Tan Republican faction, Martin's position rivaled Robert Church, Jr.'s prominence. Historians have documented Church's position in the national Republican political hierarchy. Local histories firmly follow the national narrative; however, Martin remained more connected with the city's black community daily. Church's demanding national schedule pulled him away from the city and placed him at the center of national Republican politics.

As the country's leading black politician in the 1920s and 1930s, Church spent less time on the ground in Memphis talking to the city's black population. However, Martin's pharmacy on South Florida Street, just blocks south of Beale Street, kept him in contact with the black community. The South Memphis Drug Store provided a safe space for blacks to gather and discuss the day's political issues. In addition, Martin's philanthropy included providing discounted tickets to Red Sox games at Martin Stadium. As Church's career became more national in scope, Martin became the face of the city's Black and Tan faction of the Republican Party.

The 1938 gubernatorial election signaled a shift in the city's political dynamics. A falling out between Crump and Governor Gordon Browning, whom Crump supported in his 1936 campaign, created a new dynamic in Memphis. To get black votes, Crump began to cut ties with black operatives of illegal establishments. Church advised black Memphians to protest police brutality in the city by not supporting Crump's choice for governor. Crump's candidate won.[81] Coupled with President Franklin Delano Roosevelt's reelection in 1936, the Crump

3. Black Owned and Operated

machine relied less and less on the city's black vote in state and national elections.

As the political winds shifted in the city, J.B. Martin remained true to his political roots in the black faction of the Republican Party. The 1938 gubernatorial election became another pivotal point signaling the city's demise of the Black and Tans. By 1940 J.B. Martin's Black and Tan political affiliation placed him on the wrong side of Crump's political favor. Crump turned on Martin, forcing Martin's departure from the city to Chicago during the height of the 1940 presidential campaign.

Before J.B. Martin's ouster from the city, the Martin brothers maneuvered to bring another local Memphis owner into the Negro American League. Thomas Hayes, Jr., purchased the Birmingham Black Barons following the 1939 season. The Martin brothers convinced Hayes to buy the floundering organization after only seeing Rickwood Stadium in Birmingham host barnstorming games. Hayes Jr.'s connections to the city of Memphis ran deep. Thomas Hayes, Sr., stood as one of the city's most prominent black men at the dawn of the twentieth century. The Hayes Funeral Home stood as a pillar within the community at 245 Poplar Avenue. He symbolized black economic success as president of the Tri-State Casket Company and first vice president of the Solvent Savings Bank and Trust Company. Hayes Sr. was a member of Robert Church, Jr.'s Lincoln League and a founding member of Memphis's NAACP regional office in 1917.[82] Born into black political and economic prominence, Thomas Hayes, Jr., joined the family business and ventured into ownership on the advice of fellow Memphian J.B. Martin.

Once a proud member of the Negro Southern League, Negro National League, and the Negro American League with the Red Sox, the Birmingham Black Barons had fallen on hard times. Hayes's connections with the Martins included various political and economic ties in Memphis. Hayes joined the Martins as members of the Independent Business and Civic Association, set up by prominent Memphis black businessman J.E. Walker.[83] In addition, his involvement in the local Memphis chapter of the NAACP, the Lincoln League, and the Black and Tan faction of the Republican Party bespoke his prominence among members of the city's black bourgeoisie. Over the next twelve years, Hayes's leadership reinvigorated the Black Barons. During the Hayes era, the franchise won three Negro American League pennants, appeared in three Negro League World Series, and had nearly two dozen players who went on to break the color barrier and play in Organized

The Memphis Red Sox

Ball (MLB)[84]—all while maintaining one of the healthiest rivalries in all Negro leagues baseball with the Memphis Red Sox.

With the inclusion of Thomas Hayes, Jr., in the Negro American League ownership group, the power center of the league shifted to Memphis. J.B. Martin became the league's president, and the headquarters of the league's office resided in the Bluff City.[85] At the time, J.B. Martin was the most prominent black man in the city. With Robert Church, Jr.'s forced exile in 1938, J.B. Martin stood atop the Republican party infrastructure in the city. In a public display of his newfound prominence within Blackball and the city politically, J.B. Martin presented gold watches to thirteen Red Sox players before an August 1940 game at Martin Stadium.[86] This act of appreciation of his players was an act of graft for the upcoming 1940 presidential election. Martin expected his players and the team's fans to remain loyal to the Republican Party by supporting Wendell Willkie over FDR in November.

Following J.B. Martin's forced departure from the city by Boss Crump, he maintained as much control of the franchise as he could from Chicago. Yet, by August of 1941, J.B. Martin allowed the incorporation of the team, signaling that he was officially renouncing his financial ties to the club.[87] By selling his shares to his brothers, he was no longer legally president of the Memphis Red Sox. By dissociating himself from the Red Sox, J.B. Martin freed his brothers W.S. and B.B. to operate the team under the modus operandum prevalent under Boss Crump's regime. W.S.'s position as an assimilationist ensured the club's continued operation. Although J.B. Martin's shadow hovered over the Red Sox, the daily operations and decisions now rested in the hands of W.S. Martin and B.B. Martin.

J.B. Martin's place in Negro leagues history often begins with his forced migration to Chicago. He reemerged as owner of the Chicago American Giants and president of the Negro American League. Yet, his importance to baseball in Memphis is unparalleled, and arguably his importance politically on a local level parallels that of Robert Church Junior. Historian Darius Young argues that Robert Church Junior's place in the Black Freedom Struggle is as a national political figure.[88] Church's genesis of the Lincoln Republican League of Tennessee catapulted him into the national political conversation. And, like J.B. Martin, the long arm of Boss Crump forced his departure from the Bluff City to Chicago, where he continued as one of the nation's foremost black Republican figures.

Like Church, J.B. Martin's story focuses on his legacy nationally.

3. Black Owned and Operated

Yet, J.B. Martin remained as crucial to the Black Freedom Struggle in the Bluff City as he was as owner of the South Memphis Drug Store or as a devoted leader for the Black and Tan Republicans in Memphis as he was the owner of the Red Sox. Removing J.B.'s work on the local level outside of baseball hampers his historical legacy in the city in ways foreign to the man at the time, thus relegating his role as secondary to his contemporaries, Lee and Church.

With his younger brother J.B. living in Chicago, and as the older and "more responsible" brother, W.S. took control of the club's finances, while B.B. became the team's booking agent and road manager. Longtime secretary and common-law wife of W.S. Martin, Eva Cartman, believed that the challenges of operating both Collins Chapel Hospital, the city's only black hospital, and the Red Sox placed increased pressure on W.S. to ensure the success of both.[89]

The younger B.B. Martin lost many players' confidence financially following his escapades on road trips. They watched him collect payment for games played on barnstorming tours. When the team returned home, B.B. was known for keeping more than his share when reporting to W.S.[90] B.B.'s reputation as a philandering ladies' man on Beale Street preceded him. His relaxed lifestyle led the players to question his financial responsibility. When the players needed a loan, they headed to the Martin Medical Building to speak to W.S. He never pulled out more than a player asked for, but he ensured the players had what they needed.[91]

At the onset of the 1941 season, W.S. Martin enlisted Eva Cartman's help as the Red Sox's bookkeeper. This move signaled her increased role in the daily operations of the club. Like Effa Manley, whose husband owned the Newark Eagles, Cartmen left her indelible mark on the franchise. A graduate of the nurses' training school at Collins Chapel, Cartman completed a year of postgraduate work at Chicago's Cook County Hospital before returning to Memphis. She became the chief of nursing at Collins Chapel.[92] Although thirty years younger than W.S. Martin, she earned his respect with her leadership at the hospital.

During the 1943 season, W.S. sent B.B. to Philadelphia, Pennsylvania, to retrieve players who jumped the Red Sox for the Negro National League teams on the East Coast. Verdell Mathis and Spike Keyes jumped the Red Sox for Ed Bolden's Philadelphia Stars, and William "Lefty" Burns jumped to the Baltimore Elite Giants. Struggling on the field and at the turnstile, the Red Sox ownership decided to act. The *Memphis World's* sports editor and Red Sox team press secretary

The Memphis Red Sox

Sam Brown spent most of the season attacking the unscrupulous practice of raiding Negro American League teams. Brown offered two solutions to the problem: (1) the creation of a commissioner to mediate disputes between teams in the two leagues and (2) a deposit of $1,000 as a reminder to obey the rules.[93]

In addition, J.B. Martin's ascension to the presidency of the Negro American League gave his brothers an added advantage. No longer a lone voice, the Martins asserted their prowess through J.B. Martin's negotiations with the Negro National League to bring their players back home to Memphis. When Verdell Mathis jumped to the Philadelphia Stars the Martins took action. When B.B. Martin arrived in Philadelphia, he promised Mathis a raise and permission to play in future East-West All-Star games if he came back.[94] Mathis reluctantly returned to Memphis. The team continued to struggle following the players' return, yet this incident points to the prominence of the Martin family and their growing power in black baseball.

Although J.B. Martin and his brothers now stood in the upper echelons of the Negro leagues, Boss Crump sent a potent reminder that he controlled the city of Memphis. Based on the success of the East-West All-Star game in Chicago, B.B. Martin secured Russwood Stadium for an all-star game between the Negro American League and Negro National League at the end of the 1943 season. The white *Commercial Appeal* and the black *Memphis World* announced that NNL president Tom Wilson and NAL president J.B. Martin would be present.

However, when J.B. Martin arrived at Russwood Stadium for the game, police detectives detained him. They removed him from the stadium and brought him to the police station, where Police Chief Boyle confronted J.B. Martin and made it abundantly clear that he was not welcome in Memphis and that he was not to return.[95] Even as the Martin family stood atop black baseball, Jim Crow's head reared itself in denying J.B. Martin an opportunity to shine a light upon his success in his hometown. Yet, his return was a source of pride for the black community. J.B. Martin stood up to the Crump machine in an era when segregation dictated that blacks acquiesce to the demands of the whites. Maneuvering the complicated racial structures of Jim Crow Memphis required courage and meant risking embarrassment, arrest, or possibly worse. For those blacks that remained in the city, it reminded them of the realities they faced daily.

Following World War II, the Red Sox and other professional black baseball teams became financially independent. They were among the largest black businesses in the United States during the Jim Crow Era,

3. Black Owned and Operated

a multi-million dollar operation.[96] From Chicago, J.B. Martin, now the president of the Negro American League, trumpeted that, following Jackie Robinson's signing with the Brooklyn Dodgers, Negro leagues owners "may now be in a position to sell players to the major leagues."[97]

However, the divide between the owners complaining of "Branch Rickey's piracy" and those like J.B. Martin, who openly supported reintegrating the game, caused a rift in an unstable ownership consortium in black professional baseball. Although new construction had begun in 1944, in the winter of 1947, amid this divide, W.S. Martin announced that the Red Sox intended to build a $250,000 stadium to replace the one built by R.S. Lewis in 1923.[98] Hindsight allows for the questioning of this decision. Yet, following World War II, the Martins saw the potential of a new stadium. Unfortunately, the success of Robinson's integrating white major league baseball was less than guaranteed.

The financial profitability of the Red Sox organization merited the need to accommodate its growing fan base. As a result, the renovated Martin Stadium rivaled white Memphis's Russwood Stadium following its completion. Standing on the corner of Iowa and Lauderdale, Martin Stadium symbolized the Red Sox's economic success and the Martin brothers' financial wherewithal to complete the project. In a socially conscious decision, the Martins hired Italian-American Matthew "Matty" Brescia to announce the Red Sox games and promote the team through the local media.

Appalled by the treatment of blacks in Memphis, Brescia eagerly set out to promote black athletes in the city, and readily accepted the position the Martins offered him. Advertisements for the Red Sox stopped appearing in the local white media. The relationship between many white Memphians (white Anglo-Saxon Protestants) remained distrustful of Catholic immigrants like the Italian Brescia. Hiring a socially conscious white Italian promotor cost the team.

Later in the 1947 season, Brescia greeted Branch Rickey at the Memphis Airport and escorted him to Martin Stadium. Brescia sat with Rickey as the Red Sox, with Dan Bankhead on the mound, nabbed a 7–2 victory over the Birmingham Black Barons. Later that night, the Martins agreed to sell Bankhead to the Dodgers for $15,000, making a former Memphis Red Sox player the first African American pitcher to reintegrate into the major leagues. The *Memphis World* announced the signing on its front page.[99] Jackie Robinson (Dodgers) and Larry Doby (Indians) were at the forefront of breaking racial barriers as position players. Bankhead became the first black pitcher to pitch in the major leagues in 1947.

Unfortunately, the pressure for Bankhead to succeed became

The Memphis Red Sox

overbearing, and his story is little more than a sidenote in baseball's history of integration. In 1947, the Red Sox provided the first pitcher and negotiated a buy-out of Bankhead's contract—something that the white owner of the Kansas City Monarchs did not do with Jackie Robinson. Announced over the loudspeaker, Bankhead's signing with the Dodgers led to a standing ovation, signifying the pride Memphians held in their team's breaking down the barriers of Jim Crow.[100]

Branch Rickey signed the first black major league pitcher, Dan Bankhead (shown), in August of 1947 from the Memphis Red Sox for $15,000 (A.P. Wire Service, August 1947).

3. Black Owned and Operated

The 1948 season saw the Martin brothers unveil arguably the preeminent black-owned stadium in the Negro leagues. This renovated Martin Stadium placed the Red Sox franchise at the forefront of Blackball teams. The *Memphis World* referred to the renovated stadium as "one of the finest baseball and sports arenas in the country, owned and operated by Negroes."[101] Even the conservative-minded *Commercial Appeal* noted that Martin Stadium was "the largest Negro park in the world."[102] Unfortunately for the Martin brothers and the Red Sox organization, 1948 continued black America's newfound love affair with white major league baseball.

Larry Doby joined the Cleveland Indians in July 1947 to become the first black player in the American League and second in the MLB. By the end of the 1947 season, five black players had made their way to the MLB, including the Red Sox's Dan Bankhead. Then, in July 1948, the legendary Satchel Paige made his first appearance in the MLB for the Cleveland Indians against the St. Louis Browns.[103] Black players were making their mark in the MLB, and the MLB turned to actively recruit the best black players in the Negro leagues. Black newspapers across the country followed Robinson's every move.

Memphis's black citizens could now get an excursion to St. Louis and watch Jackie Robinson play in person. The best black players were no longer competing against the Red Sox at Martin Stadium. Instead, they competed in the major leagues against the best white baseball players. Attendance figures for the 1948 season at Martin Stadium echoed declining attendance across the Negro leagues. For the Martin brothers, renovating the stadium at the height of Negro leagues play during World War II seemed like a solid business decision. Unfortunately, the desegregation of professional baseball doomed the economic paradigm that allowed for heightened success during World War II.

Racial uplift and activism shifted away from Republicanism by 1940 and towards a more active and vocal resistance in the city. Boss Crump refused to allow the Freedom Train, seen as a weapon in the global struggle between dictatorship and democracy by progressives across the nation, to stop in Memphis because of desegregated viewing, which led to a debate over freedom in the Bluff City. A group of black students from LeMoyne-Owen College voiced their disapproval by traveling the eighty miles to Jackson, Tennessee, to view the train's exhibits. However, this group comprised only a small percentage of blacks in the city.

In the coming 1948 elections, residents of black working-class neighborhoods registered protest votes against Crump candidates and

The Memphis Red Sox

their conception of freedom.[104] W.S. Martin's acceptance of the Crump machine and its segregated policies quickly became outdated. His assimilationist policies represented an era when blacks waited quietly for their piece of freedom. At the same time, Boss Crump clarified his racial position in the 1948 presidential election by declaring his support for the third-party Dixiecrat candidate, South Carolinian Strom Thurmond.[105] Sitting on the precipice of the civil rights movement of the 1950s, Negro leagues baseball maintained segregation patterns as the black community began to define freedom through the lens of integration.

White baseball continued to siphon off the best talent. W.S. Martin reinstituted the Memphis Blues as its farm club to offset the loss of talent to white baseball. The Martins still saw significant losses at the gate during the 1950 season. The sale of Bob Boyd's contract to the Chicago White Sox helped to defray Martin's mounting losses.[106] Following the 1951 season, longtime Martin family friend Thomas Hayes, Jr., sold his interest in the Black Barons. This left only six teams in the Negro American League in 1951, and by 1953 the league continued to push on with only four teams.

The death of Boss Crump in 1954 signaled the city's end of an era politically. For the Martin family, it was now safe for exiled brother and Negro American League president J.B. Martin to return home to Memphis. Accordingly, the *Memphis World* announced that J.B. Martin would throw out the season's first pitch at Martin Stadium.[107] For J.B.'s older brother W.S., 1955 became the crowning jewel in his long career as a physician in the city. A new 50-bed facility opened in North Memphis with W.S. as president and his common-law wife Eva Cartman as the superintendent. A staff of twenty-eight white and twenty-three black physicians maintained the newly constructed hospital. The city's progressive newspaper, the *Press-Scimitar*, quoted W.S. Martin saying "This new institution is a dream come true for me."[108] With the state of Negro baseball floundering around the country, W.S. Martin turned his attention more and more to the operation of the Collins Chapel Hospital. With W.S. Martin's health waning, he missed the annual league meeting in April 1958 before dying in May 1958.[109]

Left in the hands of the youngest Martin brother, B.B. Martin, the team struggled to survive in a business of a bygone era. By 1959, the team began playing all its games away from Martin Stadium. B.B., scorned by crowds as small as 400 for Sunday afternoon doubleheaders, further alienated himself and the organization from the city's black community when he refused to allow Martin Luther King, Jr., and

3. Black Owned and Operated

Mahalia Jackson in front of the W.C. Handy Statue, 1960. When B.B. Martin denied singer and political activist Mahalia Jackson's usage of Martin Stadium for civil rights activism in 1959, it marked an end of an era in the city (George Lee Collection, Memphis Public Library).

singer Mahalia Jackson to use the stadium for a political rally in July.[110] The black community questioned why B.B. Martin would not let members of the black community use the stadium. No longer the city's central space for political activism, Martin Stadium stood as a relic of a

The Memphis Red Sox

previous time. A fire that destroyed Russwood Park, home of the white minor league Memphis Chicks, diminished the city's 1960 white minor league baseball hopes.[111]

Unwilling to cross the imaginary line of segregation, the Chicks never sought to rent Martin Stadium from B.B. Martin. Martin still owed money on the mortgage for the stadium, in addition to losses totaling over $12,000 for the 1959 season, thus forcing him to put the team, the bus, the uniforms, and the stadium up for sale.[112] In 1960, B.B. Martin sold the stadium to F.A. Maddox, Sr., the president of Tri-State Mack Distributors, as the site for a truck distribution center. Maddox paid $110,000 for the property and the stadium, a far cry from the $300,000 it was appraised for two years earlier.[113] For the first time since 1928, the Martin brothers were no longer associated with professional baseball in Memphis. Their tenure also signaled the end of black professional baseball in the Bluff City.

* * *

Throughout Negro leagues baseball history, R.S. Lewis and the Martins are iconic members who forged one of the most financially secure and longest-tenured franchises. Next to the Birmingham Black Barons, the Memphis Red Sox remains the most prominent Southern franchise of that era. Without the guidance of the Martins, the Black Barons' most celebrated owner, Memphian Thomas Hayes, might not even have sought its ownership—ownership that revitalized that club's existence after an earlier demise. The strength of the story of these men speaks to the unique construction of Negro leagues baseball in the South. Unlike its Eastern and Midwestern counterparts, Negro leagues baseball in the South existed within the constructs of segregation at the height of Jim Crow. Yet, they built an organization that flourished. They did so within the conceptual framework of Booker T. Washington's idea of self-reliance. As members of the city's black bourgeoisie, they lent their respectability to the Red Sox.

4

The 1938 Championship Season

Mediocrity defined the Memphis ball club throughout the Negro leagues era. In the twenty seasons listed by Gary Ashwill on the Seamheads Negro Leagues site, their overall winning percentage is .412.[1] Winning seasons like 1926 dot the team's history as anomalies, but after securing the second-half pennant of the Negro Southern League, the Red Sox dropped a ten-game playoff to the Birmingham Black Barons.[2] Four years earlier, the *Commercial Appeal* proclaimed the Red Sox the 1922 NSL Champions in a controversial and disputed claim to the league championship. The nature of published statistics and standings in the Negro leagues creates dilemmas not only for historians researching the period but its inconsistencies led to multiple claims to league championships.

According to Negro Southern League historian William J. Plott, the Nashville Elite Giants and the Knoxville Giants finished before the Red Sox, in 1922.[3] Yet, the *Commercial Appeal* referred to the Red Sox as the winners of the Negro Southern League and that they would "soon take on Dallas in a seven-game series to determine the negro championship of the South." The *Commercial Appeal* only published a single result in the series, a 6–2 victory by the Red Sox.[4] Inconsistencies in reporting and tabulating box scores left Blackball fans in the Bluff City believing they were champions of the NSL and plausibly the champions of the "Negro Southern World Series."

Déjà vu struck again in 1933 after the Red Sox claimed the first-half championship in the Negro Southern League. The New Orleans Crescent Stars claimed the second-half title but, in a unique twist, played the Houston Black Buffalos of the Negro Texas League in a Negro Dixie Series.[5] To further complicate the playoff picture in the NSL, the *Nashville Banner* proclaimed that the Nashville Elite Giants would be opening a championship series with the New Orleans Crescents.[6] Not to be outdone, the *Arkansas Gazette* posited their version claiming that the

The Memphis Red Sox

Little Rock Stars were to travel to Memphis to play the Red Sox for the NSL title.[7] Unfortunately, the Red Sox vs. Stars game yielded no media coverage.

Of the three scenarios, the New Orleans Crescents recorded victories over the Nashville Elite Giants before defeating Rube Foster's Chicago American Giants in what the *Times-Picayune* of New Orleans labeled the Negro World Series.[8] Left at the altar as bridesmaids again in 1935, the Red Sox claimed the first-half championship before falling to their rival across the Mississippi River in Arkansas, the Claybrook Tigers.[9] The Red Sox's move to the Negro American League in 1937 provided the impetus for J.B. Martin to assemble a more potent lineup capable of capturing a championship in one of the two Negro major leagues.

Following their seventh-place finish during their inaugural 1937 season in the Negro American League, Martin took advantage of the economic collapse of the Cincinnati Tigers club to bolster the Red Sox roster. The Martins purchased the entire Cincinnati Tigers ballclub from owner DeHart Hubbard following the 1937 season. In their only NAL season, the Tigers finished behind perennial powers Kansas City Monarchs and Chicago American Giants. Hubbard, Olympic gold medalist in 1924 at the Paris Olympic Games, was hemorrhaging money as the team's owner. Ted "Double-Duty" Radcliffe managed the Tigers' successful 1937 campaign.[10]

The Tigers finished with the second-best overall record, despite losing the first half to the Monarchs and the second-half title to the American Giants. Hubbard desperately needed the playoff money to keep the Tigers afloat economically. Without the lucrative income from playoff baseball, the native Cincinnatian, Hubbard, could no longer justify club ownership. Using discarded Cincinnati Reds jerseys became the least of his worries.[11] J.B. Martin's influence as president of the Negro Southern League in 1935, where the Tigers played their first two seasons of organized league play, made him privy to the financial plight of Hubbard. Thus when Hubbard looked to unload the team financially, Martin was a trusted confidant. Eager to bring a winner to Memphis, J.B. Martin set out to bring most of the Tigers roster to Memphis.

The Red Sox acquired one of the best pitching staffs in the Negro American League when they purchased the Tigers. The Tigers' 1937 league ERA ranked second in the NAL and second in strikeout percentage. They also led the NAL in strikeout-to-walk ratio, WHIP (Walks plus Hits per Inning Pitched), and base-on-balls percentage.[12] "Double Duty's"

4. The 1938 Championship Season

reputation as one of the best pitchers in the Negro leagues preceded him. Adding sidearm hurler Porter "Ankleball" Moss vastly improved the Red Sox's pitching rotation. This submariner led the Red Sox in games started and completed in 1938. Joining Moss were Eugene Brewer and Willie Jefferson. Jefferson would emerge as the Red Sox ace.

The Martins then replaced "Goose" Curry as manager for the 1938 season. "Double Duty's" familiarity with the Tigers made him the logical choice as player-manager. Radcliffe also brought Neil "Shadow" Robinson, Olan "Jelly" Taylor, and Marlin "Pee Wee" Carter to Memphis from Cincinnati.[13] Following the influx of Tigers players to Memphis, this revamped Red Sox lineup set out to win a championship like no other team in club history had done. The narrative includes brief introductions for thirteen members of the 1938 championship squad.

DeHart Hubbard, an Olympic track star, owned the Cincinnati Tigers that played in the NSL and the NAL leagues. Following the 1937 NAL season, he sold the team and its players to J.B. Martin, forming the nucleus of the Red Sox 1938 NAL championship team (University of Michigan Library).

Mgr/P/C—Ted "Double Duty" Radcliffe

One of the most charismatic figures in Negro leagues baseball, "Double Duty" earned his nickname in 1932 when Damon Runyon of the *New York American* wrote, "It's worth the admission price of two to see 'Double Duty' Radcliffe."[14] Radcliffe's performance saw him catch Leroy "Satchel" Paige in the first half of a doubleheader and then pitch the second game in the Negro Leagues World Series games played at Yankee Stadium for the Pittsburgh Crawfords. Negro leagues historian James Riley labeled Radcliffe as one of the most colorful players in black baseball.[15]

The Memphis Red Sox

Radcliffe later claimed that catching Satch was "like trying to catch a freight train barreling at you with the brakes gone bad."[16] According to former Negro leaguer Dick Seay, he kept his teammates in stitches. "Down in Mexico, he told the owner, his mother died twice. He wanted to go back to Chicago and wanted a little advance, so he said his mother died. The owner said, 'I thought you said she died last month!'"[17] Matched only by the embellishment of his exploits on and off the field, Radcliffe's outlandish reminiscences remain entertaining.

Radcliffe was quick to jump teams if the money was better elsewhere. Following his stops for three seasons provides insight into how players controlled their destinies in Blackball. In 1931 Radcliffe played for Cum Posey's Homestead Grays as part of what many historians label as one of the greatest teams of all time. The following season he jumped across town to the Pittsburgh Crawfords, run by well-known numbers king Gus Greenlee. In 1933 "Double Duty" played for three different clubs. He started with the Columbus Blue Birds, and when the owner could not make payroll, he jumped to the New York Black Yankees owned by Harlem entertainer Bill "Bojangles" Robinson. Then Radcliffe headed to Jamestown, North Dakota, lured by a semi-pro team amid a heated rivalry with Bismarck, North Dakota. Rare for this era of baseball, both teams employed Negro leagues players on their rosters with white players.[18]

Each time Radcliffe left for more money. Bringing "Double Duty" to Memphis was risky because he risked flight for better pay. In his memoir, Radcliffe labeled the Martin brothers "cheaper than a sheepskin. They had players making $100 a month, but I wouldn't have no players making less than $250 a month."[19] Bringing in Radcliffe as the club's manager was outside the norm for the Martin brothers. Yet, if he could bring the elusive championship season to the Bluff City, it would be worth it. Radcliffe brought the Red Sox the respect of his fellow teammates, a solid arm, a quality bat, and the ability to catch. Gary Ashwill's statistics for the 1938 Red Sox championship season show that Radcliffe posted the third-best ERA on the team at 3.83 in 47 recorded innings. He hit .293, respectable numbers for a 35-year-old veteran.[20]

Radcliffe enjoyed life on the road as a professional baseball player. However, his "vice" was not liquor but women. Negro leaguer Jake Stephens claimed he "never heard 'Double Duty' swear. He wanted to be where the women were, he might have been a lady's man, but he was no drinker."[21] When "Double Duty" returned to North Dakota in 1935, he joined his friend Satch on the Bismarck team. They shared an aluminum

4. The 1938 Championship Season

trailer on the outskirts of town that he and Paige turned into a den of iniquity. Or, as "Double Duty" himself claimed, "One woman would be goin' in as one would be goin' out."[22] One summer in Bismarck, he kept company with one female friend for seventeen days. Radcliffe said, "I told her I was going to marry her, but I never did. I was a hit-and-run man."[23] Only blocks from Beale Street, Martin Stadium, filled with a winner in town, meant that "Double Duty" would be in his element.

* * *

The exhibition season for the '38 Red Sox provided a preview of the success the season would hold for the city. In a preseason interview, new manager "Double Duty" Radcliffe claimed, "Believe me, I'm going to town." The *Pittsburgh Courier* labeled Red Sox sluggers William Haskins, Neil Robinson, and Nat Rogers as the Red Sox Murderer's Row.[24] In their first preseason game, the Red Sox lost to Eastern power Homestead Grays at Martin Stadium on Sunday, April 3. Many powerful Eastern league Negro teams participated in spring training somewhere in the South. As April turned into May, these teams made their way back north by playing teams like the Red Sox on the way.

Josh Gibson's two home runs and a single powered the Grays to the 7–3 victory over the Red Sox in this early April Sunday afternoon matinee.[25] The Grays committed four errors in the game, indicative of an early spring training game. As the season wore on, reporters began referring to the Grays' Josh Gibson, Buck Leonard, Vic Harris, and Jim Williams as "Murderer's Row," as all four hit over .350 by the season's mid-point. The Grays went on to capture both the first and second-half pennants in the Negro National League.[26] A competitive game early in the preseason against the East's most potent team previewed the club's potential for a winning season. Following the loss to the Grays, the Red Sox went on to win ten of the twelve remaining exhibition games.

OF—William "Nat" Rogers

By 1938, Rogers was a fifteen-year veteran of the Negro leagues whose bat solidified the Red Sox battery. Rogers made his mark in the 1927 Negro World Series for the Chicago American Giants, where he hit .400 to lead the Giants to victory over the Bacharach Giants. His championship pedigree included world series championships with the Chicago American Giants in 1927, 1932, and 1933. Hitting out of the three and four holes, Rogers gave the Red Sox the depth in its lineup to compete against Blackball's best. William was one of nine baseball-playing Rogers brothers from Spartanburg, South Carolina. Like many in the Negro leagues, "Nat" began playing in his early teens at fourteen, playing with teams while working various jobs. In 1911, he played with a team in Norcross, Georgia, while working in Atlanta with the railroad as a water boy. The following year he played with the Cincinnati Colored Browns while working in a tannery, and in 1913 he played in Kentucky, where he was laying tracks for the railroad and developing his strong arms and shoulders by driving spikes.

After stops in Kentucky, Pennsylvania, Ohio, Illinois, and Michigan, he landed on the Brooklyn Royals roster in the Negro major leagues in 1923. A hard-nosed player known more for his bat than his defensive prowess, he was a dangerous line-drive hitter who sprayed the ball to all fields.[27] Rogers called Memphis home for thirteen years of his playing career and would remain in the city, working as an elevator operator in Memphis until he died in 1981.[28]

* * *

The weekend after opening with the Grays, the Red Sox welcomed the Baltimore Elite Giants to Martin Stadium. The *Commercial Appeal* lauded the arrival of the Nashville Negro league team to town for the hometown folks who best remembered the team's five-year tenure in Nashville as the Elite Giants. Before moving to Maryland, Tom Wilson's entry into the Negro Southern League played out of Sulphur Dell Park in Nashville, home to the city's white minor league team.[29] Following their victory over the Elite Giants, the Red Sox lost a 10–4 contest against the visiting Philadelphia Stars at Martin Stadium on Easter Sunday, April 17.[30] This game allowed the Martins to identify Red Sox fan favorite Larry Brown's unhappiness as a backup with the Stars. In a few short weeks, the Martins negotiated Brown's release from the Stars and welcomed him back to the Bluff City.

The Red Sox bounced back from the loss to the Stars by sweeping a three-game set from the San Angelo (Texas) Black Sheep Herders, coached by former Red Sox manager Reuben Jones. The first game against the Sheep Herders became a pitcher's duel between the clubs. Eugene Bremer and "Double Duty" teamed to hold the invaders from Texas to one run. Neil "Shadow" Robinson led the hitting attack for the Red Sox with a homer and a double in the game one 3–1 victory. The *Pittsburgh Courier's* Sam Brown labeled Robinson's home run as a

4. The 1938 Championship Season

"prodigious clout over the left field fence."[31] Known best as a park (Martin Stadium) where fly balls went to die because of its deep outfield wall dimensions, Robinson's power merited greater appreciation.

In the second half of the Sunday doubleheader, the Red Sox opened up the flood gates scoring three in the first inning behind the second home run of the day by Robinson and five more in the third inning. Submariner Porter Moss opened the game for the Sox in game two, followed by Radcliffe and Willie Jefferson on the mound to secure the 10–3 win.[32] The Red Sox completed the sweep on Monday. The weekend series with the Black Sheep Herders allowed the West Texas League team to play a club in the NAL. This series also demonstrates the interconnectedness of Negro leagues scheduling as former manager Reuben Jones's willingness to contact the Martin brothers to set up a preseason series—a welcome gate attraction for the Martins, who would bring back Jones to manage the club three more times over the next ten years.[33]

The Red Sox opened May with a two-game sweep against NAL opponent, the Atlanta Black Crackers. In the Sunday afternoon doubleheader, the Sox tallied two one-run victories.[34] They then took three of four from NAL rival the Kansas City Monarchs that began with a doubleheader on May 7. They played the first game in the early afternoon in Jonesboro, Arkansas, that went to the Monarchs 7–1. They then traveled the seventy miles to Memphis and played game two at Martin Stadium. The Red Sox took the second half of this doubleheader and swept the Monarchs the next day with identical scores of 2–1 in both games, to announce their presence at the onset of NAL play.[35]

Porter Moss shined in the first game for the Red Sox, holding the Monarchs to one run on four hits over eight innings. Willie Jefferson toed the rubber for the second game and equaled Moss's performance, going eight innings and only allowing four hits.[36] Then on Tuesday, May 17, the Martins advertised a doubleheader featuring the Chicago American Giants against the Kansas City Monarchs. The winner of the first game would turn around and play the Red Sox in this final game of the preseason. The Monarchs knocked off the American Giants in the opener 4–0 before falling to the Red Sox 8–7 in the nightcap.[37] J.B. Martin capitalized on the drawing power of the Monarchs and American Giants to turn the turnstiles at the gates of Martin Stadium on a Tuesday night.

With the exhibition season complete, the Red Sox held a .769 winning percentage, dropping only three games. Two losses came against Eastern powers, the Homestead Grays and the Philadelphia Stars. The

The Memphis Red Sox

Red Sox success in the preseason spoke well for their impending success in the first half of the Negro American League season. Manager Ted "Double Duty" Radcliffe had the team playing some of the best ball in all of black professional baseball. Winning games was a welcome sight to Memphians, who for years felt the absence of a championship to call their own.

P—Porter "Ankleball" Moss

Following a stellar 1937 campaign in Cincinnati (35–8), Moss moved, with many of his Tigers teammates, to Memphis as part of the 1938 championship season. Moss stood 5'11" when he took the mound with a larger-than-life personality. Negro Leagues Museum President Bob Kendrick described his arm delivery as "so low it dug up the fires of hell, then blew it by hitters throughout Negro leagues baseball."[38] "Double Duty" Radcliffe claimed to discover Moss in a Cincinnati softball league and sign him to a pro contract.[39] Yet, before Radcliffe's tenure with the Tigers, Moss made his professional debut in a one-game appearance with the Indianapolis ABCs in 1932 under the winningest manager in Negro leagues history, "Candy" Jim Taylor.[40]

The following year, the young Moss pitched for the Goodyear Shoe Repair semi-pro team. In back-to-back starts, he struck out 15 batters on his way to becoming the most prominent pitcher in Cincinnati.[41] Moss officially joined the Tigers during the 1934 season. He went undefeated in the three reported games he pitched during 1936, placing him among the best pitchers in the Negro Southern League.[42] Moss was selected for three East-West All-Star games in his career and had the goods to compete with the best in Blackball.

The *Pittsburgh Courier* described Moss as "the sensational curveball artist."[43] Moss plied his craft in the offseason in California in the integrated Californian Winter League. In the winter before the 1938 season, Moss led the league in wins, going 3–0.[44] His submarine style was equally respected among Negro leagues all-stars and white professional players. Murdered on a train carrying the Red Sox back to Memphis from Nashville at the height of his career in 1944, Moss would undoubtedly have been selected again for the East-West game.

Red Sox teammate Marlin "Pee Wee" Carter described Moss as the life of the party on and off the field. Carter claimed that once the opposing team got in town, Moss would go to their hotel and tell

4. The 1938 Championship Season

them what he would do to them the next day when pitching. Then he would go out and do it.⁴⁵ Porter Moss's ability to throw smoke from a low angle where his arm would whip low just above the dirt and flash the white of the ball just above the red of his socks and the black of his shoe leather kept Red Sox opposing hitters on their heels wondering what they were seeing. Even when someone bunted on Moss, his throw over to first was underhand, just like his "ankle ball." His Red Sox teammates recalled Moss standing before Martin Stadium on game days selling tickets. Marlin Carter referred to him as "a showman at heart."⁴⁶ Moss joined Radcliffe in what would become a formidable starting rotation.

First Half—Champions of the NAL

The Negro American League, a descendant of Rube Foster's Negro National League, was in its second season in 1938. The Red Sox were charter members in 1937 and part of the seven-team league that included the Atlanta Black Crackers, Birmingham Black Barons, Chicago American Giants, Indianapolis ABCs, Jacksonville Red Caps, and the Kansas City Monarchs. Advertising in the *Commercial Appeal*, the Red Sox touted the return of former Claybrook Tigers players pitcher George Mitchell and third baseman Johnny Lyles.⁴⁷ Only two years removed from a heated rivalry that nearly saw the Claybrook Tigers overtake the Red Sox for popularity in the city, the return of former Tigers players meant more fans at Martin Stadium. Red Sox fans would remember Mitchell as a strong right-handed pitcher with a big round-house curve and Lyles as a hustler whose efforts in the field and on the basepaths excited the crowd.⁴⁸

The Red Sox bats pounded ten or more hits in each of the first two games as the team cruised past the ABCs. Jefferson and Moss picked up the wins, with Radcliffe behind the plate for both games.⁴⁹ In the series' final game, the Sox exploded for six runs in both the third and fourth innings to secure the game 14–9 and the sweep. The ABCs never got closer than the final five-run deficit, as Red Sox hurler "Lefty" Wilson secured his first win of the season.⁵⁰ The Red Sox opened league play with a sweep and stood atop the NAL standings for the first time in years.

The Memphis Red Sox

P—Woodrow "Lefty" Wilson

The 6'2" lefthander's short Negro leagues career included a three-year stint with the Red Sox. Historian James Riley posited that "Lefty" had average control, a mediocre curve, and change-up, but his fastball lacked sufficient velocity.[51] Wilson finished the season 2–1 with the Red Sox; after his early season victory over the ABCs, he went 1–1 for the season. In essence, Wilson became the guy who faced the local nines as the team went *around the horn* during the week.

* * *

In the wake of their opening series sweep, the Red Sox were due to face the ABCs again in Marianna, Arkansas, but rain canceled the game. Negro leaguers referred to these weekday games as going *around the horn*. They traveled from town to town, playing Negro American League foes or local nines to supplement their salaries. During the 1938 season, J.B. Martin did not send the team out on the road with a statistician. Without a statistician, this created gaps between box scores for the team. A newspaper article often proclaimed that the Red Sox team had won three games in another NAL city before any returns from an exhibition game made the local papers.

Unlike white baseball's American and National Leagues, whose game coverage included box scores and articles carried on the AP and UP press outlets, Negro leagues coverage revolved around local coverage in each club's hometown. Local coverage in Memphis lost the club for two weeks after the rainout in Marianna, Arkansas. The *Commercial Appeal* picked up coverage of the club two weeks later as the team returned from Chicago following a three-game sweep of the American Giants in the Windy City on May 28–May 29. The early June article's purpose leaned more heavily into advertising the arrival of the House of David team to Martin Stadium than the previous three games with the American Giants.

The *Commercial Appeal* included another article proclaiming the Red Sox atop the NAL after winning eleven of the twelve road games since they last played at Martin Stadium on Monday, May 16.[52] The Red Sox quickly disposed of the House of David team 12–2, moving the team's overall record to nineteen and one.[53] Exhibition games like these exposed the power of this Red Sox lineup as they efficiently handled semi-pro competition.

4. The 1938 Championship Season

While in Chicago for this three-game set with the Chicago American Giants, the *Commercial Appeal* announced the signing of fan-favorite Larry Brown to the 1938 roster. The Philadelphia Stars of the Negro National League released Brown, claiming that the warmer climate of Memphis would help his ailing arm. However, Brown's sub-par performance at the plate in 1937 for the Stars, where he hit an abysmal .167, led to the Stars releasing Brown to make way for Bill Perkins to assume full-time catching duties in Philadelphia.[54] Brown returned to Memphis after stints in New York and Philadelphia with various Negro leagues teams in the East. The mainstream white media referred to Brown as one of the best catchers in the Negro leagues.

Brown's last stint with the Red Sox was in 1929. That year he resigned with the Chicago American Giants midway through the season to help aid in their quest for the 1929 Negro world series title. The following season Brown followed the money east to New York, where he played for three years: first as part of John Henry Lloyd's Lincoln Giants, then as part of the Harlem Stars in 1931, and finally with the New York Black Yankees in 1932 under the ownership of Bill "Bojangles" Robinson. Brown moved back to Chicago with the Americans Giants for the following three seasons. In 1936 Ed Bolden, a prominent Negro leagues team owner, signed Brown to replace Hall of Famer Biz Mackey behind the plate for his Philadelphia Stars. Following his designation early in the 1938 season as a backup in Philadelphia, Brown returned to Memphis reinvigorated.

Brown's return to the Bluff City allowed "Double Duty" to relinquish his catching duties and focus primarily on pitching. Radcliffe tossed 151 innings in 1938 with an ERA of 3.34 and an 11–9 overall record.[55] Appreciative of Brown's status in Blackball, Memphis fans welcomed their own back into the fold for the 1938 season. Upon Brown's return to Martin Stadium, the fans greeted him with a celebration between their doubleheader games with the Birmingham Black Barons. Always a fan favorite, the Red Sox faithful loved having one of theirs return.

Brown responded by leading the Red Sox to four straight wins over the Birmingham Black Barons at Martin Stadium.[56] Behind the dish for the opening game of the Negro American League series with the Black Barons, Brown's return allowed Radcliffe to team with "Ankleball" Moss in a 7–6 victory. The Red Sox continued their winning ways in the second game with "Iron Man" Brown behind the dish again as twenty-one-year-old Eugene Bremmer pitched a complete game for the

The Memphis Red Sox

victorious Red Sox.[57] Immediately Brown's impact on the club took the pressure off Radcliffe to be "Double Duty," and it allowed the younger Bremmer to flourish with the veteran Brown controlling the game from behind the plate.

The next day Brown again guided "Lefty" Wilson through a nine-inning affair with the Black Barons.[58] Unfortunately, Wilson's pitching repertoire was lacking, but with his fate in the hands of the crafty veteran behind home plate, Brown gave Wilson his second and last win of the season. Finally, the Red Sox and Black Barons jumped on the road, went *around the horn*, and recorded a 5–1 Red Sox exhibition victory in Clarksdale, Mississippi.[59]

Traveling south on Mississippi Route 61 to Clarksdale brought both teams into the Mississippi Delta's heartland. According to historian Laurie Green, beginning in the New Deal Era of the 1930s, boundaries distinguishing the urban and rural South became more porous. Although a large portion of migrants moved to cities farther North, many headed to cities like Memphis. Music, radio, religion, and politics cross this rural-urban divide.[60] Baseball acted as a conduit of cultural exchange between small towns throughout the Delta. Taking in a baseball game gave many in the Delta a brief glimpse into city life in Memphis.

P—Eugene Bremmer

Throughout a productive seventeen-year career, Bremmer remained one of the best fielding pitchers in Blackball, with an excellent overhand curve and the ability to utilize a no-windup delivery. Bremmer was another carryover joining the Red Sox in 1938 after a successful 1937 season in Cincinnati with the Tigers.[61] Only twenty-one during the 1938 championship season, his 4–0 mark in 1937 left him as one of Radcliffe's favorites at the onset of the season.

* * *

Early in the season, owner J.B. Martin filed a grievance with Negro National League President Gus Greenlee over three players approached by associate NNL member Buffalo Bisons (N.Y.). Martin claimed that while the Buffalo club trained in Marianna, Arkansas, during the spring, the team's manager drove to Memphis and attempted to sign three players away from the Red Sox, breaking a written agreement between the NNL

4. The 1938 Championship Season

and the Negro American League. Cumberland Posey announced in his "Posey's Corner" in the *Pittsburgh Courier* that the NNL had already agreed by letter to the NAL not to touch NAL players but had not yet received the same from the NAL concerning NNL players.[62] Disputes like these symbolized one of the significant weaknesses of Blackball. Unlike white professional baseball's reserve clause, the players could negotiate with owners and managers from other teams, often unscrupulously. Owners like the Martins had little or no recourse to protect their investments.

P—Willie Jefferson

Jefferson, a brilliant pitcher with good breaking pitches, joined his Cincinnati Tiger teammates in their move to the Bluff City. Standing 5'9" tall, the Clearview, Oklahoma, native made his professional debut with the Claybrook Tigers in 1936.[63] Radcliffe credits himself with signing Foster to the Tigers. In another "Double Duty-ism," Radcliffe claimed he signed Jefferson out of jail. Supposedly, Jefferson was in prison for speeding, and Radcliffe encouraged John C. Claybrook to give the warden $300 to get him out of jail.[64] Jefferson's signing by Radcliffe is a problematic piece of the oral history of the Negro leagues.

Nevertheless, it provides insight into the Jim Crow world these players lived and played. Overshadowed by Porter Moss and Radcliffe's personalities, Jefferson became the ace of the 1938 staff with a 3.54 ERA.[65] Jefferson played professional Blackball for another eight years after being a part of the Red Sox championship season. Then, at age 41, he combined with his younger brother George to lead the Cleveland Buckeyes to the 1945 Negro American League championship, posting a record of 9–1 and a 1.57 ERA. Jefferson's commanding performance in game one of the 1945 Negro world series against the Homestead Grays gave the Buckeyes the opening-game win in their four-game sweep of the Grays.[66]

* * *

Early June saw the return of the Chicago American Giants to Memphis. The Martins capitalized on the return of former Red Sox manager "Candy" Jim Taylor, arguably the most prolific manager in the history of Blackball. Taylor's career as a manager and player spanned forty-five years and included more than 955 documented wins, a Negro National

The Memphis Red Sox

League pennant in 1926 with the St. Louis Stars, and two Negro World Series Championships with the Homestead Grays in 1943 and 1944. Considered by most to be a master strategist with a keen eye for identifying young talent,[67] many believe Taylor's greatest miss on talent occurred during his one-year tenure in Memphis. Taylor misjudged a young player out of Pittsburgh named Josh Gibson.

While managing a Red Sox exhibition game in Scranton, Pennsylvania, he picked up the young Gibson and proclaimed that "he would never be a catcher."[68] Gibson became a larger-than-life player with the Homestead Grays and the second Negro leagues player to be inducted into the National Baseball Hall of Fame in 1972. With his slight of Gibson aside, Taylor became one of the most respected managers in Blackball. A baseball lifer, Taylor never married, and during his career, he played with, managed, or managed-against every notable player in segregated baseball.[69]

The *Commercial Appeal* trumpeted the Chicago American Giants as a legitimate challenge for the Red Sox in this series. In previewing the game, the *Commercial Appeal* noted the American Giants' 17-game win streak, which signaled a desire by the invaders from Chicago to displace the Red Sox as the NAL's premier club.[70] The first game lived up to the hype in a twelve-inning affair that ended in a 4–4 draw. The second game saw "Ankleball" Moss take the mound for the Red Sox, and he delivered a complete game 5–3 victory in game one of the Sunday doubleheader. The Red Sox repeated their 5–3 win over the American Giants in the second game behind the pitching of Willie Jefferson and "Double Duty" Radcliffe.[71]

OF—Lloyd "Ducky" Davenport

Standing at a mere 5'4" was a left-handed outfielder with outstanding speed. Extremely fast out of the box, Davenport utilized his speed in both the field and on the base paths. Ranging left field for the Red Sox in 1938, he possessed a strong arm to go with his amazing range as an outfielder. Davenport earned the nickname "Ducky" because of his distinctive walk. Only twenty-six years old during the 1938 season, Davenport made five appearances in the East-West All-Star Game. Another of Radcliffe's players from Cincinnati, "Ducky" joined the Red Sox for the 1938 campaign. Davenport returned to Memphis for the 1939 season before bolting for the Mexican League and more money in 1940.[72]

4. *The 1938 Championship Season*

* * *

By mid–June, the Red Sox remained in the hunt for the first-half pennant. But, unlike previous years when the team faded, the 1938 club continued its winning ways. Hosting the Atlanta Black Crackers the last weekend of June allowed the Red Sox to strengthen their hold on the first-half pennant. Heading into this three-game set at Martin Stadium, the Red Sox held a game-and-a-half lead in the Negro American League. The winning ways of the Red Sox began to garner attention from the city's white baseball fans. The *Commercial Appeal* noted that "a section will be reserved for white patrons."[73] In this strictly segregated Southern city, for the Negro franchise to gain the respect of baseball fans on both sides of the color line speaks to the impact sport can have in uniting the city, albeit for the brief time they are together at the ballpark.

Thirty-five years later, a duo of young African American basketball players, Larry Finch and Ronnie Robinson from Orange Mound, would bring the Bluff City together at the Mid–South Coliseum during the Memphis State University basketball team's run to the 1973 NCAA championship game. But in 1938, baseball was America's pastime, and it was the game that brought Memphians together. In front of this bi-racial crowd at Martin Stadium on Sunday afternoon, the Red Sox defeated the Black Crackers 3–2 and 4–2. The Sox completed their sweep of the Crackers with a 6–4 victory on "Ladies' Night" under the lights at Martin Stadium the following day.[74]

Heading into a weekend series in early July with the Kansas City Monarchs, the Red Sox maintained a game-and-a-half lead over the Monarchs. On Sunday afternoon, the teams split a doubleheader at Ruppert Stadium in Kansas City, with the Red Sox losing the first game and then winning the second.[75] The opening game on July 3 went to the home-standing Monarchs, who held off a late charge by the Red Sox in extra innings. Former Red Sox "Buck" O'Neil scored the go-ahead run in the bottom of the eleventh after reaching on an error. In the second game, Neil "Shadow" Robinson doubled to open the sixth inning. "Double Duty" followed with a walk to put runners on first and second. On the ensuing hit to the outfield, Monarch outfielders Willard Brown and Eldridge Mayweather collided with each other at full speed, allowing Radcliffe and Robinson to score. The Red Sox tacked on two more in the inning, winning game two 7–3.[76] With the first-half pennant all but secured, the Red Sox looked to solidify their standing the next day.

This July 4 showcased the prowess of Red Sox slugger Neil "Shadow"

The Memphis Red Sox

More than 50,000 Negro leagues fans gathered at Comiskey Park for the 1940 East-West ASG. Neil "Shadow" Robinson started in CF and was joined by teammates Larry Brown (C), Olan Taylor (1B), and Gene Bremer (P) (T.H. Hayes Collection, Memphis Public Library).

Robinson. Robinson doubled twice and tripled once to spark the offense for the visiting Red Sox. Robinson's fireworks propelled the Red Sox to a 12–5 victory over the home-standing Monarchs and secured the first-half pennant. The most dominant half of baseball that the Red Sox ever produced resulted in a 21–4 record in the Negro American League, a .840 winning percentage.[77] By clinching the first-half pennant, the Red Sox secured a spot in the NAL playoffs at the end of the season. To keep fans coming through the gates, the Negro American League, like the other Negro leagues, employed a format with two halves of the season, each with a pennant winner, followed by a playoff series at the end of the season to determine a league champion.

1B—Olan "Jelly" Taylor

Noted more for his fancy fielding than for his hitting, he kept the fans entertained with his comical antics and flashy glovework. He earned the nickname "Jelly" as a shorter rotund man with short arms,

4. The 1938 Championship Season

his appearance belying his ability on the field. According to historian James Riley, Olan also earned the nickname "Satan" because he played like the devil. But, his mother disapproved of the nickname, so "Jelly" stuck.[78] Not only did Taylor command the field defensively at first, but he also hit a respectable .297 during the '38 championship season.[79] "Jelly" made three East-West All-Star game appearances from 1939 to 1941 with the Red Sox. West manager "Candy" Jim Taylor inserted Jelly into the starting lineup in the 1941 game when he finished second in all-star balloting for first base behind only "Buck" Leonard of the Homestead Grays. "Jelly" produced, going one for two at the plate.[80] "Jelly" spent the remainder of his career in Memphis as a Red Sox through the 1946 season. After the Japanese attack on Pearl Harbor, he was one of the first Negro leagues players inducted into the Army in World War II. When he returned from military service, he was named player-manager of the Red Sox for the 1946 season, his last in professional baseball.[81]

* * *

The dog days of July brought the woes to the team after they clinched the pennant for the first half. The Red Sox opened the second half of the season in Chicago and immediately dropped a doubleheader to the American Giants.[82] The pitching that carried them through the first half began withering in the July heat. Following a weekend series with the Chicago American Giants in the Windy City, the Red Sox stayed in Chicago to meet the Cuban Stars at Shewbridge Field, home to the University of Chicago football team. Previewed as a clash of top "semi-pro" teams, the *Daily Calumet's* take on the game provides valuable insight into how white newspapers portrayed Negro leagues baseball as less than major-league caliber.[83] Yet, they proclaimed that "Cannonball" Moss, the scheduled starter for the game, ranked with Satchel Paige in Negro baseball history. They also trumpeted the Red Sox's 47 victories in 54 games played.[84]

S.S.—Cornelius Neil "Shadow" Robinson

"Shadow" had a powerful swing, placing him among the game's best power hitters. During the 1938 campaign, he played shortstop for the Red Sox, but throughout his career, he's best known for his work patrolling the outfield in center. Robinson played in nine East-West All-Star games, batting .476 and slugging at .876, which included two

The Memphis Red Sox

home runs; these are All-Star totals exceeded only by Hall of Famer "Buck" Leonard. "Shadow" won back-to-back home run titles for the Red Sox during the 1938 championship season and 1939.[85] Robinson's three-run home run in the 1938 East-West All-Star game in front of 30,000 fans at Comiskey Park sparked the West's rally and made him the game's hero, according to the *Chicago Defender*.[86] Robinson's frequent trips to the East-West All-Star game validate his talent. Yet, playing in Memphis, a smaller Southern market, away from the nation's most prominent black periodicals like the *Amsterdam News* (NYC), *Pittsburgh Courier, Chicago Defender,* and the *Baltimore Afro-American,* he never received the accolades of sluggers Josh Gibson, Oscar Charleston or George "Mule" Suttles.

* * *

With a spot secured in the Negro American League playoffs, the dog days of summer led to a paltry 8–15 record in the second half of the season.[87] Amid their July struggles in league play, the Red Sox embarked on a barnstorming tour to capitalize on their success from the first half against the Negro National League's preeminent power, the Homestead Grays. The tour's highlight would be a doubleheader at Yankee Stadium on Sunday, July 31. They opened play against the Grays on July 27 in Beckley, West Virginia, losing a close game 8–9. This series-opening game provided the most excitement for fans, going twelve innings before the Grays could finish off the Red Sox.[88] Following the extra-inning affair, the two teams jumped on the bus for the two-hundred-mile trek north to Zanesville, Ohio, for the Thursday game.

Once again, the Red Sox battled the Grays closely, this time for five innings, before slugger Josh Gibson opened a barrage of four home runs. Gibson's hitting exhibition powered the Grays to ten runs in the sixth inning en route to a 17–4 victory for the Grays.[89] Even in this small town just east of Columbus, the Gibson myth grew and again overshadowed Red Sox stars Larry Brown and Neil Robinson.

As was the norm in these Negro leagues' *around the horn* series, the Grays and Red Sox continued to New York City with a stop in Middleton, Pennsylvania. In front of 15,000 fans, the Red Sox fell to the Grays. Again, the local newspaper highlighted the exploits of Josh Gibson and "Double Duty" Radcliffe in their coverage. Yet, in a rare instance, veteran catcher Larry Brown received mention ahead of the four o'clock game at Grandview Park.[90] Touched up for three runs on six hits, Radcliffe never made it out of the first inning in this marquee matchup of

4. The 1938 Championship Season

the series. Raymond Brown kept the Red Sox at bay, scattering ten hits over nine innings but only yielding one run to the champions from the South.[91] By the end of this game and series, the preeminent team in all of Blackball in 1938 remained the Homestead Grays.

3B—Marlin "Pee Wee" Carter

The 5'7" Carter, a native of Haslam, Texas, had jumped the Red Sox following the 1934 season to join the Cincinnati Tigers. He returned to Memphis in 1938 and stayed for the next ten years except for three years in the U.S. Coast Guard during World War II. A right-handed throwing defender, Carter turned around and hit from the left side. A lifetime .256 hitter, Carter hit out of the one or two holes.[92] Carter was a dangerous hitter who earned two trips to the East-West All-Star game during his career. During the 1938 championship season, he anchored the hot corner for the Red Sox but also saw time at second base throughout his career. Carter claimed one of the highlights of his career was hitting a single right back up the middle against Satchel Paige of the Pittsburgh Crawfords as a rookie for the Monroe Monarchs of the NSL.[93]

Following the 1939 season, Carter headed west and played in the integrated California Winter League, joining Mule Settles on the Royal Giants roster and claiming the league championship.[94] After Jackie Robinson integrated baseball in 1946, Carter played two seasons with the minor-league Rochester Royals (A) of the Southern Minnesota League.[95] Memphians may remember Carter as the head locker room attendant at the Colonial Country Club, where he worked from 1972 until he died in 1993.[96]

* * *

Thankfully for the Red Sox, they finally arrived in New York City on July 31 to play at the Polo Grounds. The *New York Age* labeled the doubleheader as a clash between the Southern champions and the Negro National League champions. The Birmingham Black Barons squared off against the Newark Eagles in the matinee, followed by the Red Sox taking on the Grays in the nightcap. The winner of the final game would take home the Dunbar Loving Brothers Cup, purportedly the largest ever given at a Negro sporting event. The *New York Age* admitted to the success of the Red Sox in the South but asked whether they could compete with the Grays' all-star caliber players.[97] During this week of exhibition games, the Grays proved their prominence. Wendell Smith of the *Pittsburgh Courier* summed it best when he said, "The Memphis Red Sox, winners of Negro American League's first half, had a tough time of it with the Grays."[98]

While on their trek to New York City, the Red Sox announced the "greatest baseball matchups" of the season in the *Pittsburgh Courier*. Joining with Henry L. Moore (Black Barons), Thomas Wilson (Elite Giants), and J.L. Wilkerson (Monarchs), the Martins continued to market the club's first-half success. The twin-billing matched the Red Sox against the Monarchs, followed by the Baltimore Elite Giants taking on the Black Barons. They scheduled these matchups first in Birmingham at Rickwood Stadium on August 7, followed by the same doubleheader lineup at Martin Stadium on August 8.[99] Although the series with the Grays brought financial gains for the club, the Red Sox niche remained in the South.

In another unique twist, the Birmingham Barons did not return to Birmingham in time for the August 7 game, so the Red Sox played both halves of the doubleheader, defeating the Monarchs and dropping the nightcap to the Elite Giants.[100] On the scheduled return trip to Memphis at Martin Stadium, the Sox defeated the Black Barons under the lights. Historian Leslie Heaphy contends that by the 1930s, Negro leagues teams learned how to book games to bring in the most money. They knew which clubs brought the biggest crowds and which cities were better baseball cities.[101] Even as the club toiled through late summer in Negro American League play, it was paramount for the organization's financial stability for the exhibition series with the Grays and the scheduled doubleheader with their Southern colleagues.

OF—Cowan "Bubba" Hyde

Hyde ignited the Red Sox offense on the base paths, was an exceptional baserunner and could run a baseball down backward as fast as anyone in Blackball. Hyde spent half his career in Memphis with the Red Sox, playing twelve seasons with the club. In 1938, Hyde roamed left field for the Sox, the same position he played the year before for Radcliffe in Cincinnati. With his speed, Hyde led off during the 1938 season and rarely walked. He graduated from Morris Brown College, an HBCU in Atlanta, Georgia, where he played football and baseball, despite his smaller stature at 5'8" and 150 pounds.

4. The 1938 Championship Season

The Monarchs and Red Sox met again in late September in Lincoln, Nebraska, in an exhibition game. The *Nebraska State Journal* billed the game as a potential Negro American League playoff matchup, claiming that two Atlanta Black Cracker wins over the Monarchs were being protested to allow the Monarchs to claim the pennant for the second half.[102] Unfortunately, the ownership's focus during the second half of the NAL season remained on profiting from the club's first-half success, not on adding players for the season's stretch run. As a result, Radcliffe and the Red Sox limped to the end of the regular season. With no record of the NAL league office ever confirming the Kansas City Monarch's protest, the Atlanta Black Crackers claimed the second-half pennant. With the league office denying the Monarchs' claim to the second-half pennant, the Red Sox prepared for the NAL championship series against the Atlanta Black Crackers.

Negro American League Championship Series

The 1938 Atlanta Black Crackers played their home games at Ponce de Leon Park, famous for a colossal Magnolia tree in right-centerfield. The Negro American League Black Crackers shared the park with the independent minor league club, the Atlanta Crackers. The Magnolia tree remains above a bank of kudzu behind the stores in a strip mall where the outfield once stood.[103] Originally known as the Atlanta Cubs, the original Black Crackers were a composite of local nines from Moorehouse, Morris Brown, and Clark Colleges in Atlanta.[104] When the white Atlanta Crackers were away on road trips, the blacks played at Morehouse College and Morris Brown College. The white Crackers donated the team's uniforms, bats, baseballs, and other supplies.[105] At the onset of the 1938 Negro American League season, the Atlanta fans voted to change their club's name to the Red Sox. However, NAL president R.R. Jackson asked the Atlanta team to vacate the Red Sox name change due to conflict with the longstanding Memphis Red Sox.[106] Not only were the Memphis Red Sox competing for the NAL championship, but also, in essence, to secure their claim to the club moniker as the Red Sox.

2B—Wyman "Red" Longley

A versatile player, Longley played numerous positions in his eighteen-year professional career. He fielded each of his positions

The Memphis Red Sox

adequately and, during the 1938 campaign, anchored second base for the Sox. Longley also protected Neil "Shadow" Robinson by hitting sixth in the lineup, where his ability to hit the long ball forced pitchers to throw to Robinson.[107]

* * *

Like the Memphis Red Sox, the Black Crackers were looking for their franchise's first championship in 1938—a longstanding member of the Negro Southern League, like the Red Sox. The Black Crackers had recently reorganized under the ownership of the Reverend John Harden. The team spent the 1937 season barnstorming and, in 1938, was invited to join the Negro American League.[108] The *Sheboygan Press* (Wisconsin) described the 1938 Black Cracker squad as "a team that possesses small, but speedy ball hawks, whose keen eye at the plate make them dangerous hitters at all times, even if they do not have the sheer power that nines like to depend on."[109] Led by a trio of players, first baseman Red Moore, shortstop "Pee Wee" Butts, and catcher Joe "Pig" Greene, the 1938 Black Crackers beat out the Kansas City Monarchs for the second-half pennant of the NAL. The Atlanta Black Crackers finished the NAL season, winning four in a row from Kansas City and four more from the Red Sox.[110] Gabby Kemp managed the club, a solid second baseman who, with "Pee Wee" Butts, shored up the middle of the infield for the Black Crackers.[111]

Left off the 1938 East-West All-Star Game selections, Butts, Kemp, and Moore felt slighted, considering they conquered the Negro American League's second-half pennant.[112] Yet, the Black Crackers presented a formidable opponent for the Red Sox in the championship series. Negro leagues historian James Riley described Ross Moore as a superb, fancy-fielding first baseman who added finesse to a team, an expert at handling ground balls, a master at catching bad throws and making it look easy, and he excelled at making a 3–6–3 double-play. Moore liked to showboat and was a crowd favorite, frequently taking throws behind his back and making other trick catches to entertain fans.

Riley described "Pee Wee" Butts as an outstanding defensive shortstop who could do everything afield, a smooth gloveman with sure hands, exceptional range, and a strong and accurate throwing arm. Greene was a good, durable receiver with a quick release and powerful throwing arm. Offensively, Greene was a fastball-hitting pull hitter with good power. While with the Crackers, Greene earned the nickname "Pig" because of the quantity of food he ate.[113] The Black Crackers'

4. The 1938 Championship Season

talent matched the Red Sox's, and they had just swept the Red Sox to end the season.

The Atlanta Black Crackers finished the Negro American League season, winning eight games in a row to secure the second-half pennant from Kansas City. Entering the series as the hotter of the two teams, the Black Crackers refused to play the NAL championship series games at Martin Stadium. Neither team wanted to play in the other's ballpark. The Black Crackers had lost eight straight games in Memphis, while the Red Sox had lost five in a row in Atlanta.[114] Protests aside, the series was scheduled to begin on September 18. The opener on Sunday afternoon pitted player/manager "Double Duty" Radcliffe against the Black Crackers' Eddie Dixon. The Red Sox also picked up second-baseman Fred Bankhead and right-fielder David Whatley from the Birmingham Black Barons for the series.[115] Neil "Shadow" Robinson set the tone for the series by smashing two home runs out of Martin Stadium in the opener. Radcliffe toed the rubber for the home team, only allowing one Black Cracker run in the complete game 6–1 victory.[116] The highlight of the series opener for the Black Crackers was the play of first baseman Moore, who caught throws behind his back in between innings during warmups.[117]

Game two of the series pitted the Red Sox's "Ankleball" Moss against Berry "Bubbles" Bubber, a pitcher the Black Crackers signed from the Ethiopian Clowns for the series.[118] Searching for an answer to the potent Red Sox lineup, the Black Crackers tried Bubber, whose only season in Blackball was the 1938 season. He walked four batters, giving up eight runs in three and a third innings as the Red Sox took a commanding lead in the series. On this Monday night, the Black Crackers would get no closer than five runs as the Red Sox took a commanding 2–0 lead in the championship series.[119] Game three, scheduled to take place at Rickwood Stadium in Birmingham on Tuesday, September 20, was never played.

Both teams had agreed on playing this one game in Birmingham and then three more in Atlanta at Ponce de Leon Stadium, and if a seventh game were necessary, they would play at a neutral site.[120] According to NAL president Jackson, the Atlanta Black Crackers arrived at Rickwood Stadium an hour and a half late for game three. Jackson decided it was too late at 8:30 p.m. to start the game and that the umpires should call it off. The white Atlanta Crackers notified the Black Crackers that De Leon Park would not be available Wednesday through Friday. The Black Crackers wanted the series delayed until Sunday. According to the

The Memphis Red Sox

Birmingham News, Dr. B.B. Martin refused to keep the team in Atlanta because of the "heavy expense."[121] At an impasse, the series stopped and would not be resumed.

Baseball historian James Riley asserts that the series "was canceled because of discord between the managements of the two ballclubs."[122] Negro leagues historian Leslie Heaphy posits that the "series ran into financial conflicts, and Negro American League president Dr. R.B. Jackson canceled the series. Jackson claimed neither team was willing to play in the other club's home ballpark."[123] With neither side agreeing, the series ended with the Red Sox holding a 2–0 lead. The Red Sox claimed the 1938 Negro American League championship. After handily losing the first two games, the Black Crackers refused to play the remaining games in the series.

The Martins capitalized on their club's Negro American League championship by hosting the annual North-South All-Star games at Martin Stadium. Winning baseball turned the turnstiles at Martin Stadium, and following their championship series wins over the Black Crackers, they scheduled back-to-back all-star games for October 2 and 3. The Sunday afternoon game saw the home-standing South team defeat the North aggregation 3 to 1. Bluff City fan favorite Larry Brown managed the Southern team. Brown was joined on the team by "Bubba" Hyde (lf), Marlin Carter (3b), Neil "Shadow" Robinson (ss), and Nat Rogers (rf). The Northern team, coached by Biz Mackey, returned the favor and defeated the Southern team 10 to 0.[124]

J.B. Martin and his brothers stood atop Blackball in the South and the Midwest. The Memphis Red Sox garnered the respect of the black national press throughout the season, in this their only championship season. By placing four players on the West squad in the East-West All-Star Game, the Red Sox showed the respect the 1938 championship team earned nationally. Porter Moss and "Double Duty" Radcliffe represented the Red Sox as pitchers. Larry Brown drew the second-highest total votes for a catcher, out tallying Hall of Famers Biz Mackey and Josh Gibson. But the hero of the 1938 East-West All-Star Game was Neil "Shadow" Robinson, whose inside-the-park home run allowed the West team to pull a stunning 5 to 4 come-from-behind victory in front of 30,000 at Comiskey Park in Chicago.[125]

When the 1939 season began, the *Commercial Appeal* declared that the Red Sox, champions of the Negro American League, were ready to open the exhibition season.[126] Current historical records note that the Red Sox were champions for the 1938 NAL season. Seamheads Negro

4. The 1938 Championship Season

Leagues Database and Baseball Reference label the Red Sox as NAL champions. The *Chicago Defender* noted that during the winter meetings in December 1938, the Negro American League recognized the Red Sox as league champions.[127] Although Atlanta Black Crackers fans still debate the merit of the Red Sox's claim to the 1938 NAL championship, the overwhelming historical record points to the Red Sox's claim.

Following the 1938 season, the Black Crackers moved to Indianapolis, Indiana, where they began to play as the Indianapolis ABCs. Financial troubles remained

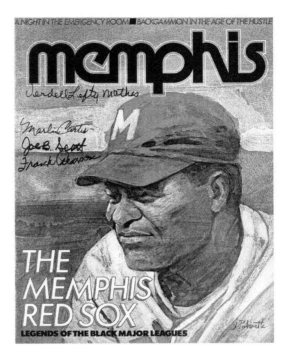

This 1979 *Memphis Magazine* cover displays a painting of Red Sox manager Larry Brown (Author's Collection—Permission from *Memphis Magazine* & John Robinette).

for team owner Harden throughout the 1939 season. Unable to stay financially solvent in Indianapolis, Harden looked to Louisville as an option mid-season. Unfortunately, the Louisville Black Caps resisted sharing their stadium with the ABCs, so Harden returned the team to Atlanta as a barnstorming team.[128] Like many other Negro leagues teams during the Great Depression, the Atlanta Black Crackers struggled to survive financially. On the other hand, the Red Sox remained one of the soundest financial clubs in the Negro American League throughout the remaining years of the Negro leagues era. Although they would never again claim a league championship, the Red Sox remained a pillar of black success in the Bluff City.

5

Boss Crump Ejects J.B. Martin

For black Memphians, professional baseball provided an avenue and space to build racial pride and change white Memphians' perceptions. Martin Stadium at Lewis Park provided a platform outside the black church for political advocacy and stood as a tool of protest against the status quo. It demonstrated black prowess and capability and served as a yardstick of accomplishment.[1] Many of the city's prominent black businesses and political leaders participated in Opening Day ceremonies to gain a larger platform.

J.B. Martin was no different as he tossed out the first pitch in the 1921 season.[2] In the years before the Martin brothers purchased the club, Martin Stadium provided an avenue for Martin and his Republican colleagues to rally political support in the black community. J.B. Martin's political involvement with Robert Church, Jr., precluded any association with the Red Sox. When his political position ran contrary to the city's white political boss, Boss Crump, it cost him dearly. Yet, even after Martin's forced departure from the city, Martin Stadium remained a focal point for political gatherings.

As a member of the Lincoln League, J.B. Martin mobilized the black community politically, starting in the 1920s. The Lincoln League organized political rallies, gave speeches, held large weekly meetings in Church Auditorium, collected donations to pay poll taxes, and eventually registered over 10,000 voters. The group's leader, and arguably the nation's most prominent black politician, Robert Church, Jr., claimed that the league's purpose was "for the race's second emancipation when it would free itself from lynching and Jim Crowism by using the ballot box."[3] Martin's political involvement also included his membership as one of the founding members of the city's NAACP (National Association for the Advancement of Colored People) branch. In addition, Martin helped Church Jr. control the city's black political machine while

5. Boss Crump Ejects J.B. Martin

Church was out of town working on national party issues. Under the social and political caste system prevalent in the city during this era, as long as the Lincoln League, Church and J.B. Martin maintained the expected decorum and deference to Crump's white political machine, they were welcome to coexist.

Longtime Memphis political aficionado George W. Lee described Dr. J.B. Martin as a "man of considerable wealth, but he never displayed it."[4] His South Memphis drugstore served as a gathering place and space for black economic pride in the community. As a member of the Lincoln League, J.B. Martin played an integral role in mobilizing the black community. His influence transcended Memphis. As part of an African American middle class, respected for his business acumen and ability to develop genuine relationships among the black working class, J.B. Martin left an indelible mark on the city. These abilities allowed him to gain a favorable position within Robert Church, Jr.'s black political regime.

When the Martin brothers obtained control of the Red Sox from R.S. Lewis, the previous owner, J.B. Martin controlled one of the city's preeminent spaces for political rallies. Like most politicians, Martin had a knack for communicating with his constituents to make them feel a part of the political process. The city's position in the heart of the Bible Belt meant that local black preachers held a prominent place in the political landscape. By 1924, 107 black churches existed in Memphis. The Church of God in Christ was headquartered in Memphis and became an international presence by the 1930s. Baptist churches and COGIC churches attracted mainly the poor and uneducated, whereas the Methodists served the poor and middle-class black communities.[5]

The black church's prominence in the city's political processes permitted Martin to use his political savvy to convince the black clergy of these gatherings' importance. Martin was on a shortlist of men whose grasp of the political landscape approached that of Robert Church Jr's. As Martin entered the fray of Negro leagues baseball, Memphis's political landscape became even more intricately connected with baseball. As his stature grew nationally within the Negro leagues, locally Martin's successes signaled an attempt to step out of the acceptable caste role that white politicians defined during this era for black men. The year 1940 became a pivotal moment for Martin, the Red Sox, and politics in Memphis.

The 1940 presidential election brought pressure upon the two political giants of Memphis: E.H. "Boss" Crump and Robert Church, Jr., son of the first black millionaire in Memphis and the most recognizable

The Memphis Red Sox

black figure in the Republican Party at the turn of the twentieth century. He believed voting served as the most pragmatic approach for African Americans to obtain full citizenship in this country. By enfranchising thousands of black Southerners and developing a substantial voting constituency, black voters could have their voices heard among the nation's most prominent policymakers.[6]

On the other side of this political struggle stood Edward Hull "Boss" Crump. Crump created one of the country's most influential and diverse political organizations. He employed tactics almost unheard of in the American South by creating a bi-racial, multi-ethnic coalition that brought special interest politics to the Jim Crow South. He changed the face of the Democratic Party in Memphis and throughout the South.[7] As both political giants, one black and one white, faced the 1940 presidential election, the divide between them grew exponentially.

For years, Crump's coalition included Robert Church, Jr., and his black constituents. Yet, by 1940 the Republican Party's power was waning nationally since the election of Democrat Franklin Delano Roosevelt as president in 1932. The black community and Church relied for years upon Republican presidents' patronage to maintain political influence in Jim Crow Memphis. When Church threw his weight behind Republican nominee Wendell Willkie in the 1940 presidential election, Crump declared war upon Church and his political lieutenants, including J.B. Martin.

As a man, Crump held a paternalistic attitude towards black Memphians but met few of their needs. He regarded black citizens as inferior to whites, white men were equal, but black men needed to stay in their place. Crump believed that black Memphians were entitled to some government care and service. He addressed some of their needs, such as building Douglass Park, appointing black medical inspectors in black schools, giving milk to young mothers, and making efforts to end the harassment of black citizens by local officials. Crump honored heroic black citizens T.O. Fuller and Tom Lee.[8]

Black citizens who practiced assimilationist and accommodationist political ideals fared much better in Crump's Memphis. Crump tolerated minor political slights from Church and Martin in the 1920s. When FDR gained control of the White House in 1932, Crump no longer needed the black vote to maintain control of his political machine in the city. Church and Martin became expendable. As blacks remained loyal to their Republican beliefs and men like Church, they experienced increased violence and repression.

5. Boss Crump Ejects J.B. Martin

During the 1940 presidential election, Crump painted Church as ungrateful for the paternalism Crump had bestowed upon him in years past. Crump believed he was as responsible for Church's success as anyone else, yet Church refused to follow Crump's lead in supporting FDR. When Church's Black and Tan faction of the Republican Party supported Republican Wendell Wilkie for president, Crump felt betrayed.[9] Church's betrayal coincided with the 1938 deaths of two of Crump's highest-ranking white lieutenants, Frank Rice and Shelby County attorney general Tyler McLain. Their deaths left a vacuum within the organization and severely restricted Crump's access to untrammeled political advice. Crump increasingly found himself surrounded by men afraid to offer candid opinions.[10]

Robert Church, Jr., faced a political challenge from within the Republican Party. During this era, the Republican Party held two factions. The Black and Tans faction, the African American party branch, included black Republicans and sympathetic whites in the South. The other is the Lily White faction. Since the end of Reconstruction, these whites wrestled with blacks for control of the Republican Party in the South. Lily Whites sought to maintain a segregated Republican Party. In 1920, Church gained control of the party for his Black and Tans faction.[11] However, after the defeat of Herbert Hoover in the 1932 presidential election, Church's power waned. A second victory for Roosevelt in 1936 signaled an opportunity for the Lily White faction to seize control of the party in the city.

Robert Church, Jr., could have acquiesced to Crump's demands in 1940 and relinquished his position nationally within the Republican Party to maintain the *modus vivendi* he enjoyed. During their earlier years of assimilationist acceptance, Crump rewarded Church with the city government waiving his property taxes.[12] Now that Church opposed Crump, Crump's machine sent a message to Church. Crump authorized the burning of the historic Church residence to erase the family's social, economic, and political legacy.[13] The *Commercial Appeal* headlines roared "LET 'ER BURN" as the Memphis Fire Department set Church's eighteen-room mansion on fire. The Memphis Fire Department wanted to "test" a new fog nozzle, and the Church family home was deemed expendable. The black community watched as water trickled from the eighteenth-century ruins.[14]

Following the fire that deliberately destroyed his mansion, Church left Memphis and headed for the safety of Chicago leaving J.B. Martin to direct Republican Party campaign activities in his absence. With

The Memphis Red Sox

Church removed, the next logical step was to remove his lieutenant, J.B. Martin. Crump's power was eroding, and he needed to regain control of the city. Crump's control of the black community's votes aided his overall control of the city. The Crump machine welcomed assimilationists such as Blair T. Hunt and J.B. Martin's brother, W.S. Martin. But if you were African American and voiced an opinion contrary to Crump, there would be a price.

Bob Himmaugh, an organizer for the United Cannery, Agriculture and Allied Packing Workers of America (CIO) and political ally of J.B. Martin, felt Crump's wrath firsthand. When he entered Dr. J.B. Martin's Drug Store on South Florida Street in Memphis, Tennessee, on Saturday, October 26, 1940, to buy stamps, Crump's cronies under Police Commissioner "Holy Joe" Boyle sent a message. "I walked into the store about 3 o'clock in the afternoon, and a policeman standing on one side of the entrance began to feel my pocket. I didn't say a word, and neither did the officers, but I felt like saying plenty. It is customary to enter a post office without being molested. The officer repeated the procedure as he left the store. I thought at first it might be my CIO button, but I watched and found out they were searching everybody who entered or left."[15] Martin's South Memphis Drug Store became the target of Crump's indignation.

By standing up to Crump's political machine with Robert Church, Jr., Martin was in a precarious situation. Martin was in direct opposition to the city's white political boss. The harassment of Martin reveals the caste system prevalent in Jim Crow Memphis. Blacks, like Martin, understood the type of paternalism that governed their lives daily. Acknowledge and consent to Crump's paternalism, and Crump served as the benevolent city father. Contradict this political father, and face the wrath of the "Red-Headed Snapper." Known for his quick temper, Crump's long history of dispatching political opponents grew even more significant at this critical political juncture.

Mayor Walter Chandler, Public Safety Commissioner Joseph Boyle, and the Memphis police department brought the machine's strong arm down upon J.B. Martin. The Memphis Police Department searched every customer who entered and exited Martin's South Memphis Drug Store. Crump's machine did not stop there. A propaganda campaign in the media followed that smeared J.B. Martin's good name, portraying him as a criminal who needed to be removed from the city and thus, adding to the harassment. Events like these were nothing new to the city's black community. For years, Crump allowed police brutality against black citizens to go unchecked.

5. Boss Crump Ejects J.B. Martin

During the 1920s, avowed Ku Klux Klan member Clifford Davis served as police commissioner, and almost seventy percent of the Memphis Police Department belonged to the Klan. Black Memphians accepted incentives from Crump but seldom challenged his machine.[16] Dr. J.E. Walker of the Universal Life Insurance Company, a political assimilationist, headed the Negro Democratic Club in Memphis for Roosevelt in 1936.[17] Crump allowed men like Walker to have a power position so long as it perpetuated his machine's strength, something Martin refused to do in 1940.

Upon departing for Chicago, Robert Church, Jr., left Martin to direct campaign activities for Republican presidential candidate Wendell Wilkie among the city's black citizens. Beale Street, the central business district for black Memphis, became Martin's location for Wilkie's campaign headquarters. Banners advertised a Monday, October 28, 1940, meeting at the Salem Baptist Church. The *Memphis World* detailed the starting time, the speakers, and other Republican officials scheduled to attend.[18] A member of the Crump machine quietly approached Martin to suggest canceling the meeting. Martin refused. Crump's agent warned Martin there would be repercussions if he did not call off the October 28 meeting. Nevertheless, the rally took place as scheduled and attracted over 500 people.[19] Martin had defiantly stood up to the Crump machine and now faced the imminent wrath of Crump.

For forty-two days, police officers stationed themselves outside Martin's Florida Street Drug Store doors. Two Memphis Police Department officers frisked everyone who entered the store, including little children.[20] The harassment began three days before the October 28 rally. Simultaneously, the Memphis Police Department harassed local black business owner and Republican Elmer Atkinson's pool hall on Beale Street. Police Commissioner Boyle insisted in an October 26 *Commercial Appeal* article that "the policing (at the South Memphis Drug Store and Atkinson's pool hall) has nothing to do with politics."[21]

Martin insisted that "his political connections were the reason for the unusual procedure." Boyle countered, citing Dr. Martin's police record, and charged Martin with complicity in a long-standing dope ring.[22] Backed by Mayor Chandler and Boss Crump, Boyle continued the harassment throughout the election campaign. Boyle searched the court records for a minor charge levied in 1938 against Martin. The case never went to trial. Martin avoided trial when the two criminals who perpetrated the crime were tried and sentenced for theft at Plough Pharmaceuticals.

The Memphis Red Sox

For years, J.B. Martin helped young blacks within the community in trouble with the law by posting bail. Boyle presumed Martin's guilt as a drug trafficker because of his relationship as a mentor to problem youths in the black community. Ironically, a respectable community member, Martin owned and operated a drugstore where he dispensed pharmaceuticals. Defiance of the Crump machine came with a hefty price tag. Martin's status as a respectable businessman, politician, and professional sports team owner meant nothing to the Crump machine. Instead, Boyle painted a picture of Martin as a black man who ran with the criminal element. Boyle continued to denounce Martin in the weeks that followed publicly.

The *Press-Scimitar* noted that Boyle urged Mayor Chandler to seek federal aid to determine the extent of Martin's involvement with narcotics in the city.[23] Martin and Atkinson's harassment became part of a "reign of terror" in Memphis that started in 1940 against the black community that opposed the machine. Police intimidation and trumped-up charges placed African Americans in peril in the city. The narrative presented to white citizens painted the regime as one that protected the city's law and order.

Residing in a city constrained by the de facto laws of Jim Crow, J.B. Martin found support in one of the local white newspapers. The *Press-Scimitar* and its editor Edward Meeman were prone to take note of Crump's denial of public and civil liberties. Rarely did Meeman miss an opportunity to attack the lack of virtue by Crump and his cronies. In the *Press-Scimitar*, the white community in Memphis would have unabridged access to the *Memphis World* articles detailing Boyle's attacks on Martin. Many of these articles that Meeman published were reprinted in national publications, including *Time* magazine, further tainting Crump's perception in the national media. Over the forty-two days of harassment at the South Memphis Drug Store, the *Commercial Appeal* published articles questioning the Crump machine's ethical stature.

J.B. Martin's most significant support in the media came from the *Memphis World.* Founded in 1931 by owner Alexander Scott and inspired by black nationalist Marcus Garvey, the *Memphis World* was a black newspaper written for and published by blacks. Scott advocated racial pride and progress by urging blacks in Memphis to coexist in a city where whites dominated the social, political, and economic landscape.[24] Louis Swingler, the editor of the *Memphis World*, often felt they were in "no position to act because of the real possibility of actual physical

5. Boss Crump Ejects J.B. Martin

violence."[25] Like Martin, they, too, faced the threat of retaliation for standing up to the Crump machine. However, the presence of the *Memphis World* and the *Press-Scimitar* kept Boyle, Chandler, and Crump in check. Crump had not anticipated the support J.B. Martin received from the *Commercial Appeal* and its editors. The *Commercial Appeal* spent as much time defending Martin as Crump expected the newspaper to denounce him.

Meeman went on the offensive against the Crump machine on October 31, 1940, when he republished an editorial, "Is this the American Way?" from the *Memphis World*. Swingler urged Memphians to come to the defense of Martin and Atkinson's civil liberties. "The spectacle of upstanding, law-abiding American men and women being subjected to unreasonable searches at the hands of the local police on the flimsy pretext of a hunt for dope peddlers smacks of what one reads about Hitler's Gestapo Police."[26] Swingler's argument foreshadowed A. Philip Randolph's Double V for Victory campaign initiated in the *Pittsburgh Courier* in 1942. Boss Crump's treatment of Martin and Atkinson mirrored methods employed by the Gestapo in Nazi-controlled Europe.

In a momentary lapse of fortitude, J.B. Martin sought to satisfy Crump's demands and cancel the meeting. Martin's liaison was Lieutenant George Lee, a black World War I veteran whose military service provided him political respect on both sides of the color line. Lee was known as a solid Republican ally of Church, yet he hedged towards assimilationist policies that placated the Crump machine. Lee was afraid of being drawn into the feud with Crump that threatened his favored status with Crump, so he refused to send the message back to Crump's envoy. Lee's failure to deliver the message to Crump strengthened Martin's resolve to hold the meeting. Local white millionaire and Republican C. Arthur Bruce urged Martin to remain resolute in his defiance of Crump by carrying out his plan to hold Wilkie's rally as planned.[27]

The Memphis Police Department continued its harassment of Martin and Atkinson in November at a cost to the city of $290 a day. Police Chief Carroll Seabrook justified the department's presence at both establishments claiming that "we have obtained some information, but not sufficient on which to make any arrests." The MPD intended to keep up the search. Police Commissioner Boyle deferred to Seabrook, asserting that Seabrook decided to maintain the police surveillance.[28] The *Memphis World's* editorials made their way as well. Mayor Chandler sent a memo to Boyle questioning the surveillance's value and clippings from the *Memphis World* criticizing the machine's tactics.[29] The divide was growing between the machine and the city. Instead of persuading Boyle to ease up on the surveillance, Chandler's letter only bolstered his conviction to continue the tactics aimed at removing Martin from the city's political landscape.

Boyle's harassment of Elmer Atkinson's pool hall led to Atkinson's filing for bankruptcy. He and his wife filed suit in Shelby County Court, claiming that the Memphis Police Department, under Boyle's direction, searched, seized, and humiliated every customer in their business. The suit also claimed that following November 11, 1940, the MPD escalated its attack by denying admittance to all customers. The case called for $50,000 in punitive and $50,000 in compensatory damages.[30] The case never made it to trial. Yet, the harassment of the Atkinson's pool hall drew national attention when Willie May Atkinson's priest, Father Bertrand's story, appeared in the December issue of *Time* magazine. Known for preaching on dead-end streets in South Memphis, Father Bertrand faced Memphis Police Department harassment that sought to limit his catechizing through anti-noise laws.[31] Bertrand's St. Augustine Parish became a focal point of the machine's ire numerous times. Unlike his previous run-ins with the Memphis Police Department, this encounter left an indelible mark on the Crump machine. *Time* extracted excerpts from the *Press Scimitar's* and the *Commercial Appeal's* description of a Catholic priest's humiliation.

Father Bertrand said he was "frisked" by two policemen, then told to take off his sandals and stockings for their inspection. "They told me I couldn't go into the restaurant without being searched. When they told me to take off my shoes, I sat in a parked taxi and obliged them. After that, I was permitted to go in and see Atkinson's wife."[32] The article included damning evidence of the Crump machine's plantation mentality. *Time* quoted Boyle as saying, "Governor Cooper was right when he said, 'This is a white man's country.'"[33] *Time's* exposé garnered national attention. For years Crump's cronies could avoid scrutiny with their strong-arm tactics. But, this time, they accosted a white man who was also a man of the cloth. This image tarnished Crump's perception nationally. The negative publicity further reinvigorated Boyle and Seabrook's desire to destroy J.B. Martin.

Time magazine reported that Crump had played ball politically with Robert Church, Jr., while there was a Republican in the White House offering patronage. But when FDR and the Democrats gained control of the White House, Crump no longer needed Church or his

5. Boss Crump Ejects J.B. Martin

Republican lieutenants. Crump adamantly denied that he played ball with a Republican boss.[34] Crump's stubbornness and propensity to strike back went unabated following his lieutenants Tyler McLain and Frank Rice's recent passing. Arguably, had McLain or Rice still been at the side of Crump, they may have been able to get Crump to acquiesce following Roosevelt's November victory. But, left alone with no one to challenge his manner of policing the situation, Crump maintained Martin's harassment.

With Atkinson destroyed financially, the machine turned its focus on Martin. Mayor Chandler wrote directly to Crump to discredit J.B. Martin. Chandler touted Martin's brothers as respectable men within the community who chose assimilation over confrontation. W.S. Martin and A.T. Martin were doctors, and B.B. served as a dentist. They were not the problem. W.S. Martin repeatedly benefited from his assimilationist political position throughout his medical career. Crump's altruism included numerous donations to the Memphis Health Department for establishing black clinics.[35] J.B. Martin's blatant opposition to the machine led to his forced departure from the city.

J.B. Martin turned to Thomas Oscar Fuller for help alleviating the pressure Police Commissioner Boyle placed on his South Memphis Drug Store. Fuller, a respected African American in the community, was known to have assimilationist tendencies and been in the Crump machine's good graces. Martin sought Fuller's help to reach out an olive branch of peace to Crump. Martin believed that his thirty years of service to the community as a pharmacist at the South Florida location merited forgiveness and an opportunity to mend broken relations between himself and the machine. However, the continued harassment of Martin's customers began to wear on his resolve. Fearful of losing a business he built from the ground up, J.B. Martin began to feel financial pressure. Martin allowed Fuller to relay a message suggesting that Martin was willing to leave politics alone to save his business.[36] Martin's appeal to Crump hinged on the notion that Crump's machine still depended on support from the city's black assimilationists.

Assimilationists, like Fuller, became the only avenue for Martin to make amends with Crump. Many prominent blacks leaned on assimilationist policies to gain favor for themselves and their constituents. Blair T. Hunt, the pastor of the prestigious Mississippi Boulevard Christian Church and principal of Booker T. Washington High School, as one of the more prominent African American community members, toed the accommodation line. A 1944 article in the *Chicago Defender* labeled Hunt as part of "the local Negro appeasement bloc that believed in the 'see no evil, hear no evil, speak no evil' approach to race relations." Crump's paternalism towards Hunt included lights for the high school football field and an appointment to the censor board for films in Memphis.

Martin encouraged Hunt to reach out to Mayor Chandler on Martin's behalf. Hunt's letter professed his loyalty to the machine while seeking a remedy that freed J.B. Martin from the harassment he faced at his South Memphis Drug Store. "Mr. Crump is almost a human idol to us." Hunt continued in a subservient fashion, asserting that black Memphians "do not condone crime," yet they "appreciate the efforts of Mr. Boyle."[37] Hunt's letter thanked Chandler for cleaning up the crime in Memphis. He also referred to the policing of Martin's drugstore as "inopportune."[38] Hunt's position as a leader in the black community placed him in an awkward situation. If he leaned too heavily on Chandler, he risked losing his favored position and the accommodations from Crump. Yet, he would lose respect within the black community if he did not defend another prominent black citizen.

As J.B. Martin sought prominent assimilationists' aid to his cause, other black leaders saw an opportunity to improve their place in city politics at Martin's expense. Joseph Edison "J.E." Walker commended Commissioner Boyle for cleaning up crime in the city in a November 1940 letter.[39] Instead of one unified voice, the black community remained divided. Martin's brother, W.S., wrote a letter to Crump expressing his disappointment with his younger brother, J.B. Martin. W.S. went out of his way to assure Crump that his friends supported Roosevelt in the upcoming election. The gratitude continued as he thanked Crump for the parks, new schools, and help with the health department Crump provided to the black community.[40] Crump's stalwart political position required assimilationists to support FDR. Although the New Deal served as persuasive legislation that lured many African American voters away from the Republican Party during FDR's tenure, closer analysis points to the tenacity of Crump's paternalistic tendencies to steer blacks in Memphis toward the Democratic ticket.

Another voice from the black community arose in support of J.B. Martin and direct opposition to the harassment blacks faced at the hands of Police Commissioner Boyle. Merah S. Stuart, a Universal Life Insurance Executive, wrote directly to Mayor Chandler, condemning Boyle's actions. Stuart noted the "keen racial interest and pride" among blacks in successful business enterprises such as the South Memphis Drug Store of J.B. Martin.[41]

5. Boss Crump Ejects J.B. Martin

> [It is] one of the show places (the South Memphis Drug Store) for colored visitors who come to Memphis; and the spectacle of a successful Negro business enterprise being crushed and closed by a powerful organization, supported by millions of dollars and white men of great influence, is a picture the result of which I contemplate with some misgivings. If it should be so closed, I am quite sure that the memory of it will rankle with bitterness for a long time in the hearts of thousands of Negroes who do not care one whit personally about Dr. J.B. Martin.[42]

Mayor Chandler responded with a paternalistic ear as he told Stuart that he "took up the matter with Commissioner Joseph P. Boyle and with other friends of yours, and there was a friendly discussion of the entire matter."[43] Chandler's administration actually cast aside Stuart's letter as meaningless and inconsequential.

On November 22, 1940, the Memphis police department maintained their vigil against J.B. Martin by arresting white salesman Milton Silberberg for refusing to be searched before entering Martin's South Memphis Drug Store.[44] Martin kept a dignified vigilance in the fight against the Crump machine through December. On the sixth of December, the *Press-Scimitar* reported that the MPD's harassment of the South Memphis Drug Store was over. Quoted in the *Press-Scimitar's* article, Boyle told reporters that the MPD would police the store differently by using periodic surveillance of the drugstore in forty-five-minute increments. The South Florida Drug Store clerks told reporters that the police were no longer searching customers.[45] The reign of terror lessened, but it was not over.

With Atkinson out of the way and J.B. Martin in his sights, Boyle raised the stakes and placed more heat upon Martin. Boyle told the *Commercial Appeal* in an article that made the December 12, 1940, headlines: "We'll Have No Race Trouble Here!" With the backing of Crump and the recent capitulation of Atkinson, Boyle reiterated his belief that "this is a white man's country, and always will be, and any Negro who doesn't agree to this better move on." He attacked the media in Memphis for copying stories from the *Pittsburgh Courier* and the *Chicago Defender*. Boyle proclaimed most blacks are good citizens in the machine's eyes, but small discordant elements are of no advantage to their race or their relation to white people.[46]

The *Commercial Appeal* noted that the police surveillance of Martin's drugstore continued without the searching of customers. Later that month, the Memphis Commission on Interracial Cooperation charged the Memphis Police Department with police intimidation against blacks in Memphis. Enraged, Boyle lashed out against the media. He attacked Louis Swingler of the *Memphis World* and two other prominent black journalists who were also members of the Memphis Commission on Interracial Cooperation. Boyle vented, "How could members of the black media in Memphis be trusted in any discussion concerning interracial cooperation?"[47] For Boyle, white was right. Anything else was not acceptable.

Martin's resistance to the Crump machine neared its final stages. Boyle dug deeper into J.B. Martin's files at city hall to find that he was posting bail bonds without having a license. For years the city allowed Martin to post bail for local blacks without a license. Boyle turned to this discrepancy to tighten the vise. When J.B. Martin heard of Boyle's plan to construct a criminal case against him, he capitulated. He told Lieutenant George Lee, "I couldn't stand a workhouse sentence," the next day, he left for Chicago.[48] The *Chicago Defender* turned Martin's arrival into front-page news on November 30, 1940, with a headline that read "Dr. J.B. Martin in City (Chicago); Silent on Persecution."[49] J.B. Martin became part of the Great Migration of African Americans to Chicago. Unlike the quiet masses that went before him, he was forced north by Crump's harassment. After J.B. Martin left the city, the Memphis Police maintained surveillance of his drugstore.

Immediately following his forced departure from Memphis, J.B. Martin pled his case to the federal government with the help of Robert Church, Jr. They sought out Representative Clifford Davis, long an ally of Crump, in his Washington, D.C., office. Davis informed Crump of their visit and how he turned the two away by claiming there was no recourse for them through his office.[50] Thus rebuffed, Church and Martin turned to the Justice Department. Amos Woodcock, the special assistant to the Attorney General, traveled to Memphis to investigate. Upon his arrival, he met with Public Safety Commissioner Boyle. Woodcock would not meet with any black leaders while he was in town and concluded that no evidence of police harassment had occurred.[51] Thus FDR's tenuous relationship with Southern Democrats became apparent to J.B. Martin. FDR understood that he needed white Southerners like Crump and Davis to maintain control of the party.

The *Press-Scimitar* reported that Woodcock was in town investigating the harassment and was turning his report over to FDR's attorney general. They included details of Boyle's intimidation of local black newspapers and the harassment at Martin's drugstore and Atkinson's pool hall.[52] They also published the Civil Rights Statute 18 so that the

5. Boss Crump Ejects J.B. Martin

citizens of Memphis would be aware of their rights, along with a glowing biography of Woodcock so that the black community would feel safe and protected by the Justice Department. Crump proceeded to attack *Press-Scimitar* reporter Clark Porteous. Crump claimed that the attacks against him and his lieutenants were all lies. Boxed into a corner, Crump compared the *Press-Scimitar* to periodicals from New York. "Agitators and saboteurs under the guise of teachers, lecturers, farm, and industrial workers with their vicious propaganda will not be tolerated by the officials of this community."[53] Crump rallied around the deeply rooted concepts inherent in the Lost Cause. In his eyes, Northern race agitators would not invade Memphis. Woodcock's visit to Memphis ended with a reprimand to Police Commissioner Joe Boyle. The federal civil rights act had not been violated, according to his assessment of the harassment of Martin.[54]

Crump claimed that Woodcock's trip to Memphis was part of his plan to further eliminate the city's narcotics problems. Church countered the Crump narrative by asserting that Woodcock's visit was intentional. Years of civil rights abuses by the Crump machine aimed at the black community were apparent in J.B. Martin and Atkinson's treatment. President Roosevelt's "black cabinet" made inroads within the black community and started to attract African Americans away from the Republican Party and into the Democratic Party. Woodcock had to make the trip to save face with black voters in the South. Crump helped to secure not only Memphis but the state of Tennessee in the 1940 election for FDR and the Democratic Party. But his hard-knuckled approach to politics directly opposed the rights of Memphians such as J.B. Martin.

J.B. Martin's political career in Memphis and the Memphis Red Sox ownership were over. When Martin returned to Memphis in October 1943, city detectives detained him and escorted him to the police chief, where they reminded him to keep out of Memphis.[55] He came to watch the inaugural North-South All-Star game, which brought large numbers of spectators to Memphis to watch some of the best Negro leagues players compete. It was an indirect challenge to Crump's authority, another jab at Crump. As Martin had been forced out of Memphis, his small act of resistance signaled to black Memphians that his dignity was still in place. By 1949 J.B. Martin was reportedly worth more than $250,000.[56] In 1955 he returned to Memphis to throw out the first baseball for the season at Martin Stadium. This triumphant return of the exiled Martin occurred after Boss Crump's death in 1954, making it safe for Martin to return to the city.

The Memphis Red Sox

J.B. Martin's political fall and exile in 1940 would be the central moment in his life. The Black and Tan Republicans, under the leadership of Robert Church, Jr., called upon Dr. J.B. Martin to lead the charge of racial uplift during the 1940 election campaign. A successful black businessman, a key player in the Memphis Red Sox organization with broad regional and national prominence, challenged the Crump machine. A longtime member of the middle-class political elites in the African American community, Martin weathered the greatest challenge of his life. The victory was in his courage to stand up to the Crump machine's paternalism.

The Crump machine succeeded in running Robert Church, Jr., and J.B. Martin out of town. The bare-knuckled approach of politics, employed by Police Commissioner "Holy Joe" Boyle, symbolized the plight of African Americans who spoke out and resisted the Jim Crow South's social constraints in Memphis. When Dr. J.B. Martin died in 1958 at 88, his obituary described him as the former Memphis pharmacist, political leader, and co-owner of the Memphis Red Sox and that his conflict with Mr. E.H. Crump forced him to leave Memphis.[57]

6

The Boys of Summer

An African American boy learned how to play ball any way he could. Southern boys worked in fields all day before turning their attention to baseball. In the Northern cities, boys made their own baseball and joined a pickup game in a vacant lot.[1] Like their counterparts on the other side of the tracks, they also dreamed of playing professional baseball. The journeys of Negro leagues players mirrored that of their white counterparts in many ways. Yet, their journeys remained unique because of the segregation that quietly kept them out of Organized Baseball. There is no single story to explain how black players made their way to the Negro leagues. What follows are the stories of three Memphis Red Sox players. By examining their lives, we can get a glimpse into what the dream of young black boys was during the Negro leagues era and how that dream panned out for Larry Brown, Verdell Mathis, and Joe B. Scott.

Who are they? In the 1970s, historian John Holway interviewed hundreds of Negro leaguers. When asked the four greatest defensive catchers of Blackball, four names predominated: Bruce Petway, Frank Duncan, Biz Mackey, and a "wavy-haired, light-skinned, chirpy-voiced little spark plug named Larry Brown."[2] Ted "Double Duty" Radcliffe claimed Brown was the best catcher he ever saw, outside of himself. Radcliffe recalled that Brown could "catch a cut ball, knuckleball, emery ball, anything."[3] Larry Brown's career covered the duration of the modern Negro leagues era. While playing winter ball in Cuba, Brown cut down Ty Cobb trying to steal on him on five consecutive attempts.

Brown told Negro leagues chronicler John Holway "that Cobb came into the clubhouse and said 'How would you like to stay down here and pick up on this *lingua* and come back to the states and pass as a Cuban?'"[4] Brown responded to Cobb by saying, "Hell, I can't do that, everybody knows me."[5] A 1961 *Pittsburgh* Courier article confirmed that the Tigers were interested in signing Brown after a two-year

The Memphis Red Sox

"retirement" in Cuba. In this version of events, Tigers owner Frank Navin offered Brown the opportunity to break into the major leagues as a white Cuban. The article said that Brown decided against passing as a "white Cuban" for fear that Cobb would discover he was indeed a Negro.[6] His talent as a catcher merited such consideration.

As Brown approached his twentieth season in Blackball, a slight and spindly Southpaw showed up for spring training. A local Memphian, Verdell Mathis, became one of the best pitchers to come out of the city. The 1945 *Negro Baseball Pictorial Yearbook* described Mathis at the height of his career as "the most overpowering pitcher now active. The Memphis left-hander who mystified the East's touted sluggers at Chicago in the East-West All-Star game of 1944." Brown described his protégé to be as good a left-hander as "Lefty" Grove, Whitey Ford, and Rube Waddell.[7]

Painting of Verdell Mathis (by Jay Caldwell). "Lefty" Mathis is remembered as one of the all-time great Red Sox pitchers. Before his arm surgery in 1946, many believed Mathis would be the first to earn an opportunity in the Major Leagues (Jay Caldwell).

A longtime Red Sox beat sports reporter for the *Memphis World* ranked Mathis among the three best pitchers to don a Red Sox uniform, along with Carl Glass and Ted Radcliffe.[8]

The last of these three, Joe B. Scott, may have been the least known. Still, his experiences growing up in Chicago, where he played on an integrated high school team and later on integrated teams in the military, provides a unique outlook on life in the Negro leagues. Scott's ability to hit landed him a spot at the prestigious Roger Hornsby camp during the height of interest in black players by Organized Baseball following

6. *The Boys of Summer*

Jackie Robinson's signing by the Brooklyn Dodgers. These men were all major-league caliber players, left behind a silent wall of segregation that compelled them to chase their dreams in the Negro leagues.

Their stories are only a scant sample from the hundreds of players who donned the Red Sox uniform from 1921 through 1959. They each encompass unique phases of the era. Each holds strong ties to the city of Memphis and made reconstructing their stories easier with sources that are more readily accessible. This chapter attempts to follow their lives and careers in four areas: early lives leading to professional baseball, stories from their Negro leagues experiences, East-West All-Star Game experiences, and finally, how they finished their careers and the lives they lived afterward.

* * *

Future Red Sox catcher and manager Ernest Larry Brown was born on September 5, 1905, in Pratt City, Alabama.[9] His parents, Charlie Brown and Viola Brannon, had one daughter before him. Larry was raised by his mother, a domestic, and did not know his father, a man of European descent about whom little is known.[10] Pratt City, a former municipality in Birmingham, Alabama, was home to miners who toiled in the state's largest coal mine and remained central to Birmingham's booming steel industry in the late nineteenth century. Brown grew up in the all-black Drifttrack neighborhood between Highway 78 and Avenue W in Pratt City. Pratt City drew people from across the South, Northern industrial centers, and foreign nations. This Southern salad bowl of ethnic industrial culture included Southerners—black and white—Englishmen, Scots, Irishmen, Frenchmen, Russians, Germans, and Austrians, living in pockets scattered around town.[11]

Children rode the streetcars to school. Community life revolved around the churches, the commissary, and the front porch.[12] Into this world was born Larry Brown. As a young boy, he delivered papers for the *Alabama Citizen* to his neighbors in Pratt City. He teamed up with future Chicago American Giant Willie Powell on Pratt City's youth baseball team. Brown developed his toughness and arm strength by brawling with and throwing rocks at Powell.[13] When Brown's mother died in 1918, he began working for the Tennessee Coal, Iron, and Railroad Company (TCI) in Birmingham. He drove a cart pulled by mules to bring laborers to and from the job site and played for the TCI baseball team in the Birmingham Industrial League.[14]

Life for Larry Brown in Pratt City as a young black boy embodied

The Memphis Red Sox

many of the struggles common at the turn of the century. Raised by a single black mother, options for Brown to get out of Pratt City were limited. In addition, limited knowledge about Charlie Brown, Larry's white father, complicates the construction of his racial identity. Yet, later in his career, his light complexion would offer a unique opportunity to break the color line in Organized Baseball.

Brown began playing baseball on the sandlots of Birmingham, like many of his peers of the age. Historian Rob Ruck has described sandlots as belonging to an epoch in sports history when a different scale of economics applied and self-organized, independent ball clubs thrived in almost every neighborhood in and around cities.[15] When a challenging situation became even harsher with the death of his mother, Brown's ability to hold his own on the sandlots of Birmingham provided an outlet for him and an alternative to a life of manual labor.

* * *

One of the most dominant pitchers to don a Memphis Red Sox uniform entered the world on November 18, 1913, in Crawfordsville, Arkansas. Verdell Jackson Mathis, the fifth child of ten born to Jackson and Sarah Mathis. When Verdell was young, Jackson Mathis worked for the Missouri-Pacific Railroad and moved his family to Memphis, Tennessee.[16] Verdell attended Kortrecht Grammar School for Negroes, built in 1873 as the first all-brick school for colored students. Kortrecht eventually served as a grammar and high school. Black teachers staffed the entire school. In 1926, the Memphis City School Board built a new high school named Booker T. Washington in South Memphis to replace Kortrecht. With Booker T. Washington remaining the only black high school in the city, all its students came from Kortrecht Grammar.[17] In grade school at Kortrecht, Mathis bought the *Pittsburgh Courier* to follow his boyhood hero Satchel Paige. He thought, "You know I'd like to be like this guy."[18]

When Mathis moved from Kortrecht to Booker T. Washington High, he was only a few hundred yards from the Red Sox's Martin Stadium. Like any boy growing up in such proximity to professional baseball, Mathis found ways to get into the stadium. One of his methods was to discover where visiting teams were, usually in boarding homes near the stadium. On the last day of the series, he waited outside the stadium to hear who the next opponent would be from the public announcer. Then on the day of the next home game, he ran down to the boarding homes on Fourth Street and Linden Avenue, sat on the front steps,

6. The Boys of Summer

and waited for the next opponent to arrive. Once they arrived, Mathis secured the team's batboy position for the series.[19] His love for the game grew stronger with his ability to mingle with professional baseball players at Martin Stadium.

As a student at Booker T. Washington High (BTW), he developed into a talented pitcher and all-around player for the Warriors. His coach was Julian Bell, a player for the Memphis Red Sox in the late 1920s. Following a seven-year Negro leagues career, where he was known for his great curveball and control, he turned to coaching high school baseball at BTW.[20] Mathis' curveball made him one of the most effective pitchers in Blackball. Mathis' curveball and changeup developed under the tutelage of Bell.[21] Mathis married his high school sweetheart, Helen Dunn, in June 1936. While working various manual labor jobs in Memphis, his biology teacher from BTW, William Lowe, signed him to play semi-pro baseball.[22]

Lowe, who spent eight seasons with the Memphis Red Sox in the 1920s and 1930s, picked up Mathis in 1937 for his barnstorming team.[23] Lowe's team, named the Brooklyn Royal Giants, evoked thoughts of their famous professional counterparts in New York; the team played numerous games against the Mineola (Texas) Black Spiders, who Reuben Jones managed. Mathis made a good impression on Jones, who later convinced Red Sox owners to sign Mathis. On this tour, Mathis cut his baseball teeth against white professional players, most notably Cleveland Indians pitcher Bob Feller. Mathis paid close attention to all his competitors as he honed his skills.[24]

Mathis's proximity to Martin Stadium as a youth in the 1920s and 1930s demonstrates the importance of the Negro leagues to the black youth of the era. Boys like Mathis would gain entry into Martin Stadium by returning foul balls outside the stadium. Often they would keep the ball as a valuable find to take back to their sandlot games in South Memphis.[25] In the Depression, the ability to have a baseball was a rarity. Attending high school a block away from the stadium gave Mathis and his teammates something to reach for. As Mathis developed into a baseball player with potential, his proximity to Martin Stadium meant that former Red Sox players developed his skills and opened doors for him. Thus Mathis's path toward professional baseball had a helping hand from the proximity of professional Blackball in Memphis.

* * *

Future outfielder and first baseman Joe Burt Scott, the second of four children to Charles H. Scott and Lucy Paine Scott, was born on

The Memphis Red Sox

October 2, 1920, in Memphis, Tennessee. When Scott turned ten, his father, Charles, a mechanic by trade, left Lucy to pursue success with a cousin.[26] His mother became a single parent, working as a maid to support her four children: Charles (1918), Joe (1920), Irma (1922), and Naomi (1923).[27] Lucy was a religious woman who did not approve of her son playing baseball. Scott would sneak out to play baseball as a young kid with older men in his Memphis neighborhood. When his mother called home, Scott's sister would tell his mother where he was and that he was playing baseball. When she got home, she would have his older brother go outside and get a switch. She firmly believed that playing baseball with older men led to gambling and other sinful acts.[28] His older brother Charles initiated his love for baseball when he gave him a broomstick so that he could play in sandlot games in Memphis. Scott's love for the game grew when the local white minor league team, the Memphis Chickasaws, allowed him to shag fly balls during batting practice at Russwood Park.[29]

Lucy moved the Scott family to Chicago, Illinois, in 1935, where she married William Gallaway and gave birth to a fifth child, Edith (1936). Scott spent his teenage years in the Bronzeville section of Chicago on Forty-sixth Street. Like many other African American families of the period, Lucy relocated her family to Chicago, hoping for a better life and less racial oppression. Bronzeville's residents toiled hard and cooperatively to establish a full-fledged community with business, culture, and community institutions. Bronzeville's institutions grew to have national influence, rivaling New York's Harlem.[30]

Growing up in Chicago, Scott was a fan of the Chicago Cardinals' Lou Lillard. Lillard was among the last two African Americans allowed to play in the NFL before the "gentleman's agreement" amongst NFL owners to keep Blacks out of the NFL from 1934 to 1945.[31] Scott watched as Lillard, whom *The Chicago Defender* described as "easily the best halfback in football," was ostracized by both opposing teams and teammates.[32] Lillard's black-listing taught the young Scott that flashy play by black athletes led to perceptions of cockiness by white teammates and eventual exclusion. Scott described attending school the following Monday as "a sad thing to hear the guys talk about how he (Lillard) got beat up and how the blocks wasn't fair."[33]

Scott attended Tilden Tech High School only blocks from his Forty-sixth Street house. Tilden became an all-boys school in 1919 when the Chicago Board of Education reorganized the district.[34] During his freshman year, Scott began his athletic career at Tilden as part of

6. *The Boys of Summer*

the junior varsity football team. In the spring, he turned his attention to the diamond, where he earned a varsity baseball roster spot as a freshman. Although twenty percent of Tilden Tech's students were black, he was the only black player on the baseball team. Under Coach Shortall, the Craftsman won the City Championship at Wrigley Field 8–5 against Shurz High. Although Scott was not in the starting lineup, he pinch-hit in the fourth inning, doubling in the go-ahead run.[35]

This game became one of Scott's early career highlights, as he was the only black player on the field that day. Following their championship victory, the Tilden Tech players met Baseball Commissioner Kenesaw Landis, who shook all their hands, including Scott's.[36] Scott played baseball all four years at Tilden, becoming one of the team's co-captains during his senior year.[37] Playing baseball in an integrated school played an important role in how he viewed race and sport. Scott, "All I was thinking about was baseball and playing. That's all. If it wasn't, it didn't make no difference."[38] This mantra would serve him well throughout his career. As an underclassman, Scott played the outfield. He played first base for Tilden during his senior year, earning All-City and All-State accolades. As a young kid in Memphis, his childhood baseball hero was Lou Gehrig, even though people told him he was too short to play first base.[39]

After graduation from Tilden Tech, Scott got a job loading beef onto boxcars, allowing him to play baseball in the Chicago industrial league. While playing in the industrial league, Scott garnered an opportunity to play one of Satchel Paige's barnstorming teams.[40] In a 1994 interview, Scott recalled his first hit off Satchel while playing with one of Dizzy Dean's barnstorming teams in Dayton, Ohio. "He struck me out the first time. Dizzy was hitting in front of me, so he walked Dizzy to pitch to me and said, 'C'mon kid, get ready for this fire.' I tripled against the left-center field fence. When I got to third, Satchel said, 'What did you hit, kid?' I said, 'That fire!'"[41] While barnstorming, he lived with his mother and stepfather in Bronzeville.

Scott's childhood journey included participating in the Great Migration north to Chicago, like many of his generation. But, unlike Brown and Mathis, who came of age in the South, Scott broke barriers by playing sports at Tilden High. His unique story places him among the early pioneers in Chicago playing on integrated baseball teams and in parks that previously did not allow blacks to play there. These experiences allowed him later to maneuver the world of barnstorming in the Negro leagues and playing in the Army during World War II. It also allowed Scott to believe he could compete against white baseball players. One that he hoped would one day make an easier transition to playing in Organized Baseball.

Each of these players faced unique childhood situations, each providing insight into how players of the era reached the Negro leagues and eventually the Memphis Red Sox. As these three came of age and began believing in their ability to play professionally, they once again took unique paths.

* * *

In oral histories conducted by historian Laurie Green in the 1990s, she uncovered the term "plantation mentality" among the vernacular of the black working class in Memphis. This idea centers around the notion that working-class African Americans struggled against white hegemony.[42] In Birmingham, Memphis, and Chicago, all three future Red Sox players confronted the daily realities of Jim Crow, as they would throughout their professional baseball careers. However, playing professional baseball provided a reprieve, albeit minor, from the struggles of the black working class. Without baseball, all three men would have to earn a living as manual laborers during the Jim Crow era. Instead, the baseball gods came down and tapped each with an opportunity to play professional baseball.

Brown's opportunity to join the ranks of professional baseball came at the age of fifteen. While playing for TCI's company team in Birmingham's Industrial League, the Knoxville (Tennessee) Giants, a Negro Southern League (NSL) club, lost two catchers to broken fingers. Brown put on his best clothes and went to the Dunbar Hotel to meet Knoxville's manager, W.M. Brooks. The skipper looked at the 5-foot-7, 162-pounder and said, "Well, I'll be doggone. You're mighty small, mighty little." When Brooks asked Brown if he thought he could handle Giants hurler John "Strong Arm" Dickey, a 240-pound behemoth of a man, he replied, "Yes, sir, I think I can catch him." The next day, July 4, 1920, Brown caught both ends of a doubleheader, and Brooks offered him $125 a month. With his mom deceased and his sister living in Philadelphia, Brown gladly accepted and began his professional baseball career.[43]

Brown remained with Knoxville until late in the 1921 season, when he signed with the Pittsburgh Keystones of the Western Independent League. In nine games, he batted .367.[44] In one contest against the Chicago American Giants, he threw out "Jelly" Gardner, Dave Malacher, and

6. The Boys of Summer

Cristobal Torriente on the base paths. Chicago manager Rube Foster told Pittsburgh's Dizzy Dismukes, "One day, I'll have him catch for me."[45]

After the 1921 season, Brown returned to the Negro Southern League, this time with the Memphis Red Sox.[46] However, his fortunes changed in 1923 when a former Keystones teammate was named manager of the Indianapolis ABCs, who competed in the Negro National League, a leading black circuit. Dismukes had been impressed by Brown in Pittsburgh, so he signed him to back up George Dixon. Brown developed his defense by studying Dixon and working with Dismukes. The latter was a crafty right-handed submariner whose mastery of various curves considered trick pitches forced Brown to handle deliveries from multiple angles.[47] Halfway through the season, Brown returned to Memphis—by then associate members of the Negro National League—to catch full-time. Although the line between minor and major league baseball in Blackball remained hazy throughout the Negro leagues era, by 1923, it was apparent that Brown was worthy of designation as a major leaguer.

For Larry Brown, introduction into the professional ranks came early, at age 14. Brown struck out on his own in the earliest days of organized Blackball. The excitement of playing against men twice his age must have been exhilarating for the young man. With his older sister no longer in Birmingham, his father no longer in the picture, and his mother deceased, the choice between staying in Birmingham and becoming a professional player became easier. However, circumstances forced Brown to make adult decisions early in life. Immediately, his career became transient, moving him from Alabama to Tennessee to Pennsylvania. Under the guidance of older professional players, Brown improved his craft. As his ability improved, others across Blackball began to take notice of his skill before his twenty-first birthday found him starting in Memphis of the Negro Southern League. Failure could not have been an option. Where was he to return? One has to wonder if he imagined playing thirty-plus years in professional baseball when he first joined the Knoxville Giants.

* * *

Mathis' route to major league status was less circuitous than Brown's and can be directly related to his proximity to Martin Stadium during his childhood. But, once again, Mathis's relationship with former Red Sox players Julian Bell and William Lowe opened doors to his

The Memphis Red Sox

discovery. Although Mathis's journey to Blackball's major league was relatively smooth, it was not without its hurdles. His love for the game kept him playing on barnstorming teams that toured the Midwest in 1937, formed by William Lowe. When he was not out barnstorming, he was earning seven dollars a week working at a liquor store delivering beer to local stores.[48] Lowe attempted to get Mathis a tryout with the Red Sox with owner J.B. Martin in 1938, to no avail. However, when Reuben Jones became the manager for the Red Sox heading into the 1940 season, Mathis' play on the barnstorming circuit remained etched in the memory of Jones, who went to J.B. Martin's office to sign the local talent before another Negro league team.

Aware of Mathis' talent and potential, Jones pleaded directly with J.B. Martin to sign him to a contract with the Red Sox. Birmingham Barons owner Thomas Haynes, Jr., a Memphis native, attempted to sign Mathis away for $60 a month from Memphis. Mathis balked at the low bid.[49] When Jones brought Mathis over to see Red Sox owner J.B. Martin, the fiscally tight Martin hesitated at Jones's suggestion that Mathis deserved a $125 a month. Jones looked J.B. Martin in the eye and said, "Sign him for what he wants. If he don't make good. I'll pay it out of my own check."[50] Jones's faith in the young Mathis paid dividends as the season went on and foreshadowed a successful career in Blackball.

Married at a young age, Mathis held responsibilities in Memphis as a husband. His ability to pitch offered opportunities to barnstorm with semi-pro teams, but how long would he be able to chase that dream without being able to support a young family? Fortunately for Mathis, his connections with the Red Sox opened doors for him that, had he not grown up in South Memphis, may not have otherwise been opened. These connections also helped ease Mathis into the life of a professional ball player and become aware of his value to professional clubs like the Red Sox.

* * *

For Joe B. Scott, baseball seemed a forgone conclusion. Although Scott's mother despised the game as immoral, Scott's success at Tilden High in Chicago provided Scott with opportunities to barnstorm during high school and play in one of Chicago's industrial leagues afterward. Like so many other baseball players with dreams of playing professionally, following the bombing of Pearl Harbor at the end of 1941, baseball would have to wait. Scott reported to the draft office in Chicago, Illinois, to enlist in the U.S. Army in February 1942. During World

6. *The Boys of Summer*

War II, Scott spent his years playing on the U.S. Army baseball teams.[51] Frequently Scott took three-day passes from his commanding officer at Wright Army Airforce Base in Dayton, Ohio, and picked up with barnstorming teams.

While playing a game in Belleville, Illinois, with the Memphis Red Sox, a player named McGill was the third baseman for the Belleville Stags that day. After Scott hit a triple, Memphis manager Larry Brown told Scott to steal home on the second pitch. The Stags heard Brown's instructions, and after figuring out that he would be out at home, Scott returned to third base, where McGill was blocking the bag. Scott slides into third base, one up and one down, spiking McGill in the leg. Later that week, when Scott returned to base, Lieutenant Colonel McGill from the Wright Airfield base team approached Scott and offered him the opportunity to leave his all-black unit and join the post's baseball team as part of the special services.[52] While stationed at Wright Airfield, the New York Black Yankees signed Scott for $500 upon his release from the service.[53]

Then, during the 1945 Negro American League season, the Red Sox visited Chicago's Comiskey Park to play the Chicago American Giants. Still serving in the Army in 1945, Scott got a call from Verdell Mathis to meet the team in Chicago. Red Sox general manager, B.B. Martin, wanted to see the young Scott hit again. Inserted in the game in the early innings by manager Larry Brown, Scott doubled.[54] Scott's pinch hit in Chicago for the Memphis Red Sox foreshadowed the best years of his playing career in Memphis. That same year, as a member of the Dizzy Dean All-stars, he played the Pittsburgh Pirates in Muncie, Indiana, where Scott went two for three at the plate with a triple against the Pirates' Truett "Rip" Sewell.[55]

Following his release from the U.S. Army, Scott reported to New York to play for manager Marvin Barker's 1946 Black Yankees. For Scott, his time in the service during World War II opened multiple doors and provided him with choices. The native Memphian chose to head East, where money in black professional baseball was higher. When the native Memphian returned to the hometown Red Sox, it allowed the careers of Brown, Mathis, and Scott to converge for the first time.

Scott spent time playing baseball in the sandlots of Chicago for industrial league teams, like Brown's time with the TCI team in Birmingham. In a similar fashion to Mathis, Scott's time in the Army during World War II allowed him to barnstorm and compete against other professional players before joining the Negro leagues full-time

The Memphis Red Sox

once the war was over. The excitement of barnstorming with Satchel Paige and Dizzy Dean opened the eyes of a young Scott to what baseball could do for him. His ability to compete on the baseball diamond kept Scott stateside during the war. He began to understand his value as a player, choosing to sign with the team that valued him the most. After making their way to Blackball's major leagues, these three became part of the fabric of black professional baseball in the Negro leagues era.

* * *

The careers of these three players converged in the 1940s when Brown's career waned, and Mathis stood atop the Negro leagues as one of the game's most feared pitchers. Scott's career in the Negro leagues is shorter than his teammates. He spent more time in Organized Baseball than Mathis. Of the three, Brown was too late to get his chance to play in Organized Baseball. Brown's career in Memphis took off in the early 1920s with Memphis still in the Negro Southern League, what white Organized Baseball has deemed as the minor leagues.[56] But Brown's rejoining the Red Sox in the middle of the 1923 season will be our starting point for this section. As was Scott's, Mathis' transition from semi-pro player to a professional is a more readily identifiable point. Rube Foster's hegemonic control of the game in the Midwest and Ed Bolton's in the East, left Southern franchises clamoring for recognition. Brown's ability radiated as the Red Sox oscillated between major and minor league status. Brown was a highly sought-after commodity by championship-level teams in the Midwest and back East.

Brown became a welcomed addition to the baseball fabric of Memphis. Brown enjoyed the lure of the nightlife on Beale Street, the Main Street of black America for many in the South. There was never a dull moment on Beale Street, and for a young baseball player like Brown, this meant that his popularity on the field carried over to the bars on Beale after the game. Brown was the calming force who kept things light as he controlled the game from behind the plate. After the games on Beale Street, he transformed into the life of the party, enjoyed the nightlife, and stayed out on Beale until they closed the place down. For Brown, Memphis became not only his baseball home but also a place where he thrived.

Over the next three years, he honed his skills behind the plate for the Red Sox to levels that brought acclaim to the young catcher. In 1925, he was reunited with Dizzy Dismukes when the Red Sox brought Dismukes to Memphis to manage the Red Sox. Pitcher Harry Salmon

6. The Boys of Summer

recalls Brown's prowess against Rube Foster's Chicago American Giants team, which prided itself on small ball and stealing bases. Salmon remembers that they never once pitched out with Brown behind the plate; this was when Foster's team included burners Jim Brown, Dave Malacher, "Jelly" Gardner, and Christobal Torriente.[57]

Six years after first seeing Brown catch for the Pittsburgh Keystones, Foster purchased Brown's contract from the Red Sox for the second half of the 1927 season. Hot-hitting Nat Rogers of the Red Sox joined Brown on his trip north to Chicago. Foster added Rogers and Brown to help the Chicago American Giants repeat as Negro World Series Champions in 1927. Brown was the defensive catcher who could slow Atlantic City Bacharach's running game. In the stretch run, Brown hit .344 for the CAG, and during the Negro World Series, he neutralized Atlantic City's running game by throwing out half of the runners attempting to steal against him. Following the world series, Negro National League president Judge William Hueston ordered Brown and Rogers to return immediately to the Red Sox.[58] The Red Sox sought compensation for the loss of Rogers and Brown, and they returned to Memphis for the 1928 season.

Brown returned to Memphis for the 1928 and 1929 seasons and settled in as the everyday catcher for the Red Sox. When the Martin brothers purchased the Memphis club, this fiscally tight ownership group led to Brown's seeking higher-paying options elsewhere at the height of his playing career.[59] Brown finished the 1929 season back in Chicago with the American Giants. Following the American Giants' third-place finish, Brown headed East to play for the New York Lincoln Giants under John Henry Lloyd. The Lincoln Giants were one of the strongest teams in the Negro Eastern League in 1929. At 25 years old, Brown was among the most sought-after players in Blackball.

Brown spent two more seasons in New York. During the 1930 season, he played in the first-ever game at Yankee Stadium, played by two black teams.[60] In this game, and many others while he played in New York, Brown played opposite Josh Gibson. In 1930 Gibson's legend grew while Brown was behind the plate for the Lincoln Giants. The two teams were in an eleven-game challenge series when Gibson purportedly hit a home run out of Yankee Stadium.[61] Brown and a teammate claimed the ball landed inside the park in a post-game interview. The *Amsterdam News* said it went 460 feet into the left field bleachers, longer than any hit by a white player that season. The *Pittsburgh Courier* echoed the *Amsterdam News's* description of Gibson's towering shot, saying, "It was the longest hit in Yankee Stadium that year." Negro leagues historian John Holway concluded that the ball did not go out of the park but instead went over the third tier in the upper deck down the third baseline.[62] Myths like these defined Josh Gibson's career and overshadowed Brown's defensive prowess behind the plate.

Brown stayed in New York for the 1931 season as the Lincoln Giants became the Harlem Stars under the guidance of Henry "Pop" Lloyd. The Stars played as an independent team during the 1931 season, so the stats for Brown are limited, showing a respectable .318 batting average.[63] After that, Brown stayed with the organization, rebranding as the New York Black Yankees. Brown remained solid behind the plate in 1932, but his batting average dropped below the Mendoza line at .171.[64] When Gus Greenlee lured Gibson across town to the Pittsburgh Crawfords for the 1932 season, the two met again at Yankee Stadium. With Connie Rector on the mound for the Black Yankees, Gibson homered through the columns of the façade over the Yankee bullpen. The Crawfords won the first game 12–8.[65] Brown's play shined on the East Coast, considered by most to be among the best in the game behind the plate.

After three years in New York, Brown moved back to Chicago to play for the American Giants. While in Chicago, the East-West All-Star Game's genesis highlighted Brown's popularity in the game. In 1936 Brown traveled to Philadelphia to play for the Stars and owner Eddie Gottlieb. Gottlieb was more of a booking agent than an owner who booked the Stars and numerous other Negro league teams along the East Coast. Unlike the Martin brothers in Memphis, Gottlieb saw Negro league baseball as solely a business enterprise.[66] Brown's 1936 statistics offensively dropped below his .292 batting average in his last three seasons in Chicago, at .266. Then in 1937, his average dipped below the Mendoza line at .190.[67] Signed to replace Biz Mackey behind the plate in 1936 for the Stars, his designation early in the 1938 season as a backup in Philadelphia led Brown to seek a return to Memphis.

Brown returned to a staunch lineup in Memphis, led by Ted "Double Duty" Radcliffe, whose move to Memphis followed the collapse of the Cincinnati Tigers. Radcliffe brought Memphis the bulk of his 1937 Tigers team and adding Brown as the daily catcher allowed "Double Duty" to focus on pitching and managing the club. When Brown returned, fans greeted Brown with a celebration between games of their doubleheader with the Birmingham Black Barons. Always a fan favorite, Brown responded by leading the Red Sox to four straight wins over the Birmingham Black Barons.[68] With Brown behind the plate, the Red Sox

6. The Boys of Summer

cruised to a 21–4 record, claiming the first-half pennant for the Negro American League. Brown and the Red Sox claimed the 1938 Negro American League championship as theirs following the disputed championship series described in Chapter 4.

Brown's career statistics necessitate serious consideration as of Hall of Fame stature. He has appeared on two Hall of Fame ballots (2006 and 2022) and remains eligible for induction. Players prohibit themselves from considering such aspirations at the height of their careers. Behind the veil of segregation, black players only hoped to play in the Major Leagues one day, much less be considered for induction into the Hall of Fame. Yet, Brown fully understood his value as a professional baseball player. Even before the Red Sox 1938 Negro American League championship, Brown played on a Negro World Series championship team, managed an East-West All-Star game, and played in the best stadiums. His play in Cuba legitimizes the claim that Brown was among the best catchers in all baseball, not just Blackball. Like other Hall of Famers from the Negro Leagues, Brown played in cities that valued his play. The Memphis Red Sox can claim Turkey Stearnes, Willie Foster, and "Buck" O'Neil as Hall of Famers who donned the colors at one point in their careers. Still, Brown is the player most closely associated with the franchise deserving of induction.

* * *

Brown's career continued with the Memphis Red Sox into the 1940s, where he oscillated between starting catcher and player-manager. By 1940, Brown, now 34 years old, remained one of Blackball's prolific catchers. Instead of merely deviating from Brown's playing career, at this point, Brown's introduction to Mathis allows us to understand the familial relationships found in the game. Brown, whose career began at the onset of the Negro leagues era, becomes a mentor and father-like figure to the younger Mathis, a player who may get an opportunity that players like Brown have longed for their entire careers, a chance to play in Organized Baseball. After signing his contract with Martin, Mathis headed to Martin Stadium for a bullpen session with Larry Brown. By 1940 Brown had established himself as one of the preeminent catchers in Negro leagues baseball. Brown instantly took a liking to young Mathis. "He's ready now," Brown told Jones following their initial bullpen.[69]

Brown relieved the worries of Mathis's wife Helen about life on the road by going over to their house and telling her, "I'll take care of this

The Memphis Red Sox

boy. You don't have anything to worry about."[70] Brown's adoption of the young Mathis as his younger brother included demanding they be roommates on the road. Brown and Mathis became battery mates for the Red Sox as young Mathis blossomed into one of the most prolific left-handed pitchers in the game. Along with scouting reports Brown shared with Mathis on nights before he pitched, Brown also coached young Mathis on the intricacies of being a professional off the field.

With Brown behind the plate and Mathis steadily improving his craft, Mathis became the ace of the Memphis staff. While they were roommates, Brown would get up every morning, sit on the side of the bed, and go over every hitter they would face that night. Brown's knowledge of the league proved invaluable to the young Mathis. Brown would tell Mathis, "Look, you can become a star, but you've gotta do what I tell you." Facing Josh Gibson, Brown coached him up against one of the Negro leagues most feared home run hitters. Brown shouted to Mathis, "Hey, Lefty, be careful with this guy. He's been hitting the ball out of all these parks." Josh fouled off the first two balls that Mathis lobbed over the plate. Brown called time and took a trip to the mound to talk to Mathis. "Don't try to trick him this, just throw the ball through the middle of the plate." Back behind the plate, Brown told Gibson what was coming. Thinking that Brown was out to trick him, Gibson missed and struck out. Then, in a matchup with Roy Campanella, Brown yelled to Mathis, "Hey, Lefty, don't try to trick him, just throw your curveball, let him see what he can do with it."

The banter between batters and catchers in the Negro leagues conversations was much livelier than in white baseball. Brown's keen understanding of the mental side of the game allowed Mathis to grow as a pitcher. Down 0–2 to Mathis, Brown called for another curveball. Fooled, Campanella swung at the ball that bounced in the dirt in front of the plate. Brown gave Mathis the confidence to strike out the biggest names in the game.[71]

Facing the game's best brought out the best in Mathis, whether that was the players stepping into the box against him or those toeing up the rubber opposite him. He cherished pitching matchups against Satchel Paige. No one player in Blackball painted a more imposing figure on the mound, nor did any other player carry the reputation for being the best in Blackball and possibly in all of baseball. Mathis' first head-to-head matchup with Paige was on May 7, 1942, in Kansas City against the Monarchs on their Opening Day. The *Commercial Appeal's* article "Red Sox Hit Paige" described how the Red Sox "managed to hand Satchel

6. The Boys of Summer

Paige a 4 to 1 defeat Sunday afternoon. Verdell Mathews [sic] was the victor over the Monarchs' ace thrower."[72]

Memphis Red Sox sports journalist Sam Brown made headway in the *Chicago Defender* following the game when he labeled Mathis as the "best left-hander in the Negro American League."[73] Paige quietly rebounded against the young Mathis with a resounding 11 to 0 performance against the Red Sox in Dallas in mid–July.[74] The Red Sox traveled north to Wrigley Field in Chicago for a doubleheader against the Monarchs. This highly publicized game pitting the cagey veteran Paige and the young gun Mathis ended with Mathis watching as Paige fanned sixteen Red Sox batters en route to a 4 to 2 victory over the Red Sox.[75]

The following season, Mathis looked to rebound against his boyhood hero on a return trip to Chicago's Wrigley Field. Only this time, Paige suited up with the Red Sox against the New York Cubans, going five hitless innings on his way to helping Memphis secure the 1 to 0 win.[76] Forced to wait another year for the rematch he desperately wanted, Mathis was granted his opportunity back in Chicago in July 1944. In an abbreviated nightcap of a doubleheader, Mathis outpitched Paige 3 to 2 to even his career record against Paige to 2–2. Then, Mathis stepped into the batter's box against Paige and laced a triple to push across the game-winning run.[77] Mathis described the crowd as "about 30-some thousand people. They had a big van to take away the stuff they had given him (for Satchel Paige Day). I got a traveling bag, a little traveling bag. But I drove in the winning run."[78] Mathis spoiled Satchel Paige Day in Chicago for the fans and earned his second victory against the iconic pitcher.

In 1946 Mathis joined Satchel Paige's barnstorming team following the Negro American League season. This iteration of the Satchel Paige All-Stars played thirteen games across the country against Bob Feller's All-Stars.[79] Mathis' ability to play the outfield and pitch against the best caught the eye of Paige and allowed Mathis to make money after the NAL season. By 1946, Mathis was only 32 years old, but the wear and tear on his arm began to take its toll. Surgery on his arm was on the horizon, a surgery that would arguably deny him the opportunity to play Organized Baseball. Following surgery, Mathis remained with the Red Sox through their final season in 1959. Although the talent level waned in the Negro leagues following the downfall of the color line in Organized Baseball, Mathis continued to pitch for the Red Sox.

Whereas Brown's playing career merits serious consideration for induction into the Hall of Fame, Mathis's career becomes one of the

135

The Memphis Red Sox

greatest what-ifs in all Blackball. Denied an opportunity to cross the color barrier in baseball because of an injury, Mathis missed his chance because of the circumstances of medicine in the Jim Crow South. Branch Rickey told Mathis, "I didn't act hastily enough. We should have got you before your arm got hurt."[80] A twenty-year career filled Mathis with pride in his accomplishments and built a bond among his teammates that withstood the test of time. Moments, where he shined on the biggest stages, stand as positive proof that, for a brief moment, Mathis was among the game's best pitchers.

* * *

Scott actively began his Negro leagues career in 1946 with the New York Black Yankees. Making only $300 a month in New York, Scott jumped teams midway through the summer and joined Gus Greenlee's Pittsburgh Crawfords, earning $750 a month.[81] Scott helped the Crawfords secure the United States League championship in 1946. Unfortunately, the USL, an attempt by Greenlee to create a league that rivaled the Negro American League and Negro National League, was short-lived, providing Scott with only a short stay in Steel City.[82] Scott figured he was out of baseball after 1946, but Verdell Mathis convinced B.B. Martin and W.S. Martin Scott to sign Scott. Having played with Scott and against Scott during World War II, Mathis urged the Martin brothers to sign Scott for the 1947 season, where he earned $500 in 1947 with the Red Sox.[83] Back with the Memphis, he patrolled the outfield while hitting .348, one of the best of his career.[84]

Scott returned for the 1948 Negro American League season as part of Memphis Red Sox manager Larry Brown's Opening-Day lineup.[85] Earlier that spring, Scott dazzled fans at Martin Stadium by racing to the left field wall and making a one-handed gem. Later in the inning, he showcased his speed, stealing second, third, and home in the bottom half of the inning in the Red Sox's 10 to 4 defeat of the Atlanta Black Crackers.[86] During the 1948 Negro American League season, Scott's career became part of the tug-of-war between Organized Baseball and the Negro leagues. Roger Hornsby recommended Scott to Poughkeepsie of the Class B Colonial League after Scott attended Hornsby's diamond school in Hot Springs, Arkansas, in the spring of 1948, the first African American to participate in the school.[87]

Scott hoped, like many of the other Memphis Red Sox, that after the Brooklyn Dodgers' signing of Dan Bankhead in 1947, they too would get an opportunity to play in Organized Baseball. The Poughkeepsie

6. *The Boys of Summer*

Chiefs offered the Red Sox $5,000 for his contract. However, W.S. Martin and B.B. Martin, the Memphis Red Sox owners, would not sell his contract for anything less than $15,000. Scott personally protested the Martins' denying the Poughkeepsie request for his contract at $5,000. He told the Martins, "I didn't cost you, not even one red penny. I'd like to go up there."[88] Unfortunately, the Martins never budged, and Scott lost an opportunity to play in the minors that year.

As Organized Baseball added more black players to their rosters, the Negro leagues continued to market themselves uniquely to bring fans to the stadium. For example, the Red Sox marketed Scott's speed in between a July doubleheader with the Cleveland Buckeyes by having him race teammate Bob Boyd and Buckeyes players Sam Jethroe, Archie Ware, and Bill Smith in the 100 and 200-yard dash.[89] By early August, Scott continued to swing a hot bat for the Red Sox, joining four other teammates hitting over .300 heading into a weekend series against the Buckeyes.[90] Unable to convince the Martins to sell his contract to Poughkeepsie, Scott completed the 1948 season with the Red Sox, finishing with a .292 batting average.[91] Scott returned to the Red Sox for the 1949 season under manager "Goose" Curry. He rapped out four hits in an early season game with the New York Cubans to secure the Red Sox 7–4 victory.[92] As Scott remained in Memphis, George Handy, his former Red Sox teammate, joined the Bridgeport Bees of the Class B Colonial League, where he hit .346 with 22 home runs and 25 stolen bases in 126 games.[93]

Negro leagues historian Jules Tygiel argues that despite rumors of the imminent signing of black players, only the Dodgers, Indians, and Browns took the fateful step.[94] Many black players who did sign were left scuttling through the minor leagues. Others, like Scott, patiently waited for the minors to offer them the same opportunity.[95] In a uniquely Negro leagues issue, during the 1949 season, W.S. Martin kept Scott on the roster without physically having Scott sign a contract. Refusing to give Scott a raise, Martin played Scott in 1949 under his 1948 contract and 1949 became Scott's last season in the Negro leagues. His career did not end in Memphis, but his best years were behind him as he ventured out into the world of white Organized Baseball.

Scott's entrance into Blackball came right as Organized Baseball began to take steps toward integrating the sport. From his earliest days of playing integrated high school baseball in Chicago, Scott believed his skills merited an opportunity to play in the Major Leagues. The political battle that surrounded the integration of baseball left Scott seeking

The Memphis Red Sox

answers. Scott remains the lone player of the three to play in Organized Baseball's minor leagues. Caught in the middle of a power struggle between the two, Scott lost the opportunity he and many other Negro leaguers desired.

* * *

The pinnacle of the Negro leagues season was the East-West All-Star Game, which almost marked the highlight of the sports calendar for black sports fans. The fans chose teams by voting through the nation's two most prominent black newspapers, the *Chicago Defender* and the *Pittsburgh Courier*.[96] The All-Star Game was an exhibition for white baseball, but according to "Buck" O'Neil, the East-West Game was more. It was a matter of racial pride. The best players came to Chicago to play in front of the season's largest crowd. They scheduled the games the weekend before school started. Kids saved up their nickels and dimes to buy tickets at any black stores in Chicago. The weekend itself was a celebration of black life. It was one big party. The nightclubs were hopping; the most prominent names performed at night and then attended the game on Sunday.

The fans at these games were rabid baseball fans and expected the players to perform. Players vied for positions on the team and understood that a good showing in Chicago could determine their value in the Negro leagues. The game's genesis in 1933 emanated from a conversation between Gus Greenlee, owner of the Pittsburgh Crawfords, and Roy Sparrow of the *Pittsburg Sun-Telegraph*. Greenlee advised that he take his idea, with his backing, to the owner of the Chicago American Giants, Robert Cole, and play the game at Chicago's Comiskey Park.[97] Both Brown and Mathis scored their marks on the game's biggest stage. What follows are the highlights from Brown and Mathis's performances in the big game.

Browsing through historian Larry Lester's definitive work on the East-West All-Star Game, *Black Baseball's National Showcase*, when you open the Appendixes and look at the top line of the first chart depicting the games, Larry Brown's name was front and center as the manager of the winning West squad in 1933.[98] Brown's prowess behind the dish led to his appearance in seven East-West All-Star games, where he routinely garnered more votes than Negro leagues legend Josh Gibson. America's love affair with the home run propelled Gibson's heroic status in the annals of Negro leagues myth, just as it did for Babe Ruth. As Brown was selected through fan balloting, his popularity

6. The Boys of Summer

in Chicago with the American Giants and in New York with the Black Yankees placed him repeatedly among the game's best players. The nation's two most prominent black newspapers, the *Chicago Defender* and the *Pittsburgh Courier*, tallied the votes, precipitating Brown's 1933 selection.[99]

On September 14, 1933, Brown served as the West team's manager in the inaugural game. He led the West All-Star voting at catcher and started at catcher opposite Josh Gibson. Brown drilled a triple over James' Cool Papa' Bell's head in the bottom of the fifth, but he was tagged out when he overran the base.[100] The *Pittsburgh Courier* described Brown's base running debacle: "Brown went on around and came into third and was prepared to stay there. He seemed to be out of run. But the coach stirred him up with a whack and sent him in, and he was out from here to the Cuban revolution."[101] Brown's West squad defeated Willie Foster's East team 11–7 to the delight of the 19,568 attendance at Comiskey Park.[102]

Brown returned for the 1934 game as the leading vote-getter for catchers in the Negro leagues in front of Tommy Dukes, Frank Duncan, and Josh Gibson. In a defensive duel between the two squads in a low-scoring affair, Brown eked out a single for the West squad in front of the 30,000 fans at Comiskey Park. The 1935 game saw Satchel Paige come in relief and keep the West bats silent as the East pushed across their lone run in the top of the eight to win the game 1–0.[103]

The following year saw Brown again top Josh Gibson as the leading vote-getter as the *Chicago Defender* proclaimed, "Larry Brown still reigns supreme with Josh Gibson coming to the front with a rush in the closing days."[104] Yet Gibson, of the Pittsburgh Crawfords, got the start for West manager Oscar Charleston, of the Pittsburgh Crawfords. Brown's departure from Chicago and the American Giants for Philadelphia in 1936 with the Stars ultimately led to a significant drop-off in his ability to tally votes for the game. Brown would make his next appearance in an East-West All-Star Game after returning to the Memphis Red Sox in 1938 at 39 years old.

During Brown's 1938 run with the Red Sox for the 1938 Negro American League championship, he earned another East-West All-Star game selection. Wendell Smith's campaign to integrate baseball was at a fever pitch in the summer of 1938 as he prodded black folks to stop spending their dollars attending white baseball games. He also interviewed forty white players and eight white managers that summer to gauge their opinions of the Negro leagues' best players.[105] Chicago welcomed black America for the sixth annual East-West All-Star Game at Comiskey Park. According to the *Chicago Defender*, Brown was inserted defensively in the seventh inning to handle Red Sox battery mate Ted "Double Duty" Radcliffe and keep runners in check.[106] Following the East-West All-Star Game, Brown and Radcliffe returned to Memphis to finish the 1938 Negro American League championship season.

Brown's defensive prowess behind the plate proved valuable to the West squad in the 1939 game. Brown replaced starter Pepper Bassett of the Chicago American Giants in the fifth inning. Radcliffe was on the mound for the West in the ninth inning, and the powerful Mules Suttles at-bat with the West clinging to a 4–2 lead. *The Chicago Defender's* Fay Young describes the action in front of 40,000 screaming fans. "Radcliffe threw the ball across the plate, past Suttles in the ninth. Suttles missed the first two strikes and looked at a pitch-out Brown called. Then came a roundhouse curve which broke under Mule's swing."[107] Once again, Brown's knowledge of the game's best hitters allowed him to call a series of pitches that secured the victory for his Western squad. His proficiency in calling a game made Brown one of the best the game has ever seen. Brown returned as a bench player to the East-West All-Star game the following season. In the game's later innings, Brown scratched out one of five singles the East allowed that day in his only at-bat.[108]

* * *

As Father Time began to catch up with Brown in 1941, a young Verdell Mathis made his first East-West All-Star Game appearance in Brown's last. Nevertheless, Brown remained popular as the third leading vote-getter among catchers heading into the game. Brown's defensive ability remained sharp as he rifled a pill down to second base cutting down the East's nineteen-year-old phenom Roy Campanella trying to steal in the top of the ninth inning.[109] Fay Young of the *Chicago Defender* questioned West manager "Candy" Jim Taylor's lineup in the fourth inning when four of the nine players wore Red Sox jerseys.[110] The Windy City's bias misses that Radcliffe, "Jelly" Taylor, Neil Robinson, and Brown represented formidable players on any squad over the previous five seasons, including the 1938 Negro American League championship season for the Red Sox. Mathis served as the fifth Red Sox player on the West squad and briefly appeared as a pinch runner for starting catcher Pepper Bassett in the second inning.[111]

The following season, in 1939, as Mathis was coming into his own as a

6. The Boys of Summer

pitcher on the major league level in Blackball, he made his first pitching appearance in the East-West All-Star game, in the third inning. After Eugene Bremmer of the Cleveland Buckeyes gave up five runs in the top of the third, Mathis came in for the next 3 1/3 innings to limit the damage for the West All-Stars.[112] Thus, Mathis's first All-Star appearance as a pitcher occurred in a 9 to 2 loss. The game raised nearly $10,000 for the United States Army and Navy Relief Fund during World War II's first summer of baseball.[113]

Returning in 1944, Mathis took the mound for the West as the game's starter. The 1944 East-West All-Star game made headlines for its absence of Satchel Paige, following his demands that the Negro American League and the Negro National League each pay him a percentage off the top of the gate fees. Negro American League, president and former Memphis Red Sox owner J.B. Martin, adamantly refused to give in to Paige.[114] Thus opening the door for Mathis to take the mound for the West squad. Although his mentor and good friend Brown was not in uniform this day, a late replacement on the West roster, "Double Duty" Radcliffe, sat behind the plate to guide "Lefty." Mathis gave up three hits and one earned run in three innings of work. Mathis worked a scoreless first, giving up a single to Ray Dandridge but leaving him stranded. In the second, Josh Gibson led off with a triple and plated on John Davis's (Newark Eagles) single to center. Mathis left Davis stranded in the top of the second after his single and worked a scoreless third inning. Mathis became part of a four-man rotation that allowed the West to win the 1944 East-West game, even without the services of Paige.[115] When Gentry Jessup of the Chicago American Giants entered in the top of the fourth, Mathis left him with a 2–1 lead.[116]

For Mathis, the 1945 campaign was the strongest of his career, including squaring off against Satchel Paige and defeating him three times, including a 1–0 defeat in Chicago at Wrigley Field in front of 30,000 fans.[117] The 1945 East-West All-Star Game saw Mathis take the hill as the West starter, going three innings, giving up no hits, one base on balls, and ringing up four strikeouts. At the plate, he helped his cause with two singles, plating one of his team's eight runs.[118] After his only walk of the game, Mathis picked off Frank Austin of the Philadelphia Stars, only moments later using the pick-off move he developed from watching Louis Tiant, Sr., play in Mexico with Veracruz.[119] By 1945, after hours of watching and mimicking Tiant, Mathis developed one of Blackball's most feared pick-off moves.

The Memphis Red Sox

Mathis's athleticism was on display on the hill and in the box. His second-inning single to center was part of the West's four-run inning, and the following inning, he beat out a slow roller up the middle for an infield single to load the bases for the West.[120] Noted sports journalist for the *Pittsburgh Courier* Wendell Smith described Mathis in his 1945 East-West game review as a "lean southpaw with a blazing fastball, tricky curve, and change-of-pace that was too much for the East."[121] Arguably, Mathis proved that in 1945, he was the best pitcher in Blackball.

Mathis's arm began giving him trouble during the 1945 pre-season, although his arm healed enough for his second straight dominant performance on the mound during the East-West All-Star Game.[122] Over the next year, the Red Sox stretched out Mathis as their ace, pitching him repeatedly. By the beginning of the 1947 season, Mathis found himself unable to throw. Mathis missed his chance to become Major League baseball's first black pitcher because of the realities of health care in Jim Crow Memphis. Mathis understood the truth he faced after surgery on his pitching arm. Doctors from the Campbell Clinic, Memphis's preeminent white surgical facility, performed the surgery at Collins Chapel Hospital. Collins Chapel, the city's black hospital, relied on inferior equipment with its limited budget. Although his white doctor was willing to risk sneaking into Collins Chapel after hours to perform the surgery, Mathis's arm was never the same.[123] Mathis watched as Branch Rickey came to Memphis and signed Dan Bankhead, the first black pitcher in the Major Leagues. Rickey later told Mathis, "I didn't act hastily enough. We should have got you before your arm got hurt."[124]

Statistically, Mathis's play in the celebrated East-West All-Star game places him among the all-time greats ever to take the Blackball mound. Negro leagues historian James Riley elevates Mathis to equal footing with Satchel Paige, claiming Mathis won two East-West games.[125] Further analysis reveals that Mathis recorded only one win, yet had Jessup not given up a run in the top of the fourth inning of the 1944 game, Mathis would have achieved this vaunted status.[126] A deeper dive into the analytics of statistics from the East-West All-Star game, one of the few places where statistics from Negro leagues baseball are on an even par with Organized Baseball's, reveals the abilities of Mathis to perform on the game's biggest stage. His walks per nine innings place him third, and his ERA stands at and fifth with a minuscule .96 against the game's best hitters. Add in that he joins an illustrious group

6. *The Boys of Summer*

of pitchers to have earned two starts in the big game, and the conclusion that Mathis is among the best rings true statistically.[127]

* * *

For ballplayers, hanging up the cleats is one of the most difficult things to do, even more challenging than facing the game's best pitchers. Each of our three players experienced the end in different ways. For Brown, he hung on to the game as long as he could, acting as the Red Sox's player-manager long after his body allowed him to catch daily. For Mathis, his surgically repaired arm was never the same. For Scott, the opportunity to break the color line and play Organized Baseball provided challenges on the field and off. Unfortunately, he, too, suffered an injury, shortening his career.

Brown's first stint as manager of the Red Sox started with the 1942 season, and over the next seven seasons, he entered an on-again, off-again relationship with the Martins as their manager. Out as manager for the 1944 season, he was back at the helm in 1945, then found himself no longer in charge during the 1946 season. In 1947 Brown returned as the manager as the Red Sox opened play in the newly renovated Martin Stadium. The Red Sox hoped to increase attendance at a moment when the eyes of black America focused on Jackie Robinson. By 1944, Brown's role as the everyday starting catcher decreased as newcomer Clinton "Casey" Jones began sharing time behind the plate.

The following season, with Brown as the team's manager, Jones became the Red Sox's everyday catcher. No longer a regular in the lineup, the pressure on Brown to win and draw fans to Martin Stadium was exacerbated by the amount of money the Martins invested in renovations. Brown understood these pressures and convinced the Martins to sign Cuban stars Pedro Formenthal (also spelled Formental) and José Colás to fortify the lineup. At this stage of his career, Brown's value revolved around his ability to manage.

The Red Sox 1947 season became a footnote to baseball's grand experiment. Born too late to enjoy the fruits of integration, Brown watched as Branch Rickey descended upon Memphis and signed Dan Bankhead to a major league contract with the Dodgers. Bankhead's signing brought great excitement to Memphis's black fans when it was announced over the loudspeaker and in the *Memphis World*.[128] Past his prime and aging to a point where he could no longer play winter ball, Brown stayed in Memphis instead of traveling to Latin America in the off-season. Instead, he worked as a waiter at local hotels, including the

The Memphis Red Sox

Hotel Gayoso on Main Street and the William Len Hotel on the corner of Main Street and Monroe Avenue.[129] Working at the hotels allowed Brown to stay connected with the community and keep his face in the crowd.[130]

Brown's son Larry Jr. became a member of the Tuskegee Airmen during World War II and served through the Korean War.[131] In 2007 he, along with the other Tuskegee Airmen, was awarded the Congressional Gold Medal by President George W. Bush.[132] Brown Sr. remained in Memphis, where he worked at the William Len Hotel until he retired in 1970. Larry Brown received consideration from a committee of nine members who elected Josh Gibson and "Buck" Leonard into the National Baseball Hall of Fame in 1972. Unfortunately, Brown passed away in April 1972, three months before Gibson's induction into the Hall of Fame.[133]

* * *

For Verdell Mathis, the continuing pain in his throwing arm meant a slow, painful decline in his playing ability. An Opening-Day victory over the Indianapolis Clowns in 1946 looked promising, but reports of his ailing arm resurfaced by mid–July.[134] Mathis's popularity among the fans allowed him to play in the North-South All-Star game but not the more prestigious East-West one. The following season proved more of the same, as his arm allowed him to shine in games against the Birmingham Black Barons in June and July, only to find himself unable to pitch in the East-West game in August.[135] By 1948 the eyes of black America were watching the travails of Jackie Robinson; meanwhile, back in Memphis, Mathis's arm continued to falter in the team's home-opening 9 to 4 loss to the Kansas City Monarchs.[136] By 1948 time was running out if Mathis was going to have any chance of playing Organized Baseball.

With the Red Sox faltering and his arm waning, Mathis took advantage of an opportunity to head north to play semi-pro baseball in Michigan. The St. Joseph Auscos played in the Michigan–Indiana League, and the team played their home games at Edgewater Park on the grounds of the Auto Specialties Company in St. Joseph, Michigan.[137] Just as the Martins had when Mathis jumped to the Philadelphia Stars earlier in his career, they once again used the office of Negro American League president J.B. Martin to persuade Mathis to return to Memphis for the remainder of the season or face a two-year suspension.[138]

Mathis held on for two more seasons with the Red Sox, but another opportunity in white baseball presented itself for the aging hurler. Venturing north, this time to Rochester, Minnesota, Mathis tried to latch

6. The Boys of Summer

on with the Rochester Royals of the Southern Minnesota League, an independent league. Following a brief stint in Rochester, he moved to Le Sueur, Minnesota, where The *Winona Republican Herald* referred to Mathis as "the dusky-chinned chucker." Racial slights aside, Mathis held his own and earned one more start with the Le Sueur club before returning south to play out the 1950 season in more familiar surroundings with the Houston Eagles.[139] Mathis then returned to the Memphis Red Sox in 1951.

Mathis's career ended abruptly when B.B. Martin folded the Red Sox organization. Taking an opportunity to work for Chock Full O' Nuts, the company that hired Jackie Robinson when he retired, Mathis moved his family to New York. Mathis spent the next nine years in New York, enjoying watching the Brooklyn Dodgers and the New York Yankees play.[140] After nine years living in New York City, Mathis returned to Memphis, where he worked at the Colonial Country Club for the next fifteen years.[141] Back home in Memphis, Mathis coached local baseball teams and maintained a close relationship with his good friend and mentor, Larry Brown. After retiring, Mathis ran into a white family vacationing at a hotel that booked Negro leagues games in Dayton, Ohio. Upon seeing Mathis, the husband's first question was, "Where's Larry?" The two were synonymous together.

Mathis found Brown and brought him back to meet and reminisce with the white family. The man gave Brown $20 when managing the Red Sox to "save Mathis to pitch here (Dayton) because the people don't want to see nobody else."[142] Mathis and Brown were no worse off for the exchange, but Mathis did tell Brown he owed him half of those $20 payoffs.[143] Mathis died in 1998 at the age of eighty-four. The *Commercial Appeal* remembered him as a quiet, unassuming individual who was shy until he got on the mound. Mathis left a legacy of twelve grandchildren and sixteen great-grandchildren.[144]

* * *

In a uniquely Negro leagues issue, during the 1949 season, the Red Sox kept Scott on the roster without physically having him sign a contract. Refusing to give Scott a raise, W.S. Martin played Scott in 1949 under his 1948 contract. Unable to get a fair contract, Scott went north to Canada to play for the Farnham Pirates in the Provincial League in 1950. W.S. Martin sought compensation for the loss of Scott and contacted George Trautman, the president of minor league baseball. When Trautman discovered that Scott had not signed a contract for the 1949 season, Trautman told Scott that Martin had no legal ground to stand on; he was free to play in Canada.[145] Scott spent the next two seasons in Canada with the Farnham Pirates in 1950 and the St. Hyacinthe Saints in 1951, playing well in this Class C minor league.[146] The Philadelphia Athletics purchased his contract from St. Hyacinthe heading into the 1952 season. However, an injury before spring training prevented Scott from making an Athletics roster in 1952.[147]

In 1954 the Hot Springs Bathers of the Class C Cotton states League picked up Scott for a brief two-game stint. A year earlier, the Bathers signed Jim and Leander Tugerson, brothers who pitched for the Indianapolis Clowns, to become the first two African Americans to play in the Cotton States League. The league expelled the Bathers, which were reinstated only upon appeal to minor league president George Trautman. Trautman's decision stated that "the right to employ any player, regardless of race, color, or creed, lay with the individual club."[148] When Charlie Williamson, the Bathers owner, brought Scott to Hot Springs in 1954, this was no longer a strike at segregation but a marketing ploy to boost sagging attendance. The *Hope Star* (Hope, Arkansas) reminded its readers that only one year earlier, the owners of the Cotton States League "bitterly opposed the use of Negroes."[149] Scott eked out two singles in his ten plate appearances for the Bathers and returned home to Memphis.[150]

Scott's last opportunity in professional baseball came in 1956 with the Knoxville Smokies of the Class A South Atlantic League. Dick Bartell offered Scott a chance on a ten-day contract. In his first game, he "got a Texas-leaguer to leftfield" to score a run in the bottom of the fifth.[151] Scott saw action, but the racial hatred that followed signaled it was time for him to retire. Whenever he came to bat, the fans chanted, "Strike that nigger out!" After three games of the same, Scott went to Bartell and told him he was returning to Memphis to get a job.[152] Historian Jules Tygiel reminds us that fan hostility further complicated the athlete's life. Hometown spectators rarely posed a problem, but Southern fans unleashed an unending racial invective against visiting players.[153] For Scott, his last two opportunities in Organized Baseball were publicity stunts, a chance for minor league franchises to offer their fans the oddity of seeing a Negro player. Marketing schemes to boost attendance exacerbated the challenge facing Negro leagues players like Scott trying to continue their careers.

After his baseball career, Scott worked as a truck driver at the Memphis Army Depot.[154] He lived with his common-law wife, Evelyn Kinney,

6. The Boys of Summer

whom he met in Memphis in the 1940s. Later in life, Scott became an ambassador for Negro leagues baseball. As a result, when Major League Baseball held a special draft for former Negro leagues players in 2008, the Milwaukee Brewers drafted Scott.[155] AutoZone Park in Memphis, home of the St. Louis Cardinals AAA organization, offered the opportunity to continue to share the story of the Memphis Red Sox and Negro leagues baseball. In July 2008, the Redbirds hosted Scott and fellow Red Sox player Ollie Brantley for "Conversations with History: Memories of the Negro Leagues." Through conversations like these, Scott kept the memory of Negro leagues baseball alive in his hometown. As a result,

With the renaissance of interest in Negro leagues baseball in the 1990s, Joe B. Scott (shown here in 2007) remained a prominent figure in Memphis, sharing the story of the Red Sox and the Negro leagues (Steve Roberts Photography).

Redbirds GM David Chase welcomed Scott to AutoZone Park, giving him a lifetime pass to games and saluting the Negro leagues yearly when the Redbirds donned Memphis Red Sox uniforms.[156]

Following his death, the *Commercial Appeal* reminded the city that Scott "was respected and admired by baseball aficionados for his accomplishments on the baseball diamond and his work promoting the sport among Greater Memphis youngsters. He was blessed to have his accomplishments recognized during his lifetime. And the city was

The Memphis Red Sox

Verdell Mathis and Joe B. Scott shake hands on the steps of the dugout at Martin Stadium. Both players would get a chance to play Organized Baseball, but neither made it to the majors (Withers Family Collection).

blessed to have him use that recognition to be a great ambassador for baseball."[157] Scott's legacy went beyond his playing days, as he became a mentor and an ambassador for baseball in the Bluff City. He died on March 21, 2013, at 92.

* * *

For these three Memphis Red Sox players, Memphis was home. Mathis and Scott were born here and remained Memphians after their careers ended. Brown, a native of Birmingham, Alabama, adopted Memphis as his own and spent the rest of his career and the remainder of his life in the Bluff City. The love of the game propelled them to chase their dreams of playing baseball. The long bus rides on road trips and barnstorming tours brought players together and created a bond. They barnstormed through a segregated America in the summer months. Then

6. The Boys of Summer

they sought opportunities to play winter baseball south of the border. Latin American countries offered opportunities to play against some of the better players in Organized Baseball and Latin American players. Denied the opportunity to play baseball at its highest level, these three players experienced professional baseball in the Negro leagues. They played in the best parks in America and against the game's best players, white and black.

7

Barnstorming

Those who did not think the Negro leagues qualified as major league baseball claimed that, unlike Organized Baseball, Negro leaguers played in obscurity. Contrary to this misconception, Negro leaguers played countless games in front of fans nationwide when white professional baseball remained primarily east of the Mississippi River. Satchel Paige once told a reporter, "People got a chance to see me play everywhere. I played all over farm fields, penitentiaries, any place in this whole country where there was a baseball diamond. They know me and see me."[1] Baseball-devoted fans, both white and black, clamored to see baseball in small towns and urban cities where the major leagues had not yet expanded. Negro league teams barnstormed before, during, and after the traditional season, allowing the fans to see baseball in their hometowns. Barnstorming was an economic necessity for Negro leagues teams. Without barnstorming, teams like the Memphis Red Sox would not have survived the turbulent economic times of the 1920s and 1930s.

Negro leagues teams played in an era when almost every small town had a semi-pro team worth boasting about. Often the entire business community closed down for the day to come out and see their local heroes take on the Red Sox.[2] The loose bindings that held Negro leagues together created the economic necessity for barnstorming. Historian Donn Rogosin emphasized that most games played by Negro leagues teams were not the bitterly contested league games but, instead, exhibitions wherever a profitable afternoon beckoned. Simple economics: white people had more money.[3] Professional baseball players, white or black, made minuscule salaries compared to today's professionals.

Joined by many of their white counterparts, black professional players took part in an economic system symbolic of the economic structure of professional baseball. In addition, white professional players faced the financial restraints of the reserve clause imposed by white

7. Barnstorming

owners in major league baseball. Unable to employ free agency to garner higher salaries, white players often joined with Negro leagues players in barnstorming tours.

In the 1920s, Babe Ruth competed against Negro leagues players on the barnstorming circuit. In the 1930s, Dizzy Dean's barnstorming all-star teams openly competed with all-star teams composed of Negro league stars. Satchel Paige's pitching duels against Dean in the 1930s and Bob Feller in the 1940s highlighted marquee matchups on the circuit. The success of Negro leaguers in these matchups further strengthened voices calling for the integration of the American pastime.

Detractors in white baseball argued that owners of professional black baseball clubs were little more than booking agents and that exhibitions against semi-pro teams demonstrated the inferiority of black professional clubs. Yet, for the owners of black clubs to survive, they were forced to transact business within the white power structure. Thus, they scheduled games with white semi-pro owners and park managers, and in some cases, established business relationships with white entrepreneurs. This symbiotic business relationship with white semi-pro clubs and loosely associated black clubs created barnstorming schedules that were both regional and national in scope.[4] As a result, the black players found themselves barnstorming throughout the season.

For example, there was no need to go South for spring training for the Red Sox, playing in a Southern city. Instead, they often set out on barnstorming tours to recruit players and establish financial stability at the beginning of the season. During the season, inconsistencies in league scheduling allowed the Red Sox to barnstorm throughout the summer. After league play concluded, the team barnstormed against willing opponents as long as the weather held out. Finally, the players returned home for the off-season or headed south for more lucrative contracts in Latin American winter leagues. This system of barnstorming accurately described Negro leagues baseball from its inception through its demise.

Rube Foster's Chicago American Giants set the standard for black professional teams to aspire to as they traveled. Foster placed his team on Pullman Porter cars as they traveled throughout the United States. Not only did this symbolize Foster's desire to elevate the black game as equal to white professional baseball, but this also offered the comforts of travel without the impediments of segregation found throughout the country in the 1920s. Unfortunately, few black teams held the financial wherewithal of Foster's American Giants. Instead, teams like the

The Memphis Red Sox

Memphis Red Sox piled players into two or three cars, hitting the road and playing all-comers.

During the club's inaugural 1922 season in the Negro Southern League, the Red Sox began barnstorming in July. First, the Red Sox hosted the Negro National League's St. Louis Stars in a series at Russwood Park, where they split a pair of games.[5] Then they hosted Foster's Chicago American Giants, sweeping them in a five-game set.[6] In the comfortable confines of Russwood Park, the Red Sox had played host to two Negro National League powers as these teams barnstormed through the South. The victories signaled the Red Sox's desire to be considered one of black baseball's most competitive clubs.

The 1922 Red Sox set out to Dallas to compete against the Texas Colored League champions at the end of the season. In a uniquely Negro leagues twist, the Red Sox played what the *Commercial Appeal* referred to as "a Dallas team." The *Commercial Appeal* claimed the Red Sox defeated this team from Dallas 6–2 in the series' first game.[7] The September 10, 1922, article was the last one posted by the *Commercial Appeal* concerning the series. With no league standings in historical records, the Dallas Black Giants barnstormed throughout the 1922 season and proclaimed themselves Texas Colored League champions. The Red Sox accepted their proclamation and offered to go to Dallas to compete for the "negro [sic] championship of the South."[8] These barnstorming series posed as attempts for the Red Sox to prove their ability to compete on a higher level. In 1922 the various Negro leagues throughout the country remained independently operated without the ties that bound the owners of white baseball's American and National Leagues. In turn, the nature of black professional baseball and the Memphis Red Sox remained regional and allowed the team to seek out a "championship" with a team from Dallas. The Memphis faithful's only view of black baseball on a national level came from its weekly appearance in the *Chicago Defender*.

As the Red Sox and R.S. Lewis continued to seek opportunities to increase revenue, the team began barnstorming against local semi-pro teams in 1923. The most memorable of these games announced the presence of future Hall of Famer Willie Foster. Foster, the younger half-brother of the Chicago American Giants owner Rube Foster, threw a no-hitter in a 4–0 defeat of the Arkansas Travelers from Hot Springs, Arkansas. Willie Foster struck out fourteen batters while walking only two.[9] Two days later, he secured his position on the Red Sox staff when he defeated the Fort Benning infantry's Black Baseball Club.[10] Foster's

7. Barnstorming

The Red Sox played the Dallas Black Giants in 1922 for the Negro championship of the South, losing all three exhibition games (Public Domain).

second game placed over 4,000 fans in the stands at Lewis Park, allowing Lewis to survive economically while maintaining membership in the Negro Southern League.

As the Red Sox did during the 1922 season, they again invited Negro National League teams south to play at Lewis Park. The Red Sox's successes in 1922 and a split with the Milwaukee Bears in 1923 positioned them for admittance into the Negro National League as an associate member.[11] In August, Willie Foster squared off against the NNL's St. Louis Stars at Lewis Park. The young hurler made waves throughout black baseball as the *Chicago Defender* claimed Foster "set the Memphis folks, as well as the entire Beale Avenue agog."[12] Hosting barnstorming games with NNL teams was a win-win for the Red Sox. Following their 1923 successes against NNL teams, the Red Sox went back on the road to play the Dallas Black Giants. Unfortunately, the Red Sox lost all three to Dallas in this series. Still, the younger Foster's showing led to Rube Foster forcing the hands of his brother and R.S. Lewis in getting Willie to "jump" to the Chicago American Giants for the remainder of the 1923 season.[13]

As an associate member of the Negro National League in 1924, the Red Sox used barnstorming as an intricate piece in the Red Sox schedule. A black-owned park was rare, but it allowed the Red Sox control of their schedule. They split a pair of games with the Cuban Stars in early May.[14] Then, as an associate member of the NNL, they played a series

The Memphis Red Sox

against the Indianapolis ABCs, the St. Louis Stars, and the Birmingham Black Barons. They continued to barnstorm against former NNL member Milwaukee Bears and an independent club, the New Orleans Segula Stars. Following a June 18, 1924, game against the Birmingham Black Barons, box scores and articles for the Red Sox disappear from the historical record.[15]

We can only assume the Red Sox continued to barnstorm and play local semi-pro teams throughout the summer. Negro leaguers claimed that numerous black baseball owners manipulated the information they provided to the media to keep salaries lower and maintain an appearance of operating a winning club. This money-saving strategy created problems for fans tracking Red Sox box scores as they barnstormed. The inconsistencies in box scores created a gap in the statistics for each season and overall records.

The ever-changing landscape of black baseball in the South birthed a unique opportunity for fans in the Bluff City to watch their Red Sox. At the onset of the 1931 season, Little Rock, Arkansas, was not yet a member of the Negro Southern League. To prove that Little Rock provided a viable fanbase value to support a franchise NSL, the Little Rock Travelers hosted several games between the Red Sox and the Birmingham Black Barons. The local newspapers heavily advertised the games, as fans could pay three dollars for a round trip "excursion" to Little Rock on the Missouri Pacific Railroad.[16] The *Arkansas Gazette* noted that the Red Sox won the first game of the doubleheader, 5–4, but the Black Barons catcher Tommy Dukes stole the show with "a sensational catch in the first inning. On a short fly down the third baseline, Dukes dove full length, caught the ball, turned a complete flip, but retained the ball for the putout."[17]

Noted as an independent team at the beginning of the 1931 season, Little Rock proved itself to be a city worthy of inclusion in the NSL. By the end of July, Little Rock considered itself an associate member of the NSL, but historical records referred to the franchise by multiple names. Earlier records listed the club as the Black Travelers. Then in July, the *Arkansas Gazette* referred to the club as the Little Rock Grays in a series with the Nashville Elite Giants, and in late July, the *Commercial Appeal* referred to the club as the Gray Travelers.[18] The line between barnstorming against independent teams and playing league games in any one season for the Red Sox was tenuous. Was the Little Rock team an affiliate NSL member or a full-fledged NSL member? Or was the team simply another semi-pro team against whom NSL members

7. Barnstorming

barnstormed? The bottom line was to place fans in the stands, keep the turnstiles moving, and use the money coming in to remain financially solvent. Keeping track of who was in the league, where they played, and who they played made tabulating league standings challenging for the media and the fan base.

The Red Sox took to the road barnstorming in late August 1931, as the *Press-Scimitar* reported that the team boarded the bus and headed south into Mississippi, seeking games throughout the state.[19] When the Red Sox returned from this tour around the Magnolia State, the Red Sox added three players to the roster. Treating the tour like a recruiting trip allowed the Red Sox to contend for the Negro Southern League second-half championship. However, both the Red Sox and the Nashville Elite Giants claimed the 1931 first-half banner, leading Nashville to schedule games with the Monroe Monarchs of the Texas-Louisiana Colored League.[20] Not to be outdone, the Red Sox scheduled a series with the Montgomery Gray Sox to determine the Negro Southern League champions, according to the *Memphis World*.[21]

Before the league office decided on the legitimacy of any of the claims to the pennant, the Gray Sox–Red Sox series was underway. The Red Sox took two of three games from the Gray Sox, thus giving the local Red Sox faithful the perception that they were on their way to becoming the Negro Southern League Champions in 1931.[22] Further muddying the waters, the *Commercial Appeal* reported that the Red Sox split a pair of games with the Gray Sox, leveling the series at three games apiece.[23] If that was the case, mathematically, the Red Sox held a three to two-game advantage in the series. No further record exists of any more games between the two teams, leaving the fans in the air as to whether their Red Sox were NSL champions.

The commencement of baseball activities for the Red Sox in 1932 began on a barnstorming trip through Texas. This trip merged the modern concept of spring training with a recruiting trip. The club picked up several players to bring back to Memphis while at the same time filling seats in small-town stadiums and on historically black college campuses throughout Texas.[24] The team completed their spring training in Memphis by hosting the Cuban House of David team, the Chicago American Giants, and the LeMoyne-Owen College nine at Martin Stadium.[25]

With the Negro Southern League in flux again in 1934, the Memphis Red Sox took to the road barnstorming throughout the 1934 campaign. Official league play did not open until late in May, and determining who was an affiliate member versus a full member remained

The Memphis Red Sox

challenging for fans. However, the owners' consensus at the February 4, 1934, meeting was that "a better circuit should be formed to include shorter mileage, larger population, and salary base to enable each team to finish with a little cash."[26]

The city's economic turbulence and political shift placed J.B. Martin in a precarious situation. As the NSL league lineup shifted, they welcomed the Chicago American Giants, Cleveland Stars, Nashville Elite Giants, and Pittsburgh Crawfords of the Negro National League as guests of NSL cities during spring training. Not only did this make economic sense for both leagues, but it also allowed the Martins to use the league's affiliation to limit contract jumping and player raiding by the Negro National League.[27]

By the middle of summer, the NSL collapsed. The only constant over the remaining months of the summer became the continual discussion of a North-South All-Star game. The venues and dates remained in flux, and a series of games never came to fruition. Instead, the Red Sox took to the road to participate in the fourteenth annual baseball tournament in Bluff Councils, Iowa.

According to the *Chicago Defender*, the Fourteenth Annual Bluff Council semi-pro tournament was a mixed-race event. The Monroe Monarchs and the Sioux City Ghosts joined the Red Sox in Council Bluffs in this 1934 tournament. The Ghosts, primarily an all-black softball team from Sioux City, Iowa, fared well as they transitioned from softball to baseball. They were easily identified by their black shirts and pants, which featured an orange skull and crossbones.[28] Under the leadership of Reuben Jones, the Red Sox awaited the Sioux City Ghosts in the semifinals. The Red Sox's success in the 1934 Council Bluffs tournament reiterates the belief the Martin brothers held that the Red Sox belonged in the Negro leagues' major leagues with teams like the Detroit Stars and Chicago American Giants.

The Red Sox quickly handled the Ghosts 7–3 behind the pitching of James "Suit Case" Mason. The Red Sox led the original House of David team 3–0 after eight innings in the finals. The *Chicago Defender* posited that "the bearded wonders scored six runs in the top of the ninth inning to win the championship game, 6–3."[29] Facing off against the House of David meant playing the quintessential barnstorming baseball team of the 1930s. The House of David considered signing Babe Ruth, the Sultan of Swat, for the 1934 season. Late in the season, in place of signing Ruth, they made a bigger splash by signing Olympian Babe Didrikson Zaharias.[30] No record exists of Zaharias playing in the Iowa tournament,

7. Barnstorming

yet the name recognition of both Ruth and Zaharias speaks to barnstorming teams' success like the House of David. Unable to compete for a championship in their own Negro Southern League, the Red Sox barnstorming tour through the Midwest allowed them to compete for a championship of another kind in Council Bluffs, Iowa.

When Wichita, Kansas, hosted the inaugural national semi-pro championship tournament in August 1935, the Memphis Red Sox were among the 32-team field. Raymond "Hap" Dumont, a newspaperman turned sports promoter, offered a $7,000 purse that enticed the Red Sox to pack their bags and head to Wichita. In addition, he provided Satchel Paige a $1,000 guarantee if his team, the North Dakota Bismarcks, played in the tournament. Bismarck's pitching staff included future Hall of Famer Hilton Smith, one-time Memphis Red Sox Ted "Double Duty" Radcliffe, and Chet Brewer.[31] The Red Sox spent August barnstorming on their way to the tournament. The *Wichita Eagle* reported that most of the 32 teams barnstormed en route to help defray the cost of travel.[32] The Red Sox opened the double-elimination tournament with a 7–5 win over another all-black team, the Texas Centennials from Dallas, Texas.[33]

Along with the Red Sox and Paige's integrated Bismarcks, the field included four other all-black teams, a Japanese team, and a Native American team from Wewoka, Oklahoma.[34] Wichita's history of hosting interracial baseball games dates back to barnstorming appearances of the Kansas City Monarchs and the Cuban Stars in the 1920s. Historian Jason Pendleton points to the Midwest's particularly small percentage of the black population in Kansas as being integral to its unique acceptance of interracial baseball.[35] The tournament drew more than 50,000 fans during its two weeks. The Bismarcks captured the title as thousands of white fans witnessed integrated baseball, most for the first time. The Red Sox bowed out to Yuma, Arizona, 4–3 in week two.[36]

The following season, the national semi-pro tournament's promotor Dumont turned the promotion over to four former major leaguers: Ty Cobb, Honus Wagner, Tris Speaker, and Fred Clarke. Due to their preconceived notion of black players, the quartet blackballed black players from playing in Wichita over the next four years.[37] Borrowing from a Satchel Paige quote, the Red Sox and the other black players playing in Dumont's inaugural 1935 National Baseball Championship "cracked another little clink in Jim Crow."[38]

The Red Sox began barnstorming the country by bus in 1928. Following its incorporation during the offseason, the club's financial stability allowed the Red Sox to improve the conditions for their players as

The Memphis Red Sox

they barnstormed.[39] Although the Red Sox had not attained the respectability of Foster's Chicago American Giants, who traveled by Pullman car, bus travel signaled a desire by ownership to attract better players. Yet, it was here on the bus that the life of a Negro leaguer can be best understood. They played schedules that rivaled the number of games played by their white counterparts, but most of these games fell under the auspices of barnstorming games.

Players described playing a weekend league series at Lewis Park and then *going around the horn*; after the Sunday doubleheader at the park, players loaded on the bus and drove to Little Rock, playing the same league opponent. Following that game, they loaded on the bus again and went to Pine Bluff, Arkansas, to play the same league opponent. Finally, after playing an opponent five or six times a week, the team bus headed to the following weekend league series.[40]

The *Commercial Appeal* followed the 1939 Red Sox on a barnstorming trip *around the horn* with the St. Louis Stars. After a three-game set in Memphis played on a Sunday and Monday, the two teams traveled to Clarksdale, Mississippi, on Tuesday. Then, on Wednesday, Greenville, Mississippi, back on the road to Little Rock, Arkansas, for a game on Thursday, and finally back to Memphis to finish with a game at Martin Stadium.[41] In the 1940s, Red Sox infielder Marlin Carter described going *around the horn* with a weekend series with the American Giants on Saturday and Sunday. "Following the doubleheader on Sunday, play them in Little Rock, Arkansas, on Monday night, maybe Greenwood, Mississippi, Tuesday night, Grenada, Mississippi, Wednesday night, and we'd turn them loose, and we would go on to Birmingham."[42] Although only the games played on the weekend counted as league contests, the barnstorming games provided the money necessary to keep the Red Sox financially afloat.

Red Sox catcher Clinton "Casey" Jones (team member 1940–1955) described life on the road barnstorming as not always fun but something you had to do. Jones recalled buying a can of sardines, a block of cheese, slices of bologna, and a few drinks for the trip. Most of the time, the team only stopped at local stores, preferably in black neighborhoods, to get something to eat. As the Red Sox did year in and year out, barnstorming throughout the South meant spending many nights sleeping on the bus. Players received a $1.50-a-day meal allowance, but restaurants maintained strict Jim Crow segregation throughout the South. If players were allowed to buy food at the restaurant, they would have to go to the back door to get their food. In some towns, the local chamber of

7. Barnstorming

commerce prearranged restaurants where the team would eat after the games. After one game in West Springfield, Illinois, Jones recalled that a local restaurant served the team, but that same owner refused the team service on their next trip through town.[43]

Teams depended on the bus drivers to safely get them from town to town on these barnstorming trips. Teasing the bus driver was a favorite pastime of many of the players. On a trip through the Ozark Mountains, the Red Sox bus driver, Sam Raif, became distracted by the chatter between himself and the players. As the bus headed down steep inclines, the bus driver would need to downshift to help the brakes handle the graded slope. On this occasion, too involved with the chatter, Raif missed his opportunity to downshift. When he attempted to do so, the bus was going too fast, and he could not get into a lower gear. A utility player, Raymond Long, took over the wheel as Raif attempted to force the bus into a lower gear. The bus got loose and tilted to its side as it was going around a curve; it then nudged a car passing by, straightening the bus back upright.

As the speed of the bus approached 70 miles per hour, Red Sox Pitcher Verdell "Lefty" Mathis saw that they were quickly approaching a bridge, and he feared the bus would crash. Mathis' anxiety reached a fevered pitch as his teammates yelled, "Don't jump, Lefty, DON'T JUMP." Mathis jumped out of the window of the decelerating bus, injuring his backside and his hands upon hitting the ground. The bus was able to stop on the other side of the bridge, and Mathis's teammates came back to gather him off the side of the road.[44]

Mathis could only lie on his stomach as the team searched for a doctor. Unfortunately, the next closest town in Missouri only had a white doctor's office, and the white doctor refused to look at Mathis. They had no choice but to get back on the bus and drive the rest of the way to Kansas City to find a black doctor to look after his injuries. It took two weeks for Mathis to stand up straight again. He eventually returned to the lineup, but W.S. Martin was liable for the damage to the car that nudged the bus back upright. Raif, known for carousing with women at the stadiums, was a changed man after that incident.[45]

On another barnstorming stretch between Louisiana and Houston, Texas, Raif needed to replace the motor on the bus. When they found a shop with an engine to go in the bus, the mechanic at the shop told Raif, "I can't put it in today." Raif replied, "I don't want you to put it in today. I got somebody to put it in." Raif found five cars to get the team to

The Memphis Red Sox

the ballpark to play the game that night. When he returned to the bus, he sent all but five of the players on to Houston; the other five stayed behind and helped Raif install the new engine. The white mechanic looked at Raif's handiwork and told him, "If you was a white man, you would be the manager of my mechanic shop right here."[46] After finishing, they loaded the bus, drove to Houston, and picked the team up to head to the next town.

For a brief period during World War II, the Red Sox barnstormed via trains. The Office of Defense Transportation's 1943 ban on gasoline for pleasure driving jeopardized black baseball. Joseph P. Eastman of the ODT interpreted the ban to preclude team buses for baseball games. Negro leagues teams would have to travel by train or by private car.[47] Following a June 16, 1944, game in Nashville against Tom Wilson's Nashville Elites, the Red Sox boarded a crowded train headed back to Memphis for a doubleheader. With Jim Crow segregation in effect on the train, all black passengers, including the Red Sox players, were placed in a car behind the mail car. A white man who was quite intoxicated walked up and down the train's aisle harassing women passengers. Porter Moss, a three-time all-star pitcher for the Red Sox, said, "Why don't you sit down and leave the women alone?" Moss headed to the back of the train, where a group of players gathered around a dice game.[48]

As the train approached its next stop, the same white man drew his pistol and fired at the conductor. The bullet went through the conductor's stomach and lodged into Moss's chest under his heart while paralyzing his legs. Jim Crow's strict social code cost Moss crucial time in his fight for life when a white doctor on the train refused to look at Moss's wounds. Sixty miles short of Jackson, Tennessee, they could only cable ahead and have an ambulance at the train depot when they arrived. Two of the Red Sox players stayed in Jackson and awaited word on Moss. Moss died that night on the operating table; his killer was later apprehended and served only ten years in prison.[49]

On a barnstorming trek through Texas in 1944, the Red Sox players decided to go on strike following the first game of a doubleheader in Houston. The team's traveling secretary and journalist phoned B.B. Martin and explained the situation to him. Brown conveyed to Martin that the team believed it should receive a higher per diem. According to Red Sox Joe B. Scott, Brown relayed a message from B.B. Martin, "If they don't want to play, leave them there." The Red Sox completed the second game in the double-header, boarded the bus, and were none the better

7. Barnstorming

for the experience.[50] Like his brothers, B.B. Martin maintained a tight budget and refused to give in to demands made by the players. Even as the economy turned the corner during World War II and most Americans' discretionary funds increased exponentially, the Martins refused to increase per diems for their players on road trips.

During the 1949 Negro American League season, the Red Sox's barnstorming tour became a family affair. Red Sox manager Larry Brown married his second wife, Sarah Bell Wood, in October 1948 after the season ended. Interested to see what life was like on the road for her husband, Sarah Bell Brown opened the first month of the 1949 season traveling on the bus with the Red Sox. Over those thirty days, the Red Sox visited thirteen cities and stayed in only one hotel on the entire trip. The rest of the nights, the team and Sarah slept on the bus while traveling to the next game.[51]

After the season, many Red Sox players barnstormed with black all-star teams, playing white all-star teams packed with major leaguers. Barnstorming tours against white teams after the end of the traditional season dated back to Rube Foster's 1915–1916 winter tour. His Chicago American Giants crisscrossed the United States, beginning in the California Winter League, then through the Deep South, and concluding in Cuba.[52] When Judge Kennesaw Landis, a Georgia native, became the commissioner of Major League Baseball following the 1920 Black Sox scandal, he banned white major league teams from playing against Negro leaguers as complete teams in major league uniforms.[53]

In the wake of Landis' mandate, white major leaguers began assembling all-star teams to compete against the Negro leaguers following the season. In the 1930s, Dizzy Dean's All-Stars competed against Satchel Paige's All-Stars in some of the most publicized duels of the decade. In the 1940s, Bob Feller replaced Dean when he rented two airplanes and crisscrossed the country, competing against Satchel Paige's team of Negro leagues all-stars. The 1946 Bob Feller–Satchel Paige Tour indicates how lucrative this brand of barnstorming became. Stan Musial received a $10,000 share for his participation in the tour, whereas his share for playing in Major League Baseball's World Series was less than $4,000. The 1946 tour played thirty-two games in twenty-six days and drew over 400,000 fans.[54]

For fans today, barnstorming across the country remains a foreign concept. But, for Negro leagues teams like the Memphis Red Sox, it was a financial necessity and an integral part of the season. White baseball players barnstormed after their MLB seasons against Negro leagues

The Memphis Red Sox

players. Paydays were lucrative, and the more games teams played before it became too cold, the higher the financial reward. The reserve clause dictated they, too, like Negro leaguers, would have to work second jobs in the off-season to make decent money. Baseball in the pre–Jackie Robinson era remained confined primarily to the East Coast. America's pastime remained vibrant in the nation's heartland and thrived on the West Coast. Fans longed to see the best players compete against each other and that town's best local nine. Small towns across America became familiar with the best players in the game through these exhibitions that included Negro leaguers, like those who played for and against the Memphis Red Sox. Red Sox teams went *around the horn* through Alabama, Arkansas, Mississippi, and Tennessee. Life on the road for the players created a special bond that lasted long past their careers on the field. Barnstorming also sheds light on the harsh realities of Jim Crowism during the Negro leagues era. As full-fledged participants in barnstorming, African Americans continued to weave their story among the likes of the game's greatest players in the nation's pastime.

8

Winterball

Following the typical Negro leagues season, black professional players headed south to ply their skills in Latin American winter leagues. Latin America provided a reprieve from the daily abuses of Jim Crowism found in the states, as well as an opportunity to make more money. Baseball has historical roots in Cuba and Puerto Rico, dating back to American imperialism on the islands that brought economic control and American culture. Cuban baseball historian Roberto González Echevarría contends that the sacredness of baseball lends itself to nationalism with parades, flags, and political leaders in attendance. The game is incorporated into popular Latin American culture, becoming spectacle, entertainment, and fun.[1]

Baseball for Latin American countries, especially those under the direct imperialistic arm of the United States, mirrors the relationship between England and the West Indies through cricket. Historian C.L.R. James argues that cricket's role is a purveyor of colonialism and that sport is not a sanctuary from the real world. Still, that liberation and oppression are inextricably bound.[2] Thus, baseball acts as a form of independence from American imperialism for Latin Americans. Similarly, playing in Latin America allowed Negro leagues players liberation from the racial oppression that relegated them to second-class status off the field and kept them out of Major League Baseball.

Cuban acceptance and importation of black professional players set the standard for winter league baseball in Latin America. Negro leaguers, like white major leaguers, were paid from April until October. The Cuban winter league ran from late December or early January to early April. Participation was by invitation only, and the Cuban clubs were limited in the number of foreigners allowed on each team. Therefore, they selected only the best players from the Negro and major leagues.[3] In the early twentieth century Cuban baseball teams barnstormed throughout the United States within the confines of the structure of black professional baseball.

The Memphis Red Sox

The norm in Latin American baseball was integration, yet when the first Cuban teams arrived to play in America, Jim Crow dictated they play against black teams. Yet, the Cincinnati Reds in 1911 signed two very light-skinned Cubans to major league contracts.[4] In the years to follow, as many of the managers in white baseball began to see the value in signing black players, teams urged light-skinned Negro leaguers to learn to speak Spanish and pass as Cubans to play in Organized Baseball. As a result, Cuban players became an integral part of Rube Foster's Negro National League in the 1920s with the admittance of the Cuban Stars as full members. Back in Latin America, the Negro leagues players competed as equals with white players from white Organized Baseball. The relationships built on baseball fields in Latin America cracked another little clink in Jim Crow.

Latin American winter baseball in Puerto Rico gained the momentum it needed to survive with the infusion of Negro leagues players in the late 1930s. Puerto Rican fans idealized the talented Negro leagues players. They lavished gifts, cash, and hospitality on stellar performers, who in turn appreciated a level of kindness often denied them in the States.[5] In addition, Puerto Rican promoters like Pedro "Pedrin" Zorilla of Santurce understood the box office appeal of the black baseball star. Zorilla, an oil executive with American conglomerate Shell, paid Satchel Paige $1,000 to appear in one game.[6] The American colonial influence of baseball touched the Dominican Republic under the auspices of the American Sugar Company, which established a league. In a well-documented series of events in 1937, Dominican dictator Rafael Trujillo persuaded Satchel Paige and several other prominent Negro leaguers to head south to the Dominican Republic to bolster Trujillo's own Ciudad Trujillo team.

Winter league baseball in Mexico offered another Southern destination where American imperialism yielding American baseball culture offered Negro leaguers the opportunity to earn a paycheck in the winter months. Thus, when Jorge Pasquel desired to elevate baseball in Mexico to the same standard played in the United States, a large number of Negro league players jumped at the opportunity to make more money. For years Mexican winter league baseball provided opportunities to make money in the off-season. But Pasquel's attempt to compete in the summer months drew the ire of Negro leagues owners and white owners.

Winter baseball in Venezuela provides an example of the prowess of black professional players against white opponents. In 1947 the New

8. Winterball

York Yankees traveled to Venezuela to play the Vargas club in Caracas. The Yankees brought with them Phil Rizzuto, Yogi Berra, and Charlie Keller. Filled with Negro leagues talent, the Vargas club outperformed the Yankees, with Ray Dandridge, Bill Cash, Hilton Smith, and Lennie Pearson leading the way.[7] Once again, another crack was placed in the armor of Jim Crow.

When the Vargas club defeated major league clubs, they began to seek out Negro leagues players over major leaguers. The reputations of Negro leaguers in Latin America surpassed their reputations back in the States. Thus the best Latin American teams regularly employed as many Negro leaguers as their league by-laws allowed. Then with national pride on the line, they competed in the Caribbean world series. This four-team event became the quintessential goal of Latin American league champions. In the late 1940s, Cuba, Puerto Rico, Venezuela, and Panama competed for the coveted crown.[8]

Returning to the club's earliest days in Memphis, Red Sox players continued playing in Latin America and the Caribbean through the winter. Playing in Latin America brought higher salaries and racial acceptance denied by Jim Crow in America for black baseball players. In Cuba, their money was as good as the next man's. They attended the best nightclubs, ate the best food, and stayed in finer hotels.[9] Red Sox catcher Larry Brown's exploits in Cuba placed him among the most prominent Negro league players during his heyday. Later in his career, Brown introduced Verdell Mathis to winter league competition in Mexico.

Neil "Shadow" Robinson, a twelve-year Red Sox veteran, displayed his speed on the basepaths in Puerto Rico, finishing with the second-most steals in the 1939–1940 winter season. He returned the following winter and joined Buck Leonard and Josh Gibson on a formidable Mayaguez club.[10] Negro leaguers in Puerto Rico were heroes to the Puerto Ricans watching winter league baseball on the island. Charles Ferrer, a Santurce fan, recalled "that nothing could top the performances of the Negro leaguers. What I admired most was their efforts to please the fans and win, [but] they didn't make great salaries."[11] Imagine Verdell Mathis, or any of his Negro leagues teammates, being treated like kings, eating at the best restaurants for free, staying at the best hotels, and being able to visit the nightclub of their choice.

Integration had always been a part of the Puerto Rican cultural construction since its annexation by the United States in 1898. During the season in Puerto Rico, each player received an invitation to dine at the governor's house. Jim Crow's social and political constructs in

The Memphis Red Sox

Memphis made the idea of a black professional athlete's invitation to the mayor's house unlikely, much less the governor's. The Homestead Gray's Wilmer Fields described Puerto Rican winter league ball as "very good for black players. If you got the opportunity to go to a Latin American country, you would go. If you didn't produce, your butt was coming back across the creek, and somebody else was on the way."[12]

Verdell Mathis played with San Juan after his 1940 rookie season with the Red Sox, posting a 1–1 record.[13] However, playing winter ball in Puerto Rico for the first time caused Mathis to become homesick. As a result, Mathis decided to return to Memphis by December, which explains his limited pitching appearances in the 1940–1941 season.[14]

Willie Wells arrived in Puerto Rico the following season to play with the Aguadilla club. Wells spent the 1940 and 1941 seasons in Mexico, earning the nickname "El Diablo" (The Devil). Between his play in the Mexican league for Jorge Pasquel and his return to Effa Manley's Newark Eagles, Wells hit .361 in Puerto Rico while driving twenty-one RBIs.[15] As Wells' skills diminished, he used the winter league season in Puerto Rico to stay sharp. Wells joined the Red Sox for a brief stint in 1944, and then in 1948, Wells returned to Memphis, where his son Willie Wells, Jr., joined the team. The pair formed the second father-son duo to play together in the Negro leagues, following the Duncans of the Kansas City Monarchs.[16]

According to Cuban baseball historian Roberto González Echevarría, baseball in Cuba is as good an index as any to exemplify the complicated relationship between Cuba and the United States. Echevarría claims that the end of the Spanish-American War in 1898 to the early 1930s marked an era known as the Golden Age in Cuban baseball—an era that created Cuban baseball heroes from José de la Caridad to Martín Dihigo. The Golden Era was when Cuban players competed regularly against the best in the world, be they major leaguers or stars from the Negro leagues. This era birthed the most prominent Cuban baseball promoters, Abel Linares, Agustín Molina, and Alejandro Pompey. Their relationship with the Negro leagues led to the creation of the Cuban Stars teams and the New York Cubans.[17]

During this Golden Era, Memphis Red Sox catcher Larry Brown was a mainstay in Cuban winter leagues. Brown began his Cuban winter league career in 1924 playing for the Santa Clara club.[18] Santa Clara, the capital of Las Villas Province, and its club provided moments of brilliance in the Cuban Winter League. Santa Clara's 1923–1924 club celebrated the league championship over foes Almendares and Habana.

8. Winterball

Unfortunately for Santa Clara, the league's financial woes forced the franchise to fold in January 1925.[19] Brown returned to Cuba with the Almendares club in 1926–1927, followed by two seasons with the Cuba club, and finally, one last season with the Almendares.[20] During these five seasons, Brown learned to speak fluent Spanish. His light-skinned complexion caused white players playing in Cuba to urge Brown to break the color line in Major League Baseball by professing to be Cuban. Brown's play in Cuba positioned him as one of the most respected players in baseball, not just on the island of Cuba but in all of baseball.

Brown's excursions to Cuba for winter league baseball took place in the 1920s, yet most Red Sox players who played on the island played after Jackie Robinson broke the color barrier in MLB. Cuban baseball declined in the 1930s, and in the early 1940s, the available number of players from Cuba diminished due to World War II. Following World War II, the Cuban league became home to young major leaguers, Negro leaguers whose circuits enjoyed wartime highs, and numerous Cubans who returned from the heyday of Jorge Pasquel's Mexican League.[21]

After Robinson's breakthrough, Cuban brothers Carlos and José Colás played with the Red Sox in the late 1940s. Carlos Colás spent the entire 1940s decade playing winter ball in Cuba, primarily with the Cienfuegos club. José Colás played for three different Cuban clubs at the end of the decade, spending two winter seasons with Carlos on the Cienfuegos Club.[22] Another Cuban national, Pedro Formenthal, spent time playing in Cuban winter leagues, Venezuela, and the Mexican Leagues in the late 1940s. Formenthal's disdain for the social constructs of Jim Crow in the South led him to remain in Cuba during many summers instead of returning to the Negro leagues.

In the 1940s, under the leadership of Jorge Pasquel, Mexican baseball set out to place itself on an even keel with Major League Baseball. Pasquel, a significant financial backer of Mexican president Miguel Alemán Valdéz, set out to strengthen the Mexican summer baseball league by bringing the best Negro leagues players to Mexico. Historian Donn Rogosin argued that a solid Mexican summer baseball league threatened the hegemony of the MLB and the Negro leagues as Pasquel enticed the best players south of the border into the Mexican league. Moreover, as the largest liquor importer in Mexico, he had the money to back his aspirations.[23] As a result, Pasquel entered a team of his own in the Mexican league in 1940, the Azules de Veracruz. The Azules featured Negro leagues stars Josh Gibson, Martin Dihigo, Ray Dandridge, Leon Day, and Cool Papa Bell. Alongside these all-stars, Pasquel enticed

The Memphis Red Sox

a former Red Sox player, Ted "Double Duty" Radcliffe, and a future Red Sox player, Willie Wells.[24]

Following the 1940 Negro American League season, Larry Brown and Verdell Mathis traveled to Mexico to play for the Tampico Alijadores Club. They joined Tampico in January, playing for manager Guillermo Ornelas. Tampico is a city 10 miles inland from the Gulf of Mexico on the northeastern shore of Mexico. Joining Brown and Mathis in Tampico was a second baseman and former Red Sox Jimmy Ford.[25] In a doubleheader with the Azules de Veracruz, Pasquel's club, Mathis pitched both games against the vaunted squad. Losing the first game 0–2, Mathis looked to redeem himself in the second. Mathis held the Azules to one run, winning 5–1 in the afternoon game. After his performance, one of Pasquel's brothers approached Mathis and offered him more money to play for the Azules.[26]

Not long after Mathis' victory over the Azules, Brown split his finger, receiving a foul ball hit straight back to his bare hand as he sat behind the plate. Tampico released Brown for the remainder of the winter season. When they did, Mathis followed Brown back to Memphis. In a foreign country, Mathis found solace in having his mentor Brown taking care of him. Alone for the first time in his playing career and without his Spanish-speaking teammate from Memphis, Mathis returned home.[27]

Brown's ability to speak Spanish fluently from his years playing in Latin America secured his role as manager while enabling him to communicate with the five players the Red Sox brought in from Cuba from 1947 to 1948. Formenthal and José Colás broke in with the Red Sox in 1947. Formenthal, unable to accept the cultural norms of the Jim Crow South, played only one season in Memphis while Colás remained through the 1951 season. Raúl Sánchez and Orlando Verona joined Colás on the Red Sox roster in 1948.

Colás' play with the Red Sox earned him a trip to the 1947 East-West All-Star Game. Capitalizing on the exposure in front of 48,000-plus fans at Comiskey Park, Colás belted out two singles that resulted in two runs batted in for the West Team in its 5–2 victory over the East.[28] Colás parlayed his playing experience in Memphis into a brief minor league career, playing two seasons before returning to Cuba to finish his playing days. Verona spent six seasons with the Red Sox; the right-handed shortstop's batting average hovered around the Mendoza line during his playing days in Memphis. Raúl Sánchez was

8. Winterball

the least successful of the five Cuban players to don Red Sox uniforms, losing his only two starts as a pitcher.[29]

Unfortunately, the reception black Red Sox players received in Latin America was not replicated in Memphis for these five Cuban players. These players suffered from the double-edged dilemma of being black and Hispanic in Memphis. The color of their skin forced them to deal with the daily realities of Jim Crow, and their inability to speak English left them unaccepted by many in the city's black community. Some lived in the apartments recently added to Martin Stadium during renovations, while others lived in local boarding houses.[30] On a barnstorming trip through Dallas, Texas, with the Memphis Red Sox, Jim Crow bothered Formenthal so much that he provided his Cuban passport to dine at a white restaurant.[31]

The loneliness of Cuban players rivaled the solitude faced by Jackie Robinson with the Brooklyn Dodgers and Larry Doby with the Cleveland Indians in white baseball. Brown's fluency made coming to the ballpark a refuge for the Cuban players, one place where they could lower their guard and be themselves on the diamond. Unlike the barnstorming Cuban Stars of the early twentieth century composed of Cuban players, these Cuban players served as two or three members of a team. Players from these earlier Cuban teams placed light-skinned players who passed as white into the major leagues. By the late 1940s, this new group of Cuban players in Memphis sought the same exposure and opportunity to play in the major leagues as their Cuban predecessors.

For Negro leaguers, taking their talents South provided opportunities that baseball in America was not ready to give. Baseball thrived in the Caribbean, and its growth during the twentieth century directly correlates to the influence of Negro leaguers in the Latin American game. Played years before the integration of Major League Baseball, winter baseball in Latin America showcased what the game could become if players were judged by their talent on the diamond, not by the color of their skin. Memphis Red Sox icon Larry Brown's travails in Cuba and Mexico echo this sentiment. Ty Cobb, the "Georgia Peach's" own admission that Brown deserved an opportunity and his willingness to suggest it to the Detroit Tigers ownership speaks volumes.

The hospitality Brown received in Latin America led to a comfort level that not only continued to bring him back but also led him to become fluent in Spanish. Then as the Negro leagues began fading into the sunset, Brown's knowledge of Spanish allowed the Red Sox to bring Hispanic players to Memphis. It was another example of a cultural exchange that

The Memphis Red Sox

showed Americans what we could be if we allowed the game of baseball to be a true meritocracy. Many of modern-day professional baseball's top-tier players are Latino players. Winterball in Latin America during the Negro leagues era laid the foundation for the game's growth in Latin America and the United States.

9

The Final Outs

The onset of the modern Negro leagues era witnessed the development of America's second-most thriving black industry, professional baseball. Competing in the only space allowed, they connected black communities and built pride in cities like Memphis. In 1920, Rube Foster created a league that would exhibit a professional level of play equal to or better than Organized Baseball so that when it came time to integrate professional baseball, Negroes would be ready. He took on the moniker "We are the ship, all else is the sea."[1] The *Chicago Defender* described Foster as the "militant fighting head of an organization that was a direct slap at the inferiority complex."[2] The Negro National League's genesis spurred the creation of the Negro Southern League in the South only months later. Memphis's inclusion in the NSL in 1921 brought the city into the fold as a professional baseball city.

As R.S. Lewis and later the Martin brothers continued to build the sport in the city, they weathered the economic storms of the Great Depression and life in Jim Crow Memphis. Although the team's oscillating status in the 1920s alternated between the major and minor leagues of Blackball, the Memphis Red Sox remained a constant. As other franchises faded from the scene, the Red Sox remained solvent, coming out of World War II stronger than ever. Their wartime success at the turnstiles led to an ambitious $250,000 renovation of Martin Stadium.[3] As the stadium renovations were underway, black America became enamored with what Negro leagues historian Jules Tygiel termed "baseball's great experiment" when Jackie Robinson joined the Brooklyn Dodgers.

Wendell Smith of the *Pittsburgh Courier,* Sam Lacey of the *Chicago Defender,* and Joe Bostic of the *People's Choice (NY)* set out on a full-fledged campaign to integrate America's pastime following World War II.[4] They asked whether America would live up to her ideals. They challenged the status quo of segregation in America through baseball. Following the defeat of Hitler and fascism in Europe, could fascism

The Memphis Red Sox

in the form of segregation be defeated here at home? They believed it could. Branch Rickey's signing of Jackie Robinson forever changed the landscape for professional black baseball players and black professional baseball. Shortly after Robinson broke through with the Dodgers, Larry Doby of the Newark Eagles joined the Cleveland Indians in the American League.

Opinions among owners in the Negro leagues varied. Could Blackball remain solvent with its best players signing contracts with Organized Baseball? Would Organized Baseball incorporate Negro leagues teams? Would the Negro leagues continue to function as an affiliated minor league system for Organized Baseball? Back in Memphis, the Martins renovated Martin Stadium, hoping to build upon their recent financial success. Engrained in an assimilationist culture that allowed the brothers to thrive, they struggled to understand the shifting paradigm. The sun began to set on Negro leagues baseball, yet the Red Sox pushed forward, remaining active longer than most.

* * *

At the end of World War II, the Red Sox welcomed Olan "Jelly" Taylor back to the fold as their player/manager. Larry Brown managed the Red Sox in 1945 and remained with the team in 1946 as the Martins honored Taylor's military service by naming him the manager for the 1946 season. The Red Sox played their home games at Russwood Park, with Martin Stadium undergoing renovations. The team finished fourteen games under .500 in fifth place in the Negro American League.[5] However, even as the team struggled on the field, the turnstiles turned better than they had in any previous year. Opening Day at Russwood saw the Red Sox split with the Cincinnati Clowns in front of 8,365 fans on Sunday afternoon.[6] Only weeks later, the Red Sox capped the city's annual Cotton Jubilee Parade in front of over 9,000 fans in a two-to-one victory over rival Birmingham Black Barons.[7] With money in their pockets, Red Sox fans continued patronizing Russwood Park to cheer on the Red Sox while the team struggled to win games. The season finale against the Black Barons drew over 6,000 fans as the Red Sox finished the season 16 games behind NAL champions, the Kansas City Monarchs.[8]

April 15, 1947, marked the day that Jackie Robinson made his Major League debut with the Brooklyn Dodgers. Back in Memphis, the political and social scenery began changing in ways that placed segregated baseball as a relic from a bygone era. Black Memphians joined union

9. The Final Outs

leaders in an integrated Labor Day parade to support FDR's Fair Employment Practices Commission (FEPC) and oppose the Taft-Hartley Bill that prohibited strikes by federal employees. The LeMoyne College NAACP branch protested the city's refusal to allow the Freedom Train because of its integrated viewing policies. The black community became more outspoken in its opposition to police brutality and the city's lack of black police officers.[9] Amidst the changing times, the Martins pushed forward with opening their renovated stadium. Majestically situated on the corner of Iowa and Wellington, Martin Stadium stood as a vestige of Negro success from an era whose time was soon to pass.

Larry Brown returned in 1947 as the manager of the Red Sox, following Olan "Jelly" Taylor's one-year tenure at the helm. On his third stint with the club, Marlin Carter described Brown's managerial style as "genius. He had a voice that he could say a word, and everybody on the ballclub could hear him." By 1947 Brown replaced himself behind the dish with the younger Clinton "Casey" Jones for the majority of the

Memphis Red Sox Players: Standing on the steps of the dugout at Martin Stadium are (left to right) Neil "Shadow" Robinson, Cowan "Bubba" Hyde, Nat Rogers, McDaniel "Red" Longley, and Larry "Iron Man" Brown (Withers Family Collection).

The Memphis Red Sox

season. But on occasion, when he placed himself in the lineup at age 47, Brown commanded the respect of his players. Carter remembered Brown, "He'd put on the shin guards, his chest protector, and his mask and say, 'Let's go fellas,' and he didn't pull it off until he got back to the dugout."[10]

Even after thirty years in Blackball, Brown commanded the respect of his players. As Organized Baseball began to sign the best players in Blackball, it became imperative that Negro leagues teams find new sources of players. Brown's return and fluency in Spanish allowed the Red Sox to sign two Cuban players, Pedro Formenthal and José Colás.[11] Branch Rickey predicted, "In the near-distant future, I expect this thing to take its natural course. The signing of a Negro will be no more than the news of white boys."[12] Bill Veeck's signing of Larry Doby from the Newark Eagles in June 1947 opened the way for other teams to follow the Dodgers' lead.

In the Negro leagues, teams like the Red Sox needed to find new pools of talent to maintain their success from the war years. Formenthal spent time in the Mexican League, posting batting averages of .345, .362, and .384 before Brown urged the Martins to sign him.[13] At 5' 11" and 200 pounds, Formenthal was a charismatic player with a flair for the flamboyant. He was a flashy dresser who sported a thin mustache when other Cuban players at the time shied away from facial hair.[14] Formenthal would come to the park with a gun placed on the inside of the front of his pants. He would take the clip out, and put the bullets into a bag with his watch and money. He then would place the gun on top of his locker. After the game, he would reload the clip and put the gun back inside his pants.[15] Formenthal's unique flair included packing a gun wherever he traveled. Arriving in a segregated Bluff City in 1947 meant that Formenthal still felt the need to protect himself. But, his eccentric style off the field matched his play on the field, which endeared him to Red Sox fans as the team's everyday right fielder.

Fellow Cuban José Colás joined Formenthal in the 1947 Red Sox outfield. The six-foot-tall Colás made an immediate impact. Named to the 1947 East-West All-Star Game, Colás went two for four with two singles and two RBIs in front of 48,112 at Comiskey Park.[16] Dan Bankhead joined Colás at the East-West game. The *Chicago Defender* considered Bankhead among the top three pitchers in the Negro American League and predicted that scouts from Organized Baseball would soon descend upon Memphis to sign the right-handed hurler.[17] Much like the rest of black America in 1947, the East-West game centered around the

9. The Final Outs

possibility of having big-league scouts in attendance. Bankhead's performance in the East-West game is considered the highlight of the 1947 season for the Red Sox faithful. The Red Sox began the season with hurlers Verdell Mathis and Felix Evans on the injury list, unable to play. Thus, by the end of the first half of the season, the club was far out of contention.[18] The club finished eleven games under .500 and 24.5 games behind eventual league champion, the Cleveland Buckeyes.[19]

Dan Bankhead's role as the first African American pitcher in the big leagues is one of the organization's most significant contributions. Lost in the iconography of the Negro leagues are both the stories of the Red Sox and that of Bankhead as baseball's first black pitcher to break the color barrier. Daniel Robert Bankhead was born in Empire, Alabama, on May 3, 1920. Empire is approximately thirty miles northwest of Alabama's largest city, Birmingham. Dan was the third of the five ballplaying Bankhead brothers. The eldest, Sam, was a top-notch Negro leaguer as a speedy, versatile, good-hitting infielder-outfielder from 1930 through 1950. Sam became a manager late in his career. The second brother, Fred, was an infielder. Joe and Garnett Jr. were both pitchers. Joe was with the Birmingham Black Barons, while Garnett pitched briefly with the Memphis Red Sox and the Homestead Grays.[20] Dan Bankhead made three East-West All-Star Game appearances, including the 1947 appearance.

Shortly after the all-star break, Branch Rickey flew into Memphis on August 22 to scout Bankhead in person, and offered him a contract. Bankhead shined again in the 7–2 Red Sox win over the Birmingham Black Barons, striking out eleven batters. Rickey offered the Martins $15,000 for Bankhead, making him the first black pitcher to sign with a major league club.[21] When announced over the loudspeaker, Bankhead's signing led to the Memphis crowd erupting with pride as one of their own became a major leaguer.[22] Following his signing with the Brooklyn Dodgers, the *Commercial Appeal* described Bankhead to white fans in Memphis as a 6'2" right-hander with a good fastball, a fair curveball, not much of a changeup, and an occasional knuckleball. They quoted Bankhead as saying, "It represents an opportunity, and I'm not going to shove it off." Red Sox general manager B.B. Martin's pretentious description of Bankhead's ability by claiming, "he is a better pitcher than Satchel Paige was at the same age," escalated the expectations for Bankhead once he got to Brooklyn.[23]

The AP wire carried the news of Bankhead's signing for the fans back in Brooklyn by reiterating the Dodgers' dire need for pitching in the stretch run of the 1947 season. Dodgers manager Burt Shotton told the AP, "If Bankhead is going to help us, the best time is right now."[24] Bankhead arrived in Pittsburgh two days later. Of the 24,000 fans in attendance, according to reports, African Americans made up one-third of the fans. Bankhead came in a relief role for the Dodgers after starter Hal Gregg gave up four runs in one-plus inning of work. Working against the Pirates outfielder Wally Westlake, Bankhead's fastball tailed inside and hit Westlake on the elbow. No racial incident followed as Westlake took his base.[25] Bankhead fared no better than Gregg, giving up ten hits and eight runs over three and one-third innings.

The highlight of Bankhead's first major league appearance came at the plate, where he hit a 375-foot two-run blast off Pittsburgh lefty Fritz Ostermueller.[26] Rickey brought Bankhead directly to the Dodgers without giving him the same seasoning Robinson experienced in Montreal in the Dodgers farm system. Rickey preferred sending Bankhead to the minors, but "We need pitchers, and we need them badly."[27] Following Bankhead's initial outing, black journalist Red Smith of the *Baltimore Afro-American* wrote that the Pirates "launched Bankhead by breaking a Louisville Slugger over his brow."[28] Without any minor league experience, Bankhead's fragile psyche and lack of control in finding the strike zone became apparent at the major league level.

After the Dodgers clinched the National League championship, Dan Bankhead pitched four scoreless innings against the New York Giants in late September. With no pressure on Bankhead, he capped off Jackie Robinson Day in Brooklyn with three strikeouts while giving up only one walk.[29] While Dan Bankhead sat in the bullpen waiting for mop-up duty in Brooklyn, his brother Sam Bankhead brought his Homestead Grays to Memphis. With $15,000 in their pockets, the Martins and the Red Sox continued to move forward, with Verdell "Lefty" Mathis getting the game-one start against Sam Bankhead's dominant Grays club.[30]

Only two months after arriving in Brooklyn, Dan Bankhead entered game six of the World Series as a pinch runner. He became the second African American player to appear in the World Series. Bankhead almost turned this opportunity against the Yankees into a catastrophe when he slipped rounding third base on a single on which he should have scored. Fortunately for Bankhead, he returned safely to his feet and back to third. Bankhead eventually scored as the Dodgers forced a game seven with their 8–6 win over the Yankees.[31]

Although the Dodgers dropped game seven to the New York

9. The Final Outs

Yankees, Bankhead returned to Memphis as a hero, one of two black players for the National League Champion Brooklyn Dodgers, when he pitched in an October exhibition game against the Birmingham Black Barons for Red Sox manager Larry Brown. Bankhead toed the rubber for three innings on the way to leading the Red Sox to their 5–0 win.[32] Soon after, like most of his peers in white and black baseball, Bankhead continued playing on the barnstorming circuit.

Bankhead spent the next two seasons in the minors before returning to the Dodgers. In 1948 he performed exceptionally well for the Nashua Dodgers of the Class B New England League for manager Al Campanis. Bankhead recorded a 20–6 record with a 2.35 ERA in 31 games, including a no-hitter.[33] The following year, his promotion to Montreal seemed merited as he once again led the team with another 20–6 record and held the team's lowest ERA at 3.76 in 38 games. The year 1949 also saw him hit .323, good enough for a top-five hitting average on the team.[34] The *Sporting News* labeled Bankhead "the wild man of the International League," as he led the team and league in base on balls.[35] In the winter of 1949–50, after barnstorming in the Southwest with a group of black players led by Luke Easter, Bankhead headed to Puerto Rico. He led the Puerto Rican Winter League in strikeouts with 131. In addition to his 10–8 record, he hit seven homers.[36]

Bankhead appeared ready to return to Brooklyn as a major league pitcher. His 1950 Brooklyn Dodgers season was his most productive as a major leaguer, as he compiled a 9–4 record despite his 5.50 ERA. Bankhead pitched his first complete game in late May against the Chicago Cubs en route to his fourth win. The only mark against him that night was a lone home run he gave up in the fourth inning.[37] In July, the *New York Times* reported that Bankhead's arm might require surgery. Bankhead continued to work out of the pen for the Dodgers for the remainder of the season.[38] Like Verdell Mathis with the Red Sox, Bankhead pushed on and continued to pitch. Pitchers, especially Negro leaguers, were so dependent upon their salaries that they put their health secondary to making the next start for their club.

The 1950 season would be the last Bankhead experienced in the majors. Bankhead continued to pitch in the minors and Mexico through 1962. Historian James Riley noted that over his career in the Negro leagues and Organized Baseball, Bankhead remained one of the higher-paid players. During his years with the Dodgers, he had an agent negotiate his contract.[39] Throughout his playing days in Organized Baseball, Bankhead faced rumors that he was older than he claimed

The Memphis Red Sox

to be. Much like Satchel Paige, Bankhead heard talk assuming he was much older in 1950, to which he replied, "Why my Pappy isn't that old."[40] Bankhead also faced racial animus corporately as the Dodgers looked to break spring training with five African American players. Ultimately, Rickey traded Sam Jethroe to the Braves to avoid further controversy. Yet even the Great Mahatma fell victim to the racial discord surrounding having too many black players on one team only three years after bringing Robinson and Bankhead to the Dodgers.[41] Back in Memphis, Dan Bankhead's signing remained a sign of pride and the possibilities in this new racial paradigm. However, Bankhead's major league career was short-lived, opening possibilities for other Red Sox players to cross the racial divide into Organized Baseball.

Heading into the 1948 season, J.B. Martin, still in exile in Chicago, speculated that integration might increase interest in Blackball.[42] He believed Robinson's entry into the major leagues created

The owner of the Harlem Globetrotters, Abe Saperstein, also briefly owned the Birmingham Black Barons. He is seen here with B.B. Martin (middle) and T.H. Hayes (right) in later years after the demise of the Negro leagues (T.H. Hayes Collection, Memphis Public Library).

9. The Final Outs

more significant interest in the Negro leagues—for white and black fans. Moreover, he believed that in the long run, the popularity of baseball among Blacks would increase as they realized the potential salaries they could earn as players.[43] In Memphis, W.S. Martin and A.B. Martin attempted to maintain a business-as-usual approach to the season. Following the subpar 1947 season, the Red Sox signed three more Cuban players: Orlando Verona, Candid Morales, and Raúl Sánchez. Verona, a shortstop, demonstrated only a fraction of his power and speed as he struggled to adjust to Negro American League pitching. Sánchez, a pitcher, lost his only two outings with the club.[44] None of the Cuban additions played up to the levels that Formenthal and Colás set the previous season, leaving the Red Sox roster depleted of the talent needed to win in the NAL.

In a sign of the times to come, the Red Sox's largest crowd of the season would be their series against the Indianapolis Clowns. A crowd of 5,200 witnessed the Red Sox defeat the comedic act of the Clowns.[45] The Clowns used comedy routines to increase fan attendance. Many of their players, like Reese "Goose" Tatum, first baseman, spent their summers with the Clowns and winters with Abe Saperstein's Harlem Globetrotters. Tatum put on a show for fans with his flashy fielding at first base, but he was skilled enough to earn a trip to the 1947 East-West All-Star game.[46] Unfortunately for the Red Sox and many other Negro leagues teams, games became entertainment based upon the comedic ideals of Stepin Fetchit. The actor Lincoln Perry portrayed Stepin Fetchit on the big screen in the 1930s. His characterization of a lazy, slow-witted, jive-talkin' coon brought the wrath of many black Americans.[47] Playing to stereotypes of blackness brought fans to the stadium, but it also diminished the athletic feats of the players.

Satchel Paige faced labeling as a Stepin Fetchit throughout his career. With arms so long they seemed to almost touch the ground, and legs also very long, he had to lift his feet high to keep from tripping. He knew whites would love his caricature the way they did Step's.[48] Paige, Perry, and Tatum knew their comedic act put fans in the stands and money in their pockets. Paige's induction into the National Baseball Hall of Fame as the first Negro Leaguer legitimized his athletic feats. Unfortunately, the harsh reality of Robinson's integration of the MLB meant that Negro leagues games became little more than a sideshow.

The 1948 season saw prominent white Negro leagues owner J.L. Wilkerson sell his stake in the game's most successful organization, the Kansas City Monarchs.[49] Effa and Abe Manley sold their shares in the

The Memphis Red Sox

Newark Eagles following the 1948 season after losing $47,000 the previous two seasons.[50] Reportedly the Manleys accepted $15,000 for the club, a fraction of the $100,000 sum Abe Manley had invested.[51] The Negro leagues continued on a trajectory toward becoming a piece of forgotten history, a remnant of a bygone era. Aiding in this process was the same black media that previously had propelled black baseball into prominence. Negro leagues teams depended on the weekly coverage to inform black fans of their team's happenings. When black players entered the major leagues, their focus shifted to following Jackie Robinson and the other black players that followed. The *Pittsburgh Courier* reported that the Homestead Grays capturing of the 1948 Negro Leagues World Series was the final championship for the Negro leagues. Hidden among a cluster of stories about the players already playing in the major leagues, it only contained two paragraphs.[52] Fans in cities where Negro leagues teams once prospered now boarded train excursions to National League cities to watch Jackie Robinson play. Marketing the product on the field became more challenging as the best black players continued to sign minor-league contracts in Organized Baseball.

Politically, black Memphians joined the growing civil rights movement by protesting for black police officers in the *Memphis World.* Following the 1948 elections, when Crump's power continued to ebb, the city hired nine black police officers to patrol Beale Street and Orange Mound.[53] The black community no longer needed to remain subservient to Crump's whims. As the black community began to wrestle power away from his machine, the political voice of Lieutenant George Lee waned as he represented assimilationist politics. The burgeoning civil rights movement shifted towards active protest instead of acquiescence. Once a space for black political expression, Martin Stadium became a symbol of the past.

At the onset of the 1949 season, the Negro American League remained the sole professional black baseball league. When the New York Black Yankees left the Negro National League to barnstorm after the 1948 season, the NAL accepted the remaining three NNL teams, the Philadelphia Stars, the Baltimore Elite Giants, and the Cuban Stars, into the NAL.[54] With the downfall of the Negro National League in the East, black professional baseball slid further toward annihilation. In Memphis, W.S. Martin asked Larry Brown to step down as manager in a ploy to get more fans to the stadium. Martin replaced Brown with the more charismatic "Goose" Curry. The *Memphis World* described Curry as "being known for his colorful performances. He is not only

9. The Final Outs

baseball-wise but is popular with fans."[55] Previously a member of the black press, Curry used his connections to garner support for the Red Sox. In addition to articles on the team, Curry provided the local media with pictures and biographies of players.[56] However, outside of the 4,500 fans that showed up for the opening weekend to witness the Memphis Red Sox defeat the Chicago American Giants, Martin Stadium remained a ghost town compared to its earlier glory days.[57]

With J.B. Martin remaining at the helm of the Negro American League, Memphis remained well represented in league matters heading towards the 1950 season. At the onset of the 1950 season, eleven black players were on major league rosters. Thomas Hayes, Jr., the owner of the Birmingham Black Barons and a fellow Memphian, suggested that the Negro American League confine itself to the South, thereby sustaining itself behind the curtain of Jim Crow.[58] In his weekly article in the *Memphis World*, Red Sox manager "Goose" Curry reiterated that the Red Sox remained the only team with a black-owned stadium. He proclaimed the Martin brothers and Martin Stadium to be a "tribute to the Negro race."[59] As Organized Baseball quickly moved in and signed the Negro leagues' best talent, "the race men" of the Negro leagues remained committed to Booker T. Washington's idea of being as separate as one's fingers in the remaining cities where professional baseball held on.

The Red Sox turned to two alternatives as the talent pool continued diminishing. First, "Goose" Curry opened the first baseball training school for African Americans in Greenville, Mississippi. Curry teamed with Greenville doctor Noble Frisbee to provide a two-week school to help identify talent in the Mississippi Delta.[60] The school became the first school of its type in the country, and the two hoped to provide talent to the Negro leagues and the major leagues. After the two-week camp, the coaching staff divided the players into two teams for a barnstorming tour before the beginning of the Negro American League season. Unfortunately, local newspapers have no accounts of any of these games.[61]

The 1950 season also saw W.S. Martin revive the Memphis Blues farm team for the Red Sox. He then positioned himself as president of the struggling Negro Southern League. The *Chicago Defender* reported that Martin believed "the Negro Southern League will eventually prove to be the salvation for our Negro baseball stars trying to make their way in our great National pastime."[62] To further bolster attendance at his stadium, Martin proscribed an all-star game between the star players of the NSL and his Memphis Red Sox of

The Memphis Red Sox

the NAL. The game was a success, by that period's standards, with a crowd of 5,396 filing into Martin Stadium to watch the Red Sox score the winning run in the bottom of the eighth inning of a six-to-five victory for the Red Sox.[63] Finding new and creative ways to fill Martin Stadium allowed the Red Sox to continue.

The 1950 Negro Southern League All-Star game also provided Memphis fans with a preview of the game's first black female professional baseball player, Toni Stone. She played in six innings, walked twice, lined a double to left field, and fielded two balls cleanly without an error.[64] Stone signed with the Negro American League's Indianapolis Clowns in 1953. *Ebony* magazine claimed that "she surprised everybody by turning in a businesslike job at both second base and at the plate." *Our World*, a nationally syndicated magazine that portrayed African Americans positively, posited that "she thinks, talks, and plays like a man."[65] The Clowns later signed two more female players; pitcher Mamie "Peanut" Johnson and Connie Morgan. Although these women were brought in initially as publicity stunts, they each proved they could play the game.[66] In this post–Robinson era, designing unique marketing schemes involved creative means to bring fans to the stadium.

Bob Boyd shakes hands with Dewey Phillips, with Elvis Presley to the left of Phillips, Casey Jones catching, and Steve Boone (far right) umpiring at Martin Stadium (Withers Family Collection).

9. The Final Outs

The 1950 Red Sox team lost the services of Bob Boyd, who reported to the Chicago White Sox after W.S. Martin sold his rights for $15,000. Boyd's sale to the White Sox was a sign of division in the Martin family. Allegedly, B.B. Martin, general manager, made a deal with Frank Lane of the White Sox, then drove Boyd to the airport at midnight to whisk him out of town before his brother, W.S. Martin, found out. After hearing of the sale, of which he did not personally approve, W.S. Martin filed a $35,000 lawsuit against the White Sox. Following the dismissal of the case, the two brothers split the $15,000 between themselves.[67] The 1950 Red Sox roster included fan favorite Neil "Shadow" Robinson from the 1938 NAL championship team. Robinson hit .283 and slugged ten home runs, but that was not enough, as the Red Sox finished in fourth place in the first half of the season.[68]

The Red Sox signed another Latin player in 1950, Panamanian third-baseman León-Kellman, a solid hitter with a good arm.[69] Kellman's play earned him an appearance in the East-West All-Star Game. Joining Kellman in Chicago for the all-star weekend were catcher Casey Jones and south-paw pitcher Vibert Clarke.[70] With only ten teams in the NAL, the probability of making the game increased. By 1950 the East-West All-Star Game became a showcase for NAL players to play in front of scouts at a major league park.

By 1951 the Red Sox became a financially losing proposition for the Martin brothers. According to records from Eva

Clinton "Casey" Jones replaced Larry Brown as the starting catcher for the Red Sox in 1944 and remained with the team through the 1959 season (Arthur Webb Collection, Memphis Public Library).

The Memphis Red Sox

Cartman, owner W.S. Martin's common-law wife, the team expenses topped $22,500 for the season. The team only brought in $4,200 on the road, with no record of the club's money during home games at Martin Stadium.[71] The Cleveland Buckeyes folded the previous July after winning only three games out of forty-two. The New York Cubans, under Alex Pompez, returned to barnstorming in 1951.[72] Baseball remained their livelihood for the remaining players on the Red Sox roster. Playing series in Martin Stadium on the weekend, going around the horn during the week before heading off on the team bus to the next stop, remained a way of life. Their dream of being signed by Organized Baseball and the love of the game kept them going. A chance to play at Comiskey Park provided extra motivation. Joining Vibert Clarke in Chicago for the 1951 All-Star Game were Casey Jones, José Colás, and Gilbert Varona.[73]

The downward spiral for the Negro American League continued as the eight-team league shrank again in 1952 to six teams. Longtime Martin family friend and owner of the Birmingham Black Barons, Thomas Hayes, Jr., sold his shares and left Blackball. Hayes left as one of the game's most influential owners in Birmingham. In his twelve years as owner, the Memphian led the Black Barons to three Negro American League pennants, three trips to the Negro World Series, and eight players who moved on to Major League Baseball,

This poster announced the Memphis Red Sox and Birmingham Black Barons game at Martin Stadium on July 27, 1952 (John Haddock Collection).

9. The Final Outs

including Willie Mays.[74] Even as the NAL shrank, the Red Sox forged on. In an editorial for the *Kansas City Call*, J.B. Martin continued to sell the NAL's worthiness. He claimed, "As far as pure baseball is concerned, the NAL operates on the same rules as organized baseball. The NAL is recognized by organized baseball as a bonafide loop."[75] Martin's passion for Blackball painted a rosier picture than the daily realities faced by its remaining clubs.

In Memphis, "Goose" Curry returned as manager for the 1952 season. The *Nashville Globe* described Curry as a Leo Durocher (NY Giants manager) type as he berated the umpires for every little thing to gain an advantage for his team.[76] The Red Sox sent five players to the East-West All-Star game: outfielder Sherman Watrous, first baseman Gilbert Varona, second baseman Manuel Valdez, and pitchers Isaiah Harris and Sam "Buddy" Woods. Woods turned in a respectable 11–7 record on the bump for the Red Sox in 1952, while Sherman Watrous earned a starting nod by hitting .328 while roaming centerfield.[77] As the talent diminished in Memphis, Martin Stadium played host to the emergence of one of baseball's greatest hitters, Hank Aaron, who, in early June, ranked as the NAL's best hitter (.483). He also led the league in runs, hits, total bases, home runs, and RBIs as a second-year player with the Indianapolis Clowns.[78] Aaron helped push the Clowns toward the 1952 Negro League World Series before he signed with the Boston Braves in June. By the start of the 1954 season, he was in the majors embarking on his Hall of Fame career.[79] The Red Sox finished the 1952 season in fifth place at 29–40. The Clowns defeated the Birmingham Black Barons in the NAL Championship series. Billed as the Negro World Series, by 1952, it simply pitted the first-half NAL pennant winners against the second-half pennant winners. The NAL declared the Clowns champions after ten games in a barnstorming championship tour.[80] The luster of a Negro leagues world series no longer garnered national attention in the black media. It became another opportunity to barnstorm around the nation with two better Blackball teams.

During spring training in 1952, Red Sox manager "Goose" Curry cut future country and western Hall of Famer Charley Pride. Born on March 18, 1934, in Sledge, Mississippi, in the Delta region, Charley was the second of eleven born to Mack and Tessie Pride. His father was a sharecropper.[81] Charley also played baseball with his brothers Mack and Ed, practicing using a henhouse for a backstop. They would sneak off on Sundays to play ball despite facing their father's punishment for dishonoring the Sabbath.[82] Hoping to follow in his older brother's footsteps

The Memphis Red Sox

DR. B. B. MARTIN
GENERAL MANAGER
PHONES: 8·2303 & 9·4914

DR. W. S. MARTIN
PRESIDENT

DR. W. B. WOODS
SECRETARY

NEGRO AMERICAN LEAGUE

MEMBERS

MEMPHIS RED SOX
CLEVELAND BUCKEYES
KANSAS CITY MONARCHS
BIRMINGHAM BLACK BARONS
CHICAGO AMERICAN GIANTS
INDIANAPOLIS CLOWNS

HOME GROUDS

MARTIN STADIUM
IOWA AT WELLINGTON
PHONE 9·9198

Official Red Sox stationery from the 1950s. Listing a 211 South Third St. address, the stationery shows W.S. Martin as president and B.B. Martin as general manager (John Haddock Collection).

and find a way out of sharecropping, Charley went to Memphis to try out for the Red Sox. Returning the following year, at age 19, Charley made the 1953 Red Sox roster.

Historian James A. Riley describes Charley Pride as a pitcher with a "pretty good little curve."[83] Pride struggled in his initial stint with the club. Pulled in the third inning of a game with Birmingham, after the Black Barons scored three early runs, described his early woes.[84] Yet amid his struggles, former Negro league Dizzy Dismukes, then a scout for the New York Yankees, saw something he liked and signed the young Pride.[85] Leaving the Memphis Red Sox, he reported to the Boise (Idaho) Yankees of the Class C Pioneer League. Unable to make the grade with Boise, the Yankees demoted him to Class D Fond Du Lac (Wisconsin) Panthers, where after being shelled in his only outing, the Yankees gave him a bus ticket back to Memphis, where he finished the 1953 season.[86]

In 1953, the Negro American League included only four teams, the Kansas City Monarchs, Indianapolis Clowns, Birmingham Black Barons, and Memphis Red Sox. Professional black baseball remained on life support. The year 1953 would see "Goose" Curry's last season at the club's helm. Following another disappointing finish, 36 games behind NAL champions Kansas City, Albert "Buster" Haywood replaced him.[87] The Red Sox's fortunes improved under the former Indianapolis Clowns catcher, as the team finished in second place in an NAL that expanded for the 1954 season to include six teams.[88] That year also marked the first

9. The Final Outs

time the white mayor of Memphis, Frank Tobey, addressed the Opening Day crowd of 3,000 at Martin Stadium. Tobey received a standing ovation when he proclaimed that "Negro baseball is an important part of our community."[89]

As the civil rights movement gained momentum, many in Memphis held onto the cultural norms of Jim Crow. Changes nationally began to take shape with the May 1954 Supreme Court decision in *Brown v. The Board of Education of Topeka*, which declared segregated schools unconstitutional, overturning the "separate but equal" doctrine found in *Plessy v. Ferguson* (1896). Legalized and *de facto* segregation created the need and space for the Negro leagues. Baseball's integration now seemed to lead toward revolutionary changes, making legalized segregation a thing of the past. As integration became the *modus operandi*, black institutions, including the Negro leagues, faded into the historical memory. Boss E.H. Crump's death in October 1954 left a power vacuum through which the city would see significant changes over the next decade.

The 1954 season began with "Goose" Curry taking Charley Pride to Louisville, where the cash-strapped team traded Pride to the Birmingham Black Barons in return for a team bus.[90] Pride struggled in Birmingham, losing the only two games recorded with him on the mound.[91] Sports journalist Sam Brown of the *Memphis World* made suggestions as fans in the Bluff City looked toward the 1955 season. First, he believed that if Organized Baseball accepted black players, it was time for Negro leagues baseball to take white players. Then, he posited that the Red Sox and other Negro American League teams should seek affiliation with major league clubs to secure financial stability.[92] Finally, Brown still believed that teams like the Red Sox remained relevant in and for the black community.

The 1955 Opening Day ceremonies marked the triumphant return of J.B. Martin, Negro American League President, and former Red Sox owner, to throw out the first pitch. Crump's death the previous fall allowed for Martin's peaceful return to Martin Stadium.[93] Unfortunately for J.B., the Opening Day crowds in the 1950s were not near where they were in 1940 during his forced departure. By 1955 the Blackball game limped through the season. "Goose" Curry returned as the manager for the Red Sox, with the additional title of scout for the St. Louis Cardinals. His baseball school in Greenville, Mississippi, moved to Columbus, Mississippi, and became an evaluation camp for Organized Baseball scouts.[94] With only five teams in the NAL, the schedules

The Memphis Red Sox

remained unbalanced, and records for games played became even more relaxed. Nevertheless, "Buck" O'Neil's Kansas City Monarchs dominated the NAL. Satchel Paige rejoined the Monarchs and, along with three future big leaguers, claimed another NAL championship for the storied franchise.[95]

With four teams in the Negro American League, the Memphis Red Sox secured the first-half pennant in 1956 and looked to close in on the second-half pennant in an early September game against the Birmingham Black Barons. Charley Pride toed the rubber in the second game of a twin billing for the Red Sox.[96] Seeking ways to fill the stands, the Martins brought back Ladies Night at the ballpark, offering free admission to women and 75¢ admission for men.[97] Following the twenty-fourth Annual East-West All-Star Game in Chicago at Comiskey Park, the Martins offered the Memphis fanbase an opportunity to see the game replayed on a Sunday afternoon with the same players at Martin Stadium.[98] This game saw Memphis manager "Goose" Curry match up against Detroit's Ed Steele. Charley Pride appeared in both 1956 games after winning 14 games for the Red Sox.[99] With only four teams in the league, the talent level continued to drop, and the *Commercial Appeal* noted that the loss in Chicago by the West team was one of the worse defeats in its 24-year history.[100]

For Pride, the 1956 season introduced him to his future wife, Rozene Cohran. "She was smart, beautiful, independent, and could explain the infield fly rule," Pride wrote. "What else could a guy want?"[101] The Red Sox closed the 1956 season with a 16–6 pounding of the Detroit Stars.[102] The Army drafted Pride during the Korean War in the fall of 1956. After 14 months, he returned to the Memphis Red Sox, where he recorded 14 wins against no losses, earning a trip to the 1958 East-West All-Star Game. Pride sat out the 1959 season in a contract dispute with B.B. Martin, making 1958 his last year in a Red Sox jersey. Charley Pride would go on to a successful country music career, entering the Country Music Hall of Fame in 2000.[103]

Despite losing money, the Red Sox survived under W.S. Martin and B.B. Martin. When W.S. Martin's health began to wane, it spelled the end for the franchise. W.S. Martin's death in 1958 left the team in the hands of B.B. Martin. The Red Sox played out the 1958 season, but with mounting debts and money still owed on the mortgage for Martin Stadium, B.B. Martin began looking for a buyer for the club. With no revenue and no future owner within reach, B.B. Martin sent the Red Sox on the road for their remaining games, leaving them as a barnstorming

9. The Final Outs

team in 1959. In June, the Memphis Red Sox took two games from the Kansas City Monarchs at Yankee Stadium, according to the *New York Times*. A reported crowd of 7,100 watched as these two teams from a bygone era continued to chase their dreams.[104]

The end arrived in the spring of 1960 for the Red Sox organization. After years of losing money, B.B. Martin sold the club, the stadium, and anything associated with the team. Claiming that he lost $12,000 during the 1959 season, the youngest Martin sold the stadium's property to F.A. Maddox, president of Tri-State Mack Distributors, for $110,000.[105] Maddox and his engineers quickly discovered that the stadium stood as structurally firm as the organization had in the Negro leagues. R.S. Lewis laid the foundation for one of Blackball's longest-tenured franchises. When the Martins renovated the stadium using steel-reinforced concrete, they structurally solidified a stadium that had stood as a symbol of pride in Memphis's black community for nearly four decades. Maddox claimed that "it would take an atomic bomb to demolish Martin Stadium because it was built more like a fort than a stadium."[106]

Another irony in the segregated baseball story in the Bluff City is that the Memphis Chicks' stadium, Russwood Park, burned to the ground in a five-alarm fire on Easter Sunday, April 17, 1960.[107] Over the years, the Red Sox played many games at Russwood Park. Yet, not once did the powers in the city or the Chicks organization seek out B.B. Martin to use Martin Stadium—another racial slight. Thus, Martin Stadium's leveling in the fall of 1960 left Memphis's Negro leagues story as part of a forgotten narrative shared among old-timers and former players.

Epilogue

The end of the Negro leagues era symbolized a shift in the racial paradigm. As a burgeoning civil rights movement began to espouse the dreams and aspirations of the African American community, one of the significant impetuses in this new struggle happened when Jackie Robinson broke the color barrier in baseball. Sportswriter Leonard Koppett said it best: "Robinson accomplished more than any other individual to focus attention on the inequities of American society. The consequences of the waves his appearance made spread far beyond baseball, far beyond sport, far beyond politics, even to the very substance of a culture."[1] With the integration of America's pastime came the emerging concept that desegregation was not only a possibility but one that could become a reality throughout the nation. The Negro leagues era became a symbol of the past. The model that allowed Martin Stadium to symbolize the autonomy of the black community during the Negro leagues era in the city, by 1960, stood demolished.

As the Memphis Red Sox waned in the 1950s, black Memphians turned from their segregated past to new forms of resistance in the Black Freedom Struggle. A vacuum existed in the city of Memphis following the death of Boss Crump. Historian Elizabeth Gritter points out that a new generation of black leaders emerged, including Maxine Smith, Jessie Turner, Sr., Laurie Sugarmon and Benjamin Hooks. Black political involvement increased with membership in the local chapter of the NAACP, lawsuits seeking the desegregation of schools in the city, and sustained political mobilization.[2] Memphis State University successfully desegregated in 1959, five years after the Supreme Court case *Brown v. Board*. The local NAACP had been challenging segregation on campus at Memphis State starting in 1956. It continued its attempts in 1957 when Maxine Smith and Laurie Sugarmon attempted to enroll in the graduate program. Two years later, in 1959, the university admitted eight students who became known as the "Memphis State 8."[3] Memphis's black

Epilogue

community embarked on a path to integrate the city much like Jackie Robinson integrated Organized Baseball.

Ten years later, sports provided the impetus for Memphis to unify when a young African American basketball player from Orange Mound's Melrose High, Larry Finch, decided to sign with Memphis State. Finch was not the first black player at Memphis State—it was Herb Hilliard (1967)—but he was the university's first black star player.[4] Likewise, Jackie Robinson's integration into Major League Baseball set a precedent for other institutions to provide social justice long denied to the black community. Sports ultimately played into the civil rights movement in richly symbolic terms. Black athletes on the baseball diamond and basketball arena reinforced race pride. They established role models for African Americans who believed the time had come to assert their claims to full participation in the nation's life.[5]

Finch's career mirrored the city's social and political peaks and valleys, much like the Memphis Red Sox did in their time. Forced to play professional baseball in a league of their own, the Red Sox navigated the segregated waters of the Negro leagues. Behind the veil of segregation, the Red Sox symbolized black success. As Finch guided his Memphis State basketball team to the 1973 NCAA championship game, he became a new symbol of black identity and success. Whereas Red Sox ownership experienced the political backlash of confronting the city's white political establishment, the same political establishment embraced Finch as a symbol of unity.

The Red Sox weathered the economic storm of the Great Depression only to come out stronger. Following the storm surrounding the Memphis State basketball program during Dana Kirk's tumultuous tenure, Finch buoyed the program as its first African American head coach and allowed Memphis State to weather the sanctions imposed by the NCAA. Following the economic boom of the world war era in the Negro leagues, the Red Sox invested in renovating Martin Stadium only to fall victim to a post–Robinson baseball paradigm that did not include Negro leagues baseball. Finally, Finch invested his life and career into Memphis State University, only to fall victim to the economic failure of a new arena, the Great American Pyramid. Its failure led to his firing as head coach.

The Red Sox organization stood as a symbol of hope for black Memphians. Seen as second-class citizens during Jim Crow, black-led ownership promoted economic stability and racial pride behind the veil of segregation. Black Memphians owned and operated a professional

Epilogue

sports franchise that thrived and outlasted most of its contemporaries. Finch was the native son who broke down the color barrier for the best black basketball players in Memphis, as Jackie Robinson did for the best black baseball players nationally. Over the twenty-eight years from his signing in 1969 to his firing in 1997, Finch was a symbol of hope to the city's black and white communities.

Sports reflect the dominant ideas of society. However, they also provide arenas for athletes to challenge racial norms and air grievances. For example, the existence of the Memphis Red Sox as a professional baseball organization meant accepting the Jim Crow norm. Yet, Red Sox players played against white teams on barnstorming tours and with white players in Latin American leagues challenging Jim Crow. Likewise, the political space created by Martin Stadium at Lewis Park allowed Black and Tan Republicans under Robert Church, Jr., and J.B. Martin to safely commune with the city's black community without the oversight of the white political leaders. In the stringent political environs of Boss Crump's Memphis, the ability to gather as a community fostered Robert Church, Jr.'s black political machine. Yet, as the Negro leagues era came to an end, the political loyalties of the black community gradually shifted, leaving the Martin family out of touch with the black community politically.

As Memphis entered the 1960s, its sports history no longer included a major league–level professional baseball team. Instead, most Memphians would have viewed the Negro American League as a minor league, secondary to the Southern Association's Memphis Chickasaws. Black Memphians now chased the exploits of former Negro leaguers through the newspapers. Unlike other Negro leagues cities, Memphis remained a minor league city. Cities like New York, Philadelphia, Pittsburgh, Chicago, Detroit, St. Louis, and Kansas City hosted major league baseball teams. When Jackie Robinson's number was retired by all major league teams in 1997, these cities remained active participants in Organized Baseball. Memphis, as a minor league city, remained distant and disconnected from its past as a prominent organization in the Negro leagues.

Many of the former Red Sox players stayed in the Bluff City. Like many professional athletes, they are soon forgotten once out of the spotlight. Players like Larry Brown and Verdell Mathis worked at local hotels to stay in touch with former fans. These Red Sox players became remnants of a bygone past that no longer included segregated professional baseball. In 1970 baseball historian John Holway set out to interview

Epilogue

and collect stories of former Negro leagues players. When he arrived in Memphis in 1970, Larry Brown, sixty-five years old, was at a public park in South Memphis watching teammate Verdell Mathis coach a black youth baseball team. Brown came to life as he shared stories from his baseball past. Holway met the next day again with the two as Mathis and Brown shared pictures from the bygone era of the Memphis Red Sox. Holway described the pictures he viewed as photos of "a husky broad-chested, beaming athlete who dominated every group picture he was in."[6] However, what Holway saw before him contradicted the pictures he saw. Life for former Negro leaguers meant returning to roles out of the spotlight and bodies worn from years of playing that took tremendous tolls. Life for former Red Sox players did not include an MLB pension or healthcare. These players held onto pictures of their glory days and the hope that someone might stop them and ask them about their time playing professional baseball.

For some who lived long enough, interest in the Negro leagues returned before their days were over. The Negro Leagues Museum opened in 1990 in Kansas City, Missouri, just down the Paseo from the YMCA, where Rube Foster organized the first Negro National League. For others, it was the opening of the Jackie Robinson movie *42*. In Memphis, a documentary chronicling the Memphis Red Sox shed new light on the Red Sox's role in Bluff City.

In the 1990s, professor John Haddock at the University of Memphis teamed with professor Steven Ross to produce the documentary *Black Diamonds, Blues City: Stories of the Memphis Red Sox*. The pair gathered together many of the Red Sox players to interview them, including Marlin Carter, Verdell Mathis, Joe B. Scott, Casey Jones, and Frank Pearson. The joy on the faces of these men, as they shared their stories, made the documentary come alive. Ross described the documentary as "more than just baseball. We tried to show in the film how baseball was a venue where the African American community could create a valid and valued life of its own, despite the short-sightedness of the larger society at the time."

When asked his opinion on the documentary, Haddock quoted Benjamin Hooks, who concludes the film with this statement: "The Red Sox were an expression that we had come a long way. We were able to build a life, to build a culture, in a rigidly segregated society that told you that you were nobody. Instead, we proved to folks, and, most of all, to ourselves, that we were somebody."[7]

In the Special Collections at the University of Memphis sit shelves

Epilogue

of interviews conducted by Ross during the production of the documentary. One of the most poignant scenes places Verdell Mathis at the corner of current-day Crump Blvd and Danny Thomas Blvd in the Tri-State Trucking Center parking lot. As Mathis walks through the parking lot, he glances over at his alma mater Booker T. Washington High School's gymnasium and then places himself on the pitcher's mound. Mathis starts reliving his days on the Red Sox mound for Ross while wearing a Memphis Red Sox jacket. Unfortunately, Mathis died a few years later at 84. But an old African proverb claims that even after a person dies, they remain alive so long as you say their name.

The Memphis Red Sox: A Negro Leagues History aims to keep the names of these talented Negro leagues baseball players alive. Verdell Mathis. Larry Brown. Joe B. Scott. Casey Jones. Neil Robinson. Porter Moss. Turkey Stearnes. Willie Foster. Over 250 players donned the Red Sox jersey and played in Memphis. "Buck" O'Neil's posthumous induction into the National Baseball Hall of Fame in 2021 sheds light on the storied past of the Negro leagues. During his life, O'Neil never complained about his omission. As we look back on this history, O'Neil reminded us frequently that he wasn't born too late; instead, he was born right on time. Maybe, if we think about it, we are the ones who are late to learning about and acknowledging this valuable piece of baseball and American history. The story of the Memphis Red Sox is not only the story of Blackball but also the story of baseball, the story of Memphis, and how Memphis was home to major league-level professional baseball.

Chapter Notes

Introduction

1. Michael Lomax, *Black Baseball Entrepreneurs, 1902–1931: The Negro National and Eastern Colored Leagues* (Syracuse: Syracuse University Press, 2014), 425.
2. Donn Rogosin, *Invisible Men: Life in Baseball's Negro Leagues* (Lincoln: University of Nebraska Press, 1983), 22.
3. *Ibid.*, 6.
4. Memphis Red Sox players group interview, interview by Steven Ross, June 1994, reel 1A, for documentary *Black Diamonds, Blues City*, Special Collections, Ned McWherter Library, University of Memphis, Memphis, TN.

Chapter 1

1. Bill Plott, "The Southern League of Colored Baseballists," SABR Research Journal Archives, accessed July 7, 2021, http://research.sabr.org/journals/southern-league.
2. *Memphis World*, June 24, 1886.
3. Plott, "The Southern League of Colored Baseballists."
4. Brian McKenna, "Biography—Bud Fowler," SABR Biography Project, accessed December 5, 2022, https://sabr.org/bioproj/person/bud-fowler/.
5. "Base Ball," *The Sporting Life*, June 1, 1887, 10.
6. James A. Riley, *The Biographical Encyclopedia of the Negro Baseball Leagues* (New York: Carroll & Graf, 1994), 380.
7. Jerry Malloy, "Out at Home," *The National Pastime #2* (Cleveland: SABR, 1983), 14–29.
8. *Ibid.*
9. Robert Peterson, *Only the Ball Was White: A History of Legendary Black Players and All-Black Professional Teams* (Oxford: Oxford University Press, 1970), 28.
10. Malloy, "Out at Home."
11. Peterson, *Only the Ball Was White*, 28.
12. G.P. Hamilton, *The Bright Side of Memphis* (Memphis: G.P. Hamilton, 1908), 109.
13. George W. Lee, *Beale Street: Where the Blues Began* (New York: Robert Ballou, 1934), 167–168.
14. *Nashville Globe*, February 22, 1907.
15. *Nashville Globe*, May 22, 1908.
16. Michael E. Lomax, *Black Baseball Entrepreneurs, 1902–1931: The Negro National and Eastern Colored Leagues* (Syracuse: Syracuse University Press, 2014), 91; Riley, *The Biographical Encyclopedia of the Negro Baseball Leagues*, 474.
17. Lomax, *Black Baseball Entrepreneurs, 1902–1931*, 110, 155.
18. Montgomery K. McBee, "They Also Played the Game: A Historical Examination of the Memphis Red Sox Baseball Organization, 1922–1959" (dissertation, University of Memphis, 2001), 44–47.
19. Lomax, *Black Baseball Entrepreneurs, 1902–1931*, 167.
20. Otis Sanford, *From Boss Crump to King Willie: How Race Changed Memphis Politics* (Knoxville: University of Tennessee Press, 2017), 20–21.
21. Elizabeth Gritter, *River of Hope: Black Politics and the Memphis Freedom Movement, 1865–1954* (Lexington:

Chapter Notes

University of Kentucky Press, 2014), 40–42.

22. *Ibid.*, 52.

23. David Tucker, *Lieutenant Lee of Beale Street* (Nashville: Vanderbilt University Press, 1971), 71.

24. Lomax, *Black Baseball Entrepreneurs, 1902–1931*, 212.

25. Leslie Heaphy, *The Negro Leagues, 1869–1960* (Jefferson, NC: McFarland, 2003), 38.

26. Kadir Nelson, *We Are the Ship: The Story of Negro League Baseball* (New York: Jump at the Sun/Hyperion Books for Children, 2008), 9.

27. Heaphy, *The Negro Leagues, 1869–1960*, 40.

28. *Ibid.*, 41.

29. Peterson, *Only the Ball Was White*, 88.

30. William J. Plott, *The Negro Southern League* (Jefferson, NC: McFarland, 2019), 8.

31. *1919 Memphis City Directory*, 908, 1750, 1149; *1922 Memphis City Directory*, 761.

32. *Commercial Appeal*, April 20, 1921.

33. *Commercial Appeal*, May 8, 1921.

34. "History of Negro Southern League," Birmingham Negro Southern League Museum, accessed July 7, 2021, http://www.birminghamnslm.org/history/.

35. Plott, *The Negro Southern League*, 204, 207, and 209.

36. John B. Holway, *Blackball Stars: Negro League Pioneers* (Westport, CT: Meckler, 1989), 251.

37. McBee, "They Also Played the Game," 58–60.

38. *Commercial Appeal*, April 30, 1922.

39. *Memphis World*, April 5, 1932.

40. *Commercial Appeal*, May 18, 1921.

41. Tom Charlier, "The CA at 175: Reporting Our Own Story," *Commercial Appeal*, accessed December 5, 2022, https://archive.commercialappeal.com/news/The-CA-at-175-Reporting-our-own-story-379252321.html/.

Chapter 2

1. Phil Dixon, *John "Buck" O'Neil: The Rookie, His Words, His Voice* (n.p.: n.p., 2022), 122.

2. "MLB Holds First Night Game," History.com, November 16, 2009, https://www.history.com/this-day-in-history/-mlb-holds-first-night-game.

3. *Memphis World*, January 1, 1950.

4. McBee, "They Also Played the Game," 65.

5. Duane Marsteller, "Martin Stadium Historical Marker," Historical Marker Database, October 12, 2020, https://www.hmdb.org/m.asp?m=148990.

6. "Around the Base Lines," *Chicago Defender*, June 26, 1920.

7. Verdell Mathis, interview by Steven Ross, June 1994, reel 56, for documentary *Black Diamonds, Blues City*, Special Collections, McWherter Library, University of Memphis, Memphis, TN.

8. Verdell Mathis, interview by Steven Ross, June 1994, reel 57, for documentary *Black Diamonds, Blues City*, Special Collections, McWherter Library, University of Memphis, Memphis, TN.

9. Paul Goldberger, *Ballpark: Baseball in the American City* (New York: Alfred A. Knopf, 2019), 146.

10. Ernest Withers, "Easter Sunday Game," 1950, courtesy Withers Family Trust.

11. Russell Sugarmon, interview by Steven Ross, June 1994, for documentary *Black Diamonds, Blues City*, Special Collections, McWherter Library, University of Memphis, Memphis, TN.

12. *Chicago Defender*, July 5, 1924.

13. Goldberger, *Ballpark*, 317.

14. Laurie Green, *Battling the Plantation Mentality: Memphis and the Black Freedom Struggle* (Chapel Hill: University of North Carolina Press, 2007), 14.

15. Goldberger, *Ballpark*, 17.

16. *Commercial Appeal*, May 13, 1923; Memphis Negro Chamber of Commerce, *1943 Negro Yearbook and Directory* (Memphis: Memphis Negro Chamber of Commerce, 1943), 55.

17. Goldberger, *Ballpark*, 33–34.

18. *Ibid.*, 71.

19. "Memphis Wins One Game, Loses Two to Am. Giants," *Chicago Defender*, July 5, 1924.

20. *Commercial Appeal*, May 13, 1923.

21. Randolph Meade Walker, "The Role of the Clack Clergy in Memphis,"

Chapter Notes

West Tennessee Historical Society Papers 33 (October 1979), 42.

22. *Commercial Appeal*, May 13, 1923.
23. *Chicago Defender*, May 19, 1923.
24. *Commercial Appeal*, July 13, 1923.
25. *Kansas City Call*, August 17, 1923.
26. James A. Riley, *The Biographical Encyclopedia of the Negro Leagues* (New York: Carroll & Graf, 1994), 293.
27. John Holway, *Voices from the Great Black Baseball Leagues* (New York: Da Capo, 1992), 191.
28. Michael Lomax, *Black Baseball Entrepreneurs: The negro National and Eastern Colored Leagues, 1902–1931* (Syracuse: Syracuse University Press, 2014), 286.
29. *Pittsburgh Courier*, April 7, 1923.
30. *Commercial Appeal*, June 19, 1924.
31. Lomax, *Black Baseball Entrepreneurs, 1902–1931*, 327.
32. *Commercial Appeal*, June 23, 1924.
33. "Ephraim Williams," Wisconsin Historical Society, February 12, 2021, https://www.wisconsinhistory.org/Records/Article/CS16485.
34. "J.A. Jackson's Page," *The Billboard* 33, no. 53 (December 1921), 43.
35. "The Theater: Mr. Green and Mr. Bean," *Time* 35, no. 18 (April 29, 1940).
36. *Commercial Appeal*, April 30, 1926.
37. LeRoy "Satchel" Paige and David Lipman, *Maybe I'll Pitch Forever* (Lincoln: University of Nebraska Press, 1993), 41–42.
38. *Ibid.*
39. *Ibid.*, 36–37.
40. Verdell Mathis, interview by Steven Ross, March 1994, reel 13–15, Special Collections, McWherter Library, University of Memphis, Memphis, TN.
41. *Ibid.*
42. Rufus Thomas, interview by Steven Ross, June 1994, reel 71, for documentary *Black Diamonds, Blues City* documentary project, Special Collections, McWherter Library, University of Memphis, Memphis, TN.
43. Verdell Mathis, interview by Steven Ross, June 1994, reel 57, for documentary *Black Diamonds, Blues City*, Special Collections, McWherter Library, University of Memphis, Memphis, TN.
44. William J. Plott, *The Negro Southern League: A Baseball History, 1920-1951* (Jefferson, NC: McFarland, 2015), 56.
45. *Commercial Appeal*, September 1, 1927.
46. *Commercial Appeal*, August 1, 1927.
47. *Commercial Appeal*, April 28, 1928.
48. David Tucker, *Lieutenant Lee of Beale Street* (Nashville: Vanderbilt University Press, 1971), 64.
49. *Commercial Appeal*, April 29, 1928.
50. Lomax, *Black Baseball Entrepreneurs, 1902–1931*, 167.
51. *Commercial Appeal*, March 17, 1929.
52. *Commercial Appeal*, May 22, 1929.
53. Patrick Miller, "To Bring the Race Along Rapidly: Sport, Student Culture, and Educational Mission at Historically Black Colleges during the Interwar Years," *The Sporting World of the Modern South* (Urbana: University of Illinois Press, 2002), 136.
54. Leslie Heaphy, "Atlanta Black Crackers," Society for American Baseball Research, August 31, 2021, https://sabr.org/journal/article/the-atlanta-black-crackers/, and Tim Darnell, "Atlanta Black Crackers," New Georgia Encyclopedia, last modified March 20, 2021, https://www.georgiaencyclopedia.org/articles/sports-outdoor-recreation/-atlanta-black-crackers/.
55. *Commercial Appeal*, July 31, 1929.
56. *Commercial Appeal*, August 6, 1929.
57. Lomax, *Black Baseball Entrepreneurs, 1902–1931*, 415.
58. Larry G. Bowman, "To Save a Minor League Team: Night Baseball Comes to Shreveport," *Louisiana History: The Journal of the Louisiana Historical Association* 38, no. 2 (1997), 193–194.
59. Lomax, *Black Baseball Entrepreneurs, 1902–1931*, 416.
60. *Memphis Press-Scimitar*, May 12, 1930.
61. Donn Rogosin, *Invisible Men: Life*

Chapter Notes

in Baseball's Negro Leagues (Lincoln: Nebraska University Press, 1983), 128.

62. Robert Peterson, *Only the Ball Was White: A History of Legendary Blac Players and All-Black Professional Teams* (New York: Oxford University Press, 1970), 124.

63. *Commercial Appeal*, May 13, 1930.

64. *Memphis Press-Scimitar*, May 9, 1931, and *Commercial Appeal*, May 8, 1931.

65. *Commercial Appeal*, July 12, 1931.

66. *Commercial Appeal*, July 19, 1931.

67. Mark Ribowsky, *A Complete History of the Negro Leagues, 1884 to 1955* (Secaucus: Carol, 1997), 169.

68. *Commercial Appeal*, August 1, 1931.

69. Larry Nager, "W.C. Handy," Memphis Music Hall of Fame, accessed August 14, 2022, https://memphismusichalloffame.com/inductee/wchandy/.

70. Elizabeth Gritter, *River of Hope: Black Politics, and the Memphis Freedom Movement, 1865–1954* (Lexington: University of Kentucky Press, 2014), 109.

71. *Memphis World*, September 18, 1931.

72. *Commercial Appeal*, September 21, 1931.

73. Lomax, *Black Baseball Entrepreneurs, 1902–1931*, 404, 417–418.

74. *Memphis World*, April 19, 1932.

75. Scotty Moore, "Russwood Park," Scotty Moore—The Official Website, accessed July 11, 2021, http://scottymoore.net/russwood56.html.

76. Verdell Mathis, interview by Steven Ross, June 1994, reel 56, for documentary *Black Diamonds, Blues City*, Special Collections, McWherter Library, University of Memphis, Memphis, TN.

77. *Memphis World*, April 26, 1932.

78. *Memphis World*, April 5, 1932; *Commercial Appeal*, June 18, 1932; *Commercial Appeal*, July 5, 1932.

79. Peterson, *Only the Ball Was White*, 122.

80. Rob Ruck, *Sandlot Seasons: Sport in Black Pittsburgh* (Urbana: University of Illinois Press, 1993), 155.

81. *Commercial Appeal*, April 10, 1933.

82. Neil Lanctot, *Negro League Baseball: The Rise and Ruin of a Black Institution* (Philadelphia: University of Pennsylvania Press, 2004), 22–23.

83. *Commercial Appeal*, September 6, 1934.

84. Plott, *The Negro Southern League*, 122–123.

85. Marlin Carter and Verdell Mathis, interview by Steven Ross, June 1994, reel 1, for documentary *Black Diamonds, Blues City*, Special Collections, McWherter Library, University of Memphis, Memphis, TN.

86. George W. Lee, *Beale Street: Where the Blues Began* (New York: Robert Ballou, 1934), 179–180; Plott, *The Negro Southern League*, 125.

87. Plott, *The Negro Southern League*, 127.

88. *Commercial Appeal*, June 2, 1935.

89. *Commercial Appeal*, June 3, 1935; *Commercial Appeal*, June 17, 1935.

90. *Commercial Appeal*, July 1, 1935.

91. *Commercial Appeal*, September 16, 1935.

92. *Commercial Appeal*, June 3, 1936.

93. Lanctot, *Negro League Baseball*, 59.

94. *Commercial Appeal*, May 10, 1937.

95. *Commercial Appeal*, May 11, 1937; *Commercial Appeal*, July 6, 1937; *Commercial Appeal*, August 11, 1937.

96. *Commercial Appeal*, August 22, 1937; *Commercial Appeal*, August 24, 1937.

97. Riley, *The Biographical Encyclopedia of the Negro Baseball Leagues*, 670.

98. *Commercial Appeal*, August 4, 1939.

99. Riley, *The Biographical Encyclopedia of the Negro Baseball Leagues*, 670–671.

100. *Commercial Appeal*, July 15, 1940.

101. McBee, "They Also Played the Game," 210.

102. James Forr, "Thomas Hayes," Society for American Baseball Research, December 18, 2015, https://sabr.org/bioproj/person/tom-hayes/.

103. *Commercial Appeal*, July 26, 1940; *Commercial Appeal*, August 9, 1940.

104. Gary Ashwill, "1941 Memphis Red Sox," Seamheads Negro Leagues Database, accessed July 19, 2021, https://www.seamheads.com/NegroLgs/team.

Chapter Notes

php?yearID=1941&teamID=MRS&LGOrd=2.

105. *Commercial Appeal*, June 19, 1941.

106. Riley, *The Biographical Encyclopedia of the Negro Baseball Leagues*, 770.

107. *Ibid.*, 157.

108. Ribowsky, *A Complete History of the Negro Leagues, 1884 to 1955*, 246–247.

109. "Memphis Red Sox," Ebbets Field Flannels, accessed July 19, 2021, https://www.ebbets.com/pages/search-results?q=memphis+red+sox. I personally have bought these jerseys from Ebbets Field Flannels and used those to describe the jerseys worn by the team during World War II.

110. *Commercial Appeal*, July 5, 1942.

111. Gary Ashwill, "1942 Memphis Red Sox," Seamheads Negro Leagues Database, accessed July 19, 2021, https://www.seamheads.com/NegroLgs/team.php?yearID=1941&teamID=MRS&LGOrd=2.

112. *Memphis World*, May 7, 1943.

113. *Commercial Appeal*, April 12, 1944.

114. Frank Pearson, interview by Steven Ross, June 1994, for documentary *Black Diamonds, Blues City*, Special Collections, McWherter Library, University of Memphis, Memphis, TN.

115. *Commercial Appeal*, April 1, 1946; *Commercial Appeal*, May 7, 1946.

116. "1947 Memphis Chicks Roster," Stats Crew, accessed July 17, 2021, https://www.statscrew.com/minorbaseball/roster/t-mc12919/y-1947. Recorded attendance at Russwood for 1946 averaged 3,595 fans, and in 1947, that number went down to 3,198 as the Chicks struggled on the field and finished in seventh place in the Southern Association.

117. Bill Nowlin, "Doc Prothro," Society for American Baseball Research, September 24, 2020, https://sabr.org/bioproj/person/doc-prothro/.

118. Frank Pearson, interview by Steven Ross, June 1994, for documentary *Black Diamonds, Blues City*, Special Collections, McWherter Library, University of Memphis, Memphis, TN.

119. Charley Pride and Jim Henderson, *Pride: The Charley Pride Story* (New York: William Morrow, 1994), 64.

120. Verdell Mathis, Joe Scott, Frank Pearson, Marlin Carter, interview by Steven Ross, June 1994, for documentary *Black Diamonds, Blues City*, Special Collections, McWherter Library, University of Memphis, Memphis, TN.

121. Eva Cartman Martin, interview by Linda Murphy from questions prepared by John Haddock, February 1994, McWherter Library, University of Memphis, Memphis, TN.

122. Rufus Thomas, transcript of interview by Steven Ross, June 1994, reel 13, for documentary *Black Diamonds, Blues City*, Special Collections, McWherter Library, University of Memphis, Memphis, TN.

123. Verdell Mathis, interview by Steven Ross, June 1994, reel 57, for documentary *Black Diamonds, Blues City*, Special Collections, McWherter Library, University of Memphis, Memphis, TN.

124. *Ibid.*

125. Charley Pride, interview by Steven Ross, June 1994, reel 69, for documentary *Black Diamonds, Blues City*, Special Collections, McWherter Library, University of Memphis, Memphis, TN.

126. Verdell Mathis, interview by Steven Ross, June 1994, reel 56, for documentary *Black Diamonds, Blues City*, Special Collections, McWherter Library, University of Memphis, Memphis, TN.

127. "Citizens Committee Formed to Support Martin Stadium," *Memphis World*, January 1, 1950.

Chapter 3

1. Neil Lanctot, *Negro League Baseball: The Rise and Ruin of a Black Institution* (Philadelphia: University of Pennsylvania Press, 2004), 149.

2. *Commercial Appeal*, March 28, 1928.

3. *Commercial Appeal*, March 17, 1929.

4. George W. Lee, *Beale Street: Where the Blues Began* (New York: Robert Ballou, 1934), 88.

5. Preston Lauterbach, *Beale Street Dynasty: Sex, Song, and the Struggle for*

Chapter Notes

the Soul of Memphis (New York: W.W. Norton, 2015), 195.

6. *Ibid.*, 88–90.

7. *Chicago Defender*, September 9, 1922.

8. David Tucker, "Black Pride and Negro Business in the 1920s: George Washington Lee of Memphis," *The Business History Review* 43, no. 4 (1969), 435–451, 435.

9. *Ibid.*, 436–437.

10. Miriam DeCosta-Willis, *Notable Black Memphians* (Amherst, NY: Cambria Press, 2008), 215–216.

11. *Ibid.*, 10.

12. Plott, *The Negro Southern League: A Baseball History, 1920-1951* (Jefferson, NC: McFarland, 2015), 43.

13. Memphis Negro Chamber of Commerce, *1943 Negro Yearbook and Directory* (Memphis: Memphis Negro Chamber of Commerce, 1943), 55.

14. Sybill Mitchell, *Tri-State Defender*, December 1, 2011.

15. Plott, *The Negro Southern League*, 44.

16. *Commercial Appeal*, July 25, 1963.

17. Plott, *The Negro Southern League*, 48.

18. *Ibid.*, 49.

19. DeCosta-Willis, *Notable Black Memphians*, 269–270.

20. Darius Young, *Robert R. Church Jr. and the African American Political Struggle* (Gainesville: University of Florida Press, 2019), 1.

21. Plott, *The Negro Southern League*, 49–50.

22. *Chicago Defender*, July 17, 1926.

23. *Pittsburgh Courier*, July 24, 1926.

24. Phil Dixon, *The Negro Leagues Baseball: A Photographic History* (New York: Amereon, 1992), 142.

25. Neil Lanctot, *Fair Dealing & Clean Playing: The Hilldale Club and the Development of Black Professional Baseball, 1910–1932* (Syracuse: Syracuse University Press, 1994), 148.

26. *Chicago Defender*, January 14, 1927.

27. Plott, *The Negro Southern League*, 69.

28. *Commercial Appeal*, May 15, 1927.

29. *Commercial Appeal*, March 25, 1928.

30. Lauterbach, *Beale Street Dynasty*, 195 and 273.

31. *Memphis City Directories* 1927, 1929, 1931, 1932, and 1933.

32. *Commercial Appeal*, March 25, 1928.

33. *Chicago Defender*, April 14, 1928.

34. *Commercial Appeal*, June 1, 1928.

35. Phil Dixon, *The Negro Baseball Leagues: A Photographic History* (Mattituck, NY: Amereon House, 1992), 138.

36. *Commercial Appeal*, March 17, 1929.

37. *Commercial Appeal*, March 31, 1929.

38. *Chicago Defender*, May 25, 1929.

39. Eva Cartman Martin, interview by Linda Murphy from questions prepared by John Haddock, February 1994, Special Collections, McWherter Library, University of Memphis, Memphis, TN.

40. DeCosta-Willis, *Notable Black Memphians*, 237.

41. Eva Cartman Martin, interview by Linda Murphy from questions prepared by John Haddock, February 1994, Special Collections, McWherter Library, University of Memphis, Memphis, TN.

42. DeCosta-Willis, *Notable Black Memphians*, 236; *Nashville Globe*, April 5, 1907; Eva Cartman Martin, interview by Linda Murphy from questions prepared by John Haddock, February 1994, Special Collections, McWherter Library, University of Memphis, Memphis, TN; and Meherry Medical School Archives, Nashville, TN.

43. David Oshinsky, *Bellevue: Three Centuries of Medicine and Mayhem at America's Most Storied Hospital* (New York: Doubleday, 2016), 4–5.

44. *Ibid.*, 196.

45. "History—Bluff City Medical Association," Bluff City Medical Society, accessed October 17, 2021, https://bluffcitymedicalsociety.org/about/.

46. Gene Gill, "Memphis Hospitals and Medical Centers," Historic Memphis, accessed October 17, 2021, http://historic-memphis.com.

47. Marcus Stewart, *History of Medicine in Memphis* (Jackson, TN: McCowan-Mercer Press, 1971), 132.

48. Lee, *Beale Street*, 169.

Chapter Notes

49. Keith Wood, "The Harassment of Dr. J.B. Martin: A Story of Southern Paternalism in the 1940 Memphis," *Black Ball Journal* 8 (2016), 75.
50. Ethan Michaeli, *The Defender: How the Legendary Black Newspaper Changed America* (New York: Houghton Mifflin Harcourt, 2016), xii.
51. Keith Wood, "The Harassment of Dr. J.B. Martin: A Story of Southern Paternalism in the 1940 Memphis," *Black Ball Journal* 8 (2016), 75.
52. Elizabeth Gritter, *River of Hope: Black Politics and the Memphis Freedom Movement, 1865–1954* (Lexington: University of Kentucky Press, 2014), 141.
53. *Ibid.*
54. *Ibid.*
55. Phil Dixon, *John "Buck" O'Neil: The Rookie, His Words, His Voice* (n.p.: n.p., 2022), 76.
56. DeCosta-Willis, *Notable Black Memphians*, 237.
57. Lee, *Beale Street*, 224.
58. Verdell Mathis, Marlin Carter, Frank Pearson, and Joe Scott, interview by Steven Ross, June 1994, reel 1, for documentary *Black Diamonds, Blues City*, Special Collections, McWherter Library, University of Memphis, Memphis, TN.
59. Gary Ashwill, "Memphis Red Sox 1930 Season," Seamheads Negro Leagues Database, accessed October 21, 2021, https://www.seamheads.com/NegroLgs/year.php?yearID=1930.
60. William Plott, *Black Baseball's Last Team Standing: The Birmingham Black Barons, 1919–1962* (Jefferson, NC: McFarland, 2019), 82.
61. *Ibid.*, 93–94.
62. *1933 Memphis City Directory* (Memphis: R.L. Polk and Company, 1933), 218.
63. Plott, *The Negro Southern League*, 106.
64. Lee, *Beale Street*, 293.
65. *Commercial Appeal*, April 22, 1934, and *New Orleans Times-Picayune*, September 1, 1933.
66. *Commercial Appeal*, May 25, 1934.
67. *Pittsburg Courier*, March 3, 1934.
68. Plott, *The Negro Southern League*, 114.
69. *Chicago Defender*, April 7, 1934.
70. Plott, *The Negro Southern League*, 119.
71. *Commercial Appeal*, July 15, 1934.
72. Lanctot, *Negro League Baseball*, 39.
73. Donn Rogosin, *Invisible Men: Life in Baseball's Negro Leagues* (Lincoln: University of Nebraska Press, 1983), 18.
74. Mark Ribowsky, *A Complete History of the Negro Leagues, 1884 to 1955* (Secaucus: Carol, 1997), 204.
75. Alexander Klein, "William Dehart Hubbard," BlackPast, January 20, 2020, https://www.blackpast.org/african-american-history/hubbard-william-dehart-1903-1976/.
76. "The Tigers' Tale," MLB.com, accessed November 7, 2021, https://www.mlb.com/reds/hall-of-fame/history/cincy-tigers.
77. Dixon, *The Negro Baseball Leagues*, 164, and Riley, *The Biographical Encyclopedia of the Negro Baseball Leagues*, 171.
78. "The Tigers' Tale," MLB.com, accessed November 7, 2021, https://www.mlb.com/reds/hall-of-fame/history/cincy-tigers.
79. Lonnie Wheeler and John Baskin, "In the Shadows: Cincinnati's Black Baseball Players," *Journal of the Cincinnati Historical Society* 46, no. 2 (1998), 35.
80. Gary Ashwill, "1937 NAL Season," Seamheads Negro Leagues Database, accessed November 7, 2021, https://www.seamheads.com/NegroLgs/year.php?yearID=1937&lgID=NAL.
81. Elizabeth Gritter, *River of Hope: Black Politics and the Memphis Freedom Movement, 1865–1954* (Lexington: University of Kentucky Press, 2014), 134.
82. DeCosta-Willis, *Notable Black Memphians*, 162–163.
83. Gritter, *River of Hope*, 118.
84. Plott, *Black Baseball's Last Team Standing*, 208.
85. "Memphian Buys Baseball Club," Thomas J. Hayes Jr. Collection, Memphis Shelby County Room, Memphis Public Library, Memphis, TN.
86. *Commercial Appeal*, August 30, 1940.
87. *Commercial Appeal*, August 12, 1941.

88. Darius Young, *Robert R. Church Jr. and the African American Political Struggle* (Gainesville: University of Florida Press, 2019), 135.

89. Eva Cartman Martin, interview by Linda Murphy from questions prepared by John Haddock, February 1994, Special Collections, McWherter Library, University of Memphis, Memphis, TN.

90. Verdell Mathis, Marlin Carter, Frank Pearson, and Joe Scott, interview by Steven Ross, June 1994, reel 1, for documentary *Black Diamonds, Blues City*, Special Collections, McWherter Library, University of Memphis, Memphis, TN.

91. *Ibid.*

92. Ida Clemens, "Medical History in Memphis Opens New Chapter," *Commercial Appeal*, May 8, 1955.

93. *Memphis World*, May 7, 1943.

94. Verdell Mathis, interview by Steven Ross, June 1994, reel 57, for documentary *Black Diamonds, Blues City*, Special Collections, McWherter Library, University of Memphis, Memphis, TN.

95. Roger Biles, *Memphis in the Great Depression* (Knoxville: University of Tennessee Press, 1996), 38.

96. Rogosin, *Invisible Men*, 6.

97. Peterson, *Only the Ball Was White*, 192.

98. *Ibid.*, 197.

99. *Memphis World*, August 26, 1947.

100. William O. Little, interview by Steve Ross, April 1994, for documentary *Black Diamonds, Blues City*, Special Collections, McWherter Library, University of Memphis, Memphis, TN.

101. *Memphis World*, April 30, 1948.

102. *Commercial Appeal*, May 13, 1948.

103. Jules Tygiel, *Baseball's Great Experiment: Jackie Robinson and His Legacy* (Oxford: Oxford University Press, 1983), 227–228.

104. Laurie Green, *Battling the Plantation Mentality: Memphis and the Black Freedom Struggle* (Chapel Hill: University of North Carolina Press, 2007), 113–115, 136.

105. Sally Thomason, "The Three Eds in Memphis, 1948," *West Tennessee Historical Society Papers* 52 (1998), 157.

106. Riley, *The Biographical Encyclopedia of the Negro Baseball Leagues*, 98–99.

107. *Memphis World*, April 29, 1955.

108. *Press-Scimitar*, April 21, 1955, and *Press-Scimitar*, May 8, 1955.

109. *Tri-State Defender*, April 12, 1958.

110. *Memphis World*, April 22, 1959, and *Tri-State Defender*, July 25, 1959.

111. *Commercial Appeal*, April 23, 1960.

112. *Memphis World*, May 28, 1960.

113. *Commercial Appeal*, October 6, 1960.

Chapter 4

1. Gary Ashwill, "Memphis Red Sox," Seamheads Negro Leagues Database, accessed June 12, 2022, https://www.seamheads.com/NegroLgs/organization.php?franchID=MRS&first=1923&last=1948&tab=seasons.

2. William J. Plott, *The Negro Southern League: A Baseball History, 1920–1951* (Jefferson, NC: McFarland, 2015), 62–64.

3. *Ibid.*, 41.

4. *Commercial Appeal*, August 7, 1922, and Plott, *The Negro Southern League*, 41.

5. *Pittsburgh Courier*, August 26, 1933.

6. *Nashville Banner*, September 9, 1933.

7. *Arkansas Gazette*, September 9, 1933.

8. Plott, *Black Baseball's Last Team Standing*, 112.

9. Plott, *The Negro Southern League*, 131.

10. "The Cincinnati Tigers' Tale," MLB.com, accessed March 15, 2021, https://www.mlb.com/reds/hall-of-fame/history/cincy-tigers.

11. *Ibid.*

12. Gary Ashwill, "1937 Cincinnati Tigers," Seamheads Negro Leagues Database, accessed March 16, 2021, https://www.seamheads.com/NegroLgs/team.php?yearID=1937&teamID=CT&LGOrd=2&tab=pit.

Chapter Notes

13. Gary Ashwill, "1938 Memphis Red Sox," Seamheads Negro Leagues Database, accessed March 16, 2021, https://www.seamheads.com/NegroLgs/team.php?yearID=1938&teamID=MRSLGOrd=2&tab=bat.

14. Kyle P. McNary, *Ted "Double Duty" Radcliffe: 36 Years of Pitching and Catching in Baseball's Negro Leagues* (Minneapolis: McNary, 1994), 71.

15. Riley, *The Biographical Encyclopedia of the Negro Baseball Leagues* (New York: Carroll & Graf, 1994), 648.

16. Timothy M. Gay, *Satch, Dizzy, and Rapid Robert: The Wild Saga of Interracial Baseball Before Jackie Robinson* (New York: Simon & Schuster, 2010), 13.

17. John Holway, *Voices from the Great Black Baseball Leagues* (New York: Da Capo, 1992), 169–170.

18. McNary, *Ted "Double Duty" Radcliffe*, 75–76, 79.

19. *Ibid.*, 140.

20. Gary Ashwill, "1938 Memphis Red Sox," Seamheads Negro Leagues Database, accessed June 14, 2022, https://www.seamheads.com/NegroLgs/team.php?yearID=1938&teamID=MRSLGOrd=2&tab=fld.

21. John Holway, *Voices from the Great Black Baseball Leagues* (New York: De Capo, 1992), 170–171.

22. Timothy M. Gay, *Satch, Dizzy, and Rapid Robert: The Wild Saga of Interracial Baseball Before Jackie Robinson* (New York: Simon & Schuster, 2010), 111.

23. Kyle McNary, *Ted "Double Duty" Radcliffe* (Minneapolis: McNary, 1994), 115.

24. *Pittsburgh Courier*, March 26, 1938.

25. *Commercial Appeal*, April 4, 1938.

26. Buck Leonard with James Riley, *Buck Leonard: The Black Lou Gehrig* (New York: Carroll & Graf, 1995), 93–94.

27. Riley, *The Biographical Encyclopedia of the Negro Baseball Leagues*, 679–680.

28. Gary Ashwill, "1938 Memphis Red Sox," Seamheads Negro Leagues Database, accessed June 14, 2022, https://www.seamheads.com/NegroLgs/team.php?yearID=1938&teamID=MRS&LGOrd=2&tab=fld, and Riley, *The Biographical Encyclopedia of the Negro Baseball Leagues*, 680.

29. Plott, *The Negro Southern League*, 10.

30. *Pittsburgh Courier*, April 23, 1938.

31. *Pittsburgh Courier*, April 30, 1938.

32. *Ibid.*

33. Gary Ashwill, "1938 Memphis Red Sox," Seamheads Negro Leagues Database, accessed June 14, 2022, https://www.seamheads.com/NegroLgs/team.php?yearID=1938&teamID=MRSLGOrd=2&tab=fld.

34. *Commercial Appeal*, May 2, 1938.

35. Dixon, *John "Buck" O'Neil*, 122–123.

36. *Pittsburgh Courier*, May 14, 1938.

37. *Commercial Appeal*, May 11, 1938.

38. Bob Kendrick, host, "The Murder of Porter Moss," *Black Diamonds* (SXM podcast), May 26, 2022, accessed June 14, 2022, https://podcasts.apple.com/us/podcast/the-murder-of-porter-moss/id1561015600?i=1000563970355.

39. McNary, *Ted "Double Duty" Radcliffe*, 139.

40. Kendrick, "The Murder of Porter Moss."

41. *Cincinnati Enquirer*, May 1, 1933.

42. Plott, *The Negro Southern League*, 140.

43. *Pittsburgh Courier*, March 26, 1938.

44. William McNeil, *The California Winter League: America's First Integrated Professional Baseball League* (Jefferson, NC: McFarland, 2002), 248.

45. Kendrick, "The Murder of Porter Moss."

46. Verdell Mathis, Marlin Carter, Frank Pearson, and Joe Scott, interview by Steven Ross, June 1994, reel 1, for documentary *Black Diamonds, Blues City*, Special Collections, McWherter Library, University of Memphis, Memphis, TN.

47. *Commercial Appeal*, May 14, 1938.

48. Riley, *The Biographical Encyclopedia of the Negro Baseball Leagues*, 499 and 557.

49. *Commercial Appeal*, May 16, 1938.

50. *Commercial Appeal*, May 17, 1938.

51. Riley, *The Biographical Encyclopedia of the Negro Baseball Leagues*, 875.

52. *Commercial Appeal*, June 2, 1938.

Chapter Notes

53. *Commercial Appeal*, June 5, 1938.
54. *Pittsburgh Courier*, May 28, 1938, and Gary Ashwill, "1938 Philadelphia Stars," Seamheads Negro Leagues Database, accessed June 21, 2022, https://www.seamheads.com/NegroLgs/team.php?yearID=1938&teamID=PS&LGOrd=1.
55. Gary Ashwill, "1938 Memphis Red Sox," Seamheads Negro Leagues Database, accessed June 7, 2019, http://www.seamheads.com/NegroLgs/team.php?yearID=1938&teamID=MRS&LGOrd=1.
56. *Commercial Appeal*, June 3, 1938; June 5, 1939; June 6, 1938; and June 7, 1938.
57. *Commercial Appeal*, June 6, 1938.
58. *Commercial Appeal*, June 7, 1938.
59. *Commercial Appeal*, June 9, 1938.
60. Laurie Green, *Battling the Plantation Mentality: Memphis and the Black Freedom Struggle* (Chapel Hill: University of North Carolina Press, 2007), 8–9.
61. Riley, *The Biographical Encyclopedia of the Negro Baseball Leagues*, 104–105.
62. *Pittsburgh Courier*, May 7, 1938.
63. Riley, *The Biographical Encyclopedia of the Negro Baseball Leagues*, 421.
64. McNary, *Ted "Double Duty" Radcliffe*, 140.
65. Gary Ashwill, "1938 Memphis Red Sox," Seamheads Negro Leagues Database, accessed June 7, 2019, http://www.seamheads.com/NegroLgs/team.php?yearID=1938&teamID=MRS&LGOrd=1.
66. Riley, *The Biographical Encyclopedia of the Negro Baseball Leagues*, 421.
67. Kendrick, "The Murder of Porter Moss."
68. Riley, *The Biographical Encyclopedia of the Negro Baseball Leagues*, 766.
69. Bill Johnson, "Jim Taylor," Society for American Baseball Research, September 17, 2021. https://sabr.org/bioproj/person/jim-taylor/.
70. *Commercial Appeal*, June 10, 1938.
71. *Commercial Appeal*, June 11, 1938.
72. Riley, *The Biographical Encyclopedia of the Negro Baseball Leagues*, 212–213.
73. *Commercial Appeal*, June 25, 1938.
74. *Commercial Appeal*, June 27–28, 1938.
75. *Commercial Appeal*, July 4, 1938.
76. Phil Dixon, *John "Buck" O'Neil: The Rookie, His Words, His Voice* (n.p.: n.p., 2022), 177.
77. *Ibid.*, 178–179.
78. Riley, *The Biographical Encyclopedia of the Negro Baseball Leagues*, 770.
79. Gary Ashwill, "1938 Memphis Red Sox," Seamheads Negro Leagues Database, accessed June 7, 2019, http://www.seamheads.com/NegroLgs/team.php?yearID=1938&teamID=MRS&LGOrd=1.
80. Larry Lester, *Black Baseball's National Showcase: The East-West All-Star Game, 1933–1953* (Lincoln: University of Nebraska Press, 2001), 165, 169–170.
81. Riley, *The Biographical Encyclopedia of the Negro Baseball Leagues*, 770.
82. *Commercial Appeal*, July 11, 1938.
83. *The Daily Calumet* (Chicago), July 11, 1938.
84. *Ibid.*
85. Riley, *The Biographical Encyclopedia of the Negro Baseball Leagues*, 670–671.
86. *Chicago Defender*, August 27, 1938.
87. McBee, "They Also Played the Game," 191.
88. *Hinton Daily News* (Hinton, West Virginia), July 28, 1938.
89. *The Zanesville Signal*, July 29, 1938.
90. *The Evening News* (Harrisburg, Pennsylvania), July 30, 1938.
91. *New York Age*, August 1, 1938.
92. Gary Ashwill, "Marlin Carter," Seamheads Negro Leagues Database, accessed June 26, 2022, https://www.seamheads.com/NegroLgs/player.php?playerID=carte01mar.
93. Malcolm Allen, "Marlin Carter," Society for American Baseball Research, April 4, 2022, https://sabr.org/bioproj/person/marlin-carter/.
94. William McNeil, *The California Winter League: America's First Integrated Professional Baseball League* (Jefferson, NC: McFarland, 2002), 199–200.
95. Lester, *Black Baseball's National Showcase*, 159–160.
96. Allen, "Marlin Carter."
97. *New York Age*, July 9, 1938.
98. *Pittsburgh Courier*, August 6, 1938.

Chapter Notes

99. *Pittsburgh Courier*, July 30, 1938.
100. *Commercial Appeal*, August 9, 1938.
101. Leslie Heaphy, *The Negro Leagues, 1869–1960* (Jefferson, NC: McFarland, 2003), 138–139.
102. *Nebraska State Journal*, September 14, 1938.
103. Philip J. Lowry, *Green Cathedrals: The Ultimate Celebration of Major League and Negro League Ball Parks* (New York: Walker, 2006), 7–8.
104. Plott, *The Negro Southern Leagues*, 9.
105. Tim Darnell, "Atlanta Black Crackers," New Georgia Encyclopedia, last modified March 20, 2021, https://www.georgiaencyclopedia.org/articles/sports-outdoor-recreation/atlanta-black-crackers/.
106. Plott, *The Negro Southern Leagues*, 143.
107. Riley, *The Biographical Encyclopedia of the Negro Baseball Leagues*, 493.
108. Darnell, "Atlanta Black Crackers."
109. *Sheboygan Press*, August 3, 1938.
110. Heaphy, "Atlanta Black Crackers."
111. *Ibid.*
112. Lester, *Black Baseball's National Showcase*, 118.
113. Riley, *The Biographical Encyclopedia of the Negro Baseball Leagues*, 564, 139, and 337.
114. Darnell, "Atlanta Black Crackers."
115. *Commercial Appeal*, September 18, 1938.
116. *Commercial Appeal*, September 19, 1938.
117. McNary, *Ted "Double Duty" Radcliffe*, 145.
118. Riley, *The Biographical Encyclopedia of the Negro Baseball Leagues*, 80, and *Commercial Appeal*, September 20, 1938.
119. *Commercial Appeal*, September 20, 1938.
120. *Commercial Appeal*, September 11, 1938.
121. *Birmingham News*, October 1, 1938.
122. Riley, *The Biographical Encyclopedia of the Negro Baseball Leagues*, 545.
123. Heaphy, "Atlanta Black Crackers."
124. *Commercial Appeal*, October 3 and 4, 1938.
125. Lester, *Black Baseball's National Showcase*, 112, 118, and 119.
126. *Commercial Appeal*, March 25, 1939.
127. *Chicago Defender*, December 17, 1938.
128. Heaphy, "Atlanta Black Crackers."

Chapter 5

1. McBee, "They Also Played the Game," 52.
2. *Commercial Appeal*, April 20, 1921.
3. David Tucker, *Lieutenant Lee of Beale Street* (Nashville: Vanderbilt University Press, 1971), 71.
4. George Lee, *Beale Street: Where the Blues Began* (New York: Robert Ballou, 1934), 169–170.
5. Elizabeth Gritter, *River of Hope: Black Politics and the Memphis Freedom Movement, 1865–1954* (Lexington: University of Kentucky Press, 2014), 96.
6. Darius Young, "The Gentleman from Memphis: Robert R. Church Jr. and the Politics of the Early Civil Rights Movement" (PhD. Diss., University of Memphis, 2011), vii and viii.
7. Wayne Dowdy, *Mayor Crump Don't Like It* (Jackson: University of Mississippi Press, 2006), xii.
8. Sharon Wright, *Race, Power and Political Emergence in Memphis* (New York: Garland, 2000), 33.
9. Darius Young, "The Gentleman from Memphis: Robert R. Church Jr. and the Politics of the Early Civil Rights Movement." (PhD. Diss., University of Memphis, 2011), 210.
10. Dowdy, *Mayor Crump Don't Like It*, 98.
11. Young, "The Gentleman from Memphis," 116.
12. *Ibid.*, 212.
13. *Ibid.*, 201.
14. *Ibid.*, 200.
15. *Commercial Appeal*, October 27, 1940.
16. Wright, *Race, Power and Political Emergence in Memphis*, 33.
17. Ralph Bunche, *The Political Status*

Chapter Notes

of the Negro in the Age of FDR (Chicago: University of Chicago Press, 1973), 500.

18. Church, *The Robert R. Churches of Memphis*, 181.

19. Tucker, *Lieutenant Lee*, 126–128.

20. *Press-Scimitar*, February 19, 1942.

21. *Commercial Appeal*, October 26, 1940.

22. *Commercial Appeal*, October 27, 1940.

23. *Press-Scimitar*, October 28, 1940.

24. Mariana Pacini, *Photographs from the Memphis World, 1949–1964* (Oxford: University of Mississippi Press, 2008), 16–17.

25. Green, *Plantation Mentality*, 54.

26. *Press-Scimitar*, October 31, 1940.

27. David Tucker, *Lieutenant Lee of Beale Street* (Nashville: Vanderbilt University Press, 1971), 129.

28. *Press-Scimitar*, November 8, 1940.

29. Walter Chandler to Joseph Boyle, November 5, 1940, Box 14, Walter Chandler Papers.

30. *Elmer Atkinson and Willie Mae Atkinson v. Joseph Boyle et al.*, declaration filed 30 October 1941, in Circuit Court of Shelby County, Tennessee, Walter Chandler Papers.

31. Joel FSC McGraw, *Between the Rivers: The Catholic Heritage of West TN* (Memphis: JR Sanders, 1996), 110–114.

32. Church, *The Robert R. Churches of Memphis*, 182–183.

33. *Ibid.*, 183–184.

34. *Ibid.*

35. Mayor Walter Chandler to E.H. Crump, November 27, 1940, Crump Papers.

36. J.B. Martin to T.O. Fuller, November 7, 1940, Box 14, Walter Chandler Papers.

37. Green, *Battling the Plantation Mentality*, 42, 43, 78, 159.

38. Blair T. Hunt to Mayor Walter Chandler, November 4, 1940, Box 14, Walter Chandler Papers.

39. J.E. Walker to Commissioner Boyle, November 21, 1940, Box 14, Walter Chandler Papers.

40. W.S. Martin to E.H. Crump, November 1, 1940, Box 177, Crump Papers.

41. Gloria Brown Melton, "Blacks in Memphis 1920–1955: A Historical Study" (PhD. Diss., Washington State University, 1982), 193.

42. M.S. Stuart to Mayor Walter Chandler, November 1, 1940, Box 13, Mayor Walter Chandler Papers.

43. *Ibid.*

44. *Press-Scimitar*, November 23, 1940.

45. *Press-Scimitar*, December 6, 1940.

46. *Commercial Appeal*, December 12, 1940.

47. *Commercial Appeal*, December 5, 1940.

48. David M. Tucker, *Lieutenant Lee of Beale Street* (Nashville: Vanderbilt University Press, 1971), 129.

49. *Chicago Defender*, November 30, 1940.

50. Clifford Davis to E.H. Crump, January 23, 1941, Box 177, Crump Papers.

51. Melton, "Blacks in Memphis 1920–1955," 198.

52. *Press-Scimitar*, January 8, 1941.

53. *Press-Scimitar*, January 10, 1941.

54. *Press-Scimitar*, January 9, 1941.

55. *Ibid.*

56. Neil Lanctot, *Negro League Baseball: The Rise and Ruin of a Black Institution* (Philadelphia: University of Pennsylvania Press, 2004), 124–125.

57. *Press-Scimitar*, May 2, 1973.

Chapter 6

1. Robert Peterson, *Only the Ball Was White* (Oxford: Oxford University Press, 1970), 8.

2. John Holway, *Voices from the Great Black Baseball Leagues* (New York: Da Capo, 1992), 205.

3. Kyle McNary, *Ted "Double Duty" Radcliffe: 36 Years of Pitching and Catching in Baseball's Negro Leagues* (Minneapolis: McNary, 1994), 240–241.

4. Holway, *Voices from the Great Black Baseball Leagues*, 208–209.

5. Larry Brown, Jr., interview by Steven Ross, April 1994, Reel 85, for documentary *Black Diamonds, Blues City*, Special Collections, McWherter Library, University of Memphis, Memphis, TN.

6. *Pittsburgh Courier*, July 29, 1961.

7. John B. Holway, *Black Diamonds:*

Chapter Notes

Life in the Negro Leagues from the Men Who Lived It (Westport, CT: Meckler, 1989), 147.

8. McNary, *Ted "Double Duty" Radcliffe*, 144.

9. Larry Brown, National Baseball Hall of Fame Biographical Clippings File, accessed June 2022.

10. Byron Motley, "Brown, Larry," Oxford American Studies Center, https://oxfordaasc.com/browse;jsessionid=F477BC46E32B935C909BEB13066B1FA2?pageSize=20&sort=titlesort&t=AASC_Eras%3A5&t_1=AASC_Occupations%3A1169&type_0=primarytext&type_1=subjectreference (last accessed July 10, 2022); Delores Brown, interview by author, June 22, 2022.

11. *Two Industrial Towns: Pratt City and Thomas* (Birmingham: Birmingham Historical Society, 1988), 3.

12. *Ibid.*, 6.

13. Holway, *Black Diamonds*, 43.

14. Larry Brown, interview by John Holway, National Baseball Hall of Fame Biographical Clippings File, 1970, accessed June 2022.

15. Rob Ruck, *Sandlot Seasons: Sport in Black Pittsburgh* (Urbana: University of Illinois Press, 1987), 39.

16. Frederick Bush, "Verdell Mathis," Society for American Baseball Research, September 17, 2021. https://sabr.org/bioproj/person/verdell-mathis/.

17. Verdell Mathis, National Baseball Hall of Fame Biographical Clippings File, accessed January 2023; "Early Black Education in Memphis," Historic Memphis, accessed January 27, 2023, http://www.historic-memphis.com/memphishistoric/blackeducation/blackeducation.html.

18. Holway, *Black Diamonds*, 148.

19. Verdell Mathis, interview by Steven Ross, March 1, 1994, reel 13–15, for documentary *Black Diamonds, Blues City*, Special Collections, McWherter Library, University of Memphis, Memphis, TN.

20. Riley, *The Biographical Encyclopedia of the Negro Baseball Leagues*, 74.

21. Verdell Mathis, National Baseball Hall of Fame Biographical Clippings File, accessed January 2023.

22. Prentice Mills, *Black Ball News Revisited: Interviews and Essays Drawn from the* Journal of Negro League Baseball History (Nashville: Red Opel Books, 2019), 72–73.

23. Riley, *The Biographical Encyclopedia of the Negro Baseball Leagues*, 496; Verdell Mathis, interview by Steven Ross, March 1994, reel 13–15, for documentary *Black Diamonds, Blues City*, Special Collections, McWherter Library, University of Memphis, Memphis, TN.

24. Bush, "Verdell Mathis."

25. Verdell Mathis, interview by Steven Ross, June 1994, reel 57, for documentary *Black Diamonds, Blues City*, Special Collections, McWherter Library, University of Memphis, Memphis, TN.

26. Jim Burgess, "Joe B. Scott Biography," Baseball in Living Color, accessed January 1, 2023, https://www.baseballinlivingcolor.com/html2014/player.php?card=147.

27. 15 U.S. Census § (1930).

28. Joe B. Scott, interview by Curt Hart, March 2008.

29. *Ibid.*

30. Bob Glaze, "Exploring the Historic Bronzeville Neighborhood in Chicago," *Classic Chicago Magazine*, August 15, 2021, https://classicchicagomagazine.com/exploring-the-historic-bronzeville-neighborhood-in-chicago/#:~:text=Bronzeville%20is%20an%20historic%20neighborhood%20on%20Chicago%E2%80%99s%20South,as%20an%20early-20th-century%20African-American%20business%20and%20cultural%20hub.

31. John Eisenberg, *The League: How Five Rivals Created the NFL and Launched a Sports Empire* (New York: Basic Books, 2018), 103.

32. Thomas G. Smith, "Outside the Pale: The Exclusion of Blacks from the NFL, 1934–1946," *Journal of Sport History* 15, no. 3 (Winter 1988), 257.

33. Joe B. Scott, interview by Steven Ross, April 1994, reel 4, for documentary *Black Diamonds, Blues City*, Special Collections, Ned McWherter Library, University of Memphis, Memphis, TN.

34. *Chicago Tribune*, June 12, 1919.

Chapter Notes

35. Jim Burgess, "Joe B. Scott Biography," Baseball in Living Color, accessed January 1, 2023, https://www.baseballinlivingcolor.com/html2014/player.php?card=147.

36. Joe B. Scott, interview by Curt Hart, April 27, 2009.

37. "Tilden Technical HS 1937 Yearbook," E-Yearbook.com, accessed December 29, 2022, http://www.e-yearbook.com/sp/eybb, and "Joe B. Scott," Negro Leagues baseball emuseum, accessed December 27, 2022, https://nlbemuseum.com/history/players/scottj.html.

38. Joe B. Scott, video interview by Steven Ross, April 1994, reel 4, for documentary *Black Diamonds, Blues City*, Special Collections, McWherter Library, University of Memphis, Memphis, TN.

39. Joe B. Scott, interview by Curt Hart, March 2008.

40. Burgess, "Joe B. Scott Biography."

41. Joe B. Scott, video interview by Steven Ross, April 1994, reel 4, for documentary *Black Diamonds, Blues City*, Special Collections, McWherter Library, University of Memphis, Memphis, TN.

42. Laurie Green, *Battling the Plantation Mentality: Memphis & the Black Freedom Struggle* (Chapel Hill: University of North Carolina Press, 2007), 4–5.

43. *Ibid.*

44. Gary Ashwill, "Larry Brown," Seamheads Negro Leagues Database, accessed June 28, 2022, https://www.seamheads.com/NegroLgs/player.php?playerID=brown01lar.

45. Larry Brown, National Baseball Hall of Fame Biographical Clippings File, accessed June 2022.

46. *Ibid.*

47. Riley, *The Biographical Encyclopedia of the Negro Baseball Leagues*, 236–238.

48. Verdell Mathis, interview by Steven Ross, March 1994, reel 56, for documentary *Black Diamonds, Blues City*, Special Collections, McWherter Library, University of Memphis, Memphis, TN.

49. *Ibid.*

50. Verdell Mathis, National Baseball Hall of Fame Biographical Clippings File, accessed January 2023.

51. Gary Bedingfield, "Negro Leaguers Who Served in the Armed Forces in WWII," Baseball in Wartime—Negro League Baseball in World War II, accessed December 27, 2022, https://www.baseballinwartime.com/negro.htm.

52. Joe B. Scott, interview by Curt Hart, April 27, 2009.

53. Phil Dixon, *The Negro Baseball Leagues: A Photographic History* (Mattituck, NY: Amereon House, 1992), 293.

54. Joe B. Scott, interview by Steven Ross, April 1994, reel 4, for documentary *Black Diamonds, Blues City*, Special Collections, McWherter Library, University of Memphis, Memphis, TN.

55. Joe B. Scott, National Baseball Hall of Fame Biographical Clippings File, accessed January 2023.

56. "MLB Officially Designates the Negro Leagues as 'Major League,'" MLB.com, December 16, 2020, https://www.mlb.com/press-release/press-release-mlb-officially-designates-the-negro-leagues-as-major-league. When MLB Commissioner Rob Manfred honored the legacy of the Negro leagues in December of 1920, he named seven Negro leagues as major league. These seven leagues from 1920 to 1948 were the Negro National League (I) (1920–1931); the Eastern Colored League (1923–1928); the American Negro League (1929); the East-West League (1932); the Negro Southern League (1932); the Negro National League (II) (1933–1948); and the Negro American League (1937–1948). Thus, many years Brown plays in Memphis will be labeled "minor."

57. Larry Brown, interview by John Holway, National Baseball Hall of Fame Biographical Clippings File, 1970, accessed June 2022.

58. Gary Ashwill, "1927 Chicago American Giants," Seamshead Database, accessed June 28, 2022, and Riley, *The Biographical Encyclopedia of the Negro Baseball Leagues*, 122.

59. Keith Wood, "The Harassment of Dr. J.B. Martin: A Story of Southern Paternalism in 1940 Memphis," *Black Ball Journal* 8 (2016), 75.

60. Riley, *The Biographical Encyclopedia of the Negro Baseball Leagues*, 488.

61. Dick Clark and John Holway, "1930

Chapter Notes

Negro National League," *History Studies International Journal of History* 10, no. 7 (2018); http://research.sabr.org/journals/1930-negro-national-league.

62. Rob Neyer, "Did Gibson Hit One Out of Yankee Stadium," ESPN, May 19, 2008, accessed June 13, 2019, https://www.espn.com/mlb/columns/story?columnist=neyer_rob&id=3403111.

63. Gary Ashwill, "1931 Harlem Stars," Seamheads Negro Leagues Database, accessed June 29, 2022, https://www.seamheads.com/NegroLgs/team.php?yearID=1931&teamID=HAR&LGOrd=2.

64. Gary Ashwill, "New York Black Yankees," Seamheads Negro Leagues Database, accessed June 29, 2022, https://www.seamheads.com/NegroLgs/organization.php?franchID=NBY.

65. Larry Brown, interview by John Holway, National Baseball Hall of Fame Biographical Clippings File, 1970, accessed June 2022.

66. Stan Hochman, "Five Surviving Philly Stars, Negro Leagues to Be Honored Finally," *Philadelphia Daily News*, May 27, 2008.

67. Gary Ashwill, "Larry Brown," Seamheads Negro Leagues Database, accessed June 29, 2022, https://www.seamheads.com/NegroLgs/player.php?playerID=brown01lar&tab=bat.

68. *Commercial Appeal*, June 6, 7, 8, 9, 1938.

69. Verdell Mathis, interview by Steven Ross, April 1994, reel 2, for documentary *Black Diamonds, Blues City*, Special Collections, McWherter Library, University of Memphis, Memphis, TN.

70. Verdell Mathis, National Baseball Hall of Fame Biographical Clippings File, accessed January 2023.

71. Holway, *Black Diamonds*, 147–149.

72. *Commercial Appeal*, May 18, 1942.

73. *Chicago Defender*, June 6, 1942.

74. *Dallas Morning News*, July 13, 1942.

75. *Commercial Appeal*, July 28, 1942.

76. *Commercial Appeal*, July 19, 1943.

77. *The Chicago Defender*, August 4, 1944.

78. Holway, *Black Diamonds*, 148.

79. Verdell Mathis, National Baseball Hall of Fame Biographical Clippings File, accessed January 2023.

80. Verdell Mathis, interview by Steven Ross, April 1994, reel 1, for documentary *Black Diamonds, Blues City*, Special Collections, McWherter Library, University of Memphis, Memphis, TN.

81. Dixon, *John "Buck" O'Neil*, 293.

82. Rob Ruck, *Sandlot Season: Sport in Black Pittsburgh* (Urbana: University of Illinois Press, 1987), 175.

83. Joe B. Scott, interview by Curt Hart, April 27, 2009.

84. *Commercial Appeal*, March 20, 1948.

85. *Commercial Appeal*, March 21, 1948.

86. *Commercial Appeal*, March 22, 1948.

87. *Commercial Appeal*, April 15, 1948.

88. Joe B. Scott, interview by Steven Ross, April 1994, reel 4, for documentary *Black Diamonds, Blues City*, Special Collections, McWherter Library, University of Memphis, Memphis, TN.

89. *Commercial Appeal*, July 11, 1948.

90. *Commercial Appeal*, August 1, 1948.

91. *Commercial Appeal*, April 2, 1949.

92. *Ibid.*

93. Riley, *The Biographical Encyclopedia of the Negro Baseball Leagues*, 352.

94. Jules Tygiel, *Baseball's Great Experiment: Jackie Robinson and His Legacy* (Oxford: Oxford University Press, 1983), 224.

95. *Commercial Appeal*, October 6, 1949.

96. Larry Lester, *Black Baseball's National Showcase: The East-West All-Star Game, 1933–1953* (Lincoln: University of Nebraska Press, 2001), 1.

97. *Ibid.*, 22.

98. *Ibid.*, 401.

99. *Ibid.*, 1.

100. Frank A. Young, "First East vs. West Game, Chicago, IL," *Kansas City Call*, September 14, 1933.

101. "West Triumphs Over East in 11–7 Thriller," *Pittsburg Courier*, September 16, 1933.

Chapter Notes

102. Lester, *Black Baseball's National Showcase*, 401.
103. *Ibid.*, 61.
104. *Chicago Defender*, August 10, 1935.
105. Lester, *Black Baseball's National Showcase*, 110.
106. *Chicago Defender*, August 27, 1938.
107. *Chicago Defender*, August 12, 1939.
108. Lester, *Black Baseball's National Showcase*, 151.
109. John C. Day, *Chicago Defender*, August 2, 1941.
110. Fay Young, *Chicago Defender*, August 2, 1941.
111. Lester, *Black Baseball's National Showcase*, 171.
112. *Ibid.*, 202–204.
113. *Cleveland Call-Post*, August 22, 1942.
114. Fay Young, *Chicago Defender*, August 12, 1944.
115. Wendell Smith, *Pittsburgh Courier*, August 19, 1944.
116. Lester, *Black Baseball's National Showcase*, 238.
117. Riley, *The Biographical Encyclopedia of the Negro Baseball Leagues*, 521.
118. Lester, *Black Baseball's National Showcase*, 255.
119. Fay Young, *Chicago Defender*, August 4, 1945; Verdell Mathis, National Baseball Hall of Fame Biographical Clippings File, accessed January 2023.
120. *Chicago Defender*, August 4, 1945.
121. Wendell Smith, *Pittsburgh Courier*, August 4, 1945.
122. *Memphis World*, April 20, 1945.
123. Verdell Mathis, interview by Steven Ross, April 1994, reel 1, for documentary *Black Diamonds, Blues City*, Special Collections, McWherter Library, University of Memphis, Memphis, TN.
124. *Ibid.*
125. Riley, *The Biographical Encyclopedia of the Negro Baseball Leagues*, 521.
126. Lester, *Black Baseball's National Showcase*, 449.
127. *Ibid.*
128. *Memphis World*, August 26, 1947, and William O. Little, interview by Steve Ross, April 1994, Special Collections, Ned McWherter Library, University of Memphis, Memphis, TN.
129. *Memphis City Directory* (Memphis: R.L. Polk, 1941), 136, and *Memphis City Directory* (Memphis: R.L. Polk, 1951), 131.
130. Larry Brown, Jr., interview by Steven Ross, April 1994, reel 86, for documentary *Black Diamonds, Blues City*, Special Collections, McWherter Library, University of Memphis, Memphis, TN.
131. Delores Brown, interview by author, June 22, 2022.
132. Bryan Kirk, "Larry Brown, Legendary Tuskegee Airman, Speaks to High School Students," *The Patch,* November 18, 2016, https://patch.com/texas/houston/-larry-brown-legendary-tuskegee-airman-speaks-high-school-students?fbclid=-IwAR1hj2NicrJlwlmrIlHcJU-m-bXdjFng7xIMOJ6mYAEyswzlYSuzp8HICbw.
133. *New York Times*, April 10, 1972.
134. *Chicago Defender*, April 27, 1946, and *Chicago Defender*, July 6, 1946.
135. Frederick C. Bush, "Verdell Mathis," Society for American Baseball Research, September 17, 2021, https://sabr.org/bioproj/person/verdell-mathis/#_ednref68.
136. *Chicago Defender*, May 8, 1948.
137. "St. Joseph Auscos," Baseball Reference, accessed January 31, 2023, https://www.baseball-reference.com/bullpen/St._Joseph_Auscos#:~:text=The%20St.%20Joseph%20AUSCOS%20were%20a%20semipro%20baseball,Park%2C%20which%20was%20located%20on%20the%20factory%20grounds.
138. Bush, "Verdell Mathis."
139. *Ibid.*
140. Mills, *Black Ball News Revisited*, 83.
141. Riley, *The Biographical Encyclopedia of the Negro Baseball Leagues*, 522.
142. Holway, *Black Diamonds*, 153–154.
143. *Ibid.*
144. *Commercial Appeal*, October 31, 1998.
145. Joe B. Scott, interview by Steven Ross, April 1994, reel 4, for documentary *Black Diamonds, Blues City*, Special Collections, McWherter Library, University of Memphis, Memphis, TN.

Chapter Notes

146. "Joe B. Scott Minor League Statistics," Stats Crew, accessed December 31, 2022, https://www.statscrew.com/minorbaseball/stats/p-064b01d7. The website correctly identifies Joe B. Scott as the player, but it inaccurately lists his birth date and place of birth. If you cross reference Joe B. Scott with Joe Scott, who played for the Birmingham Black Barons, the website lists Joe Scott's birthplace and birthdate in lieu of Joe B. Scott's. Joe Scott, played in Chicago with the CAG in 1950, and then returned to Los Angeles, California, where he worked on the railroad for the next 28 years (per SABR Bio Project).

147. Joe B. Scott, National Baseball Hall of Fame Biographical Clippings File, accessed January 2023.

148. Tygiel, *Baseball's Great Experiment*, 274.

149. *Hope Star*, September 1, 1954.

150. "Joe B. Scott Minor League Statistics," Stats Crew, accessed December 31, 2022, https://www.statscrew.com/minorbaseball/stats/p-064b01d7.

151. *Knoxville News-Sentinel*, July 4, 1956.

152. Joe B. Scott, interview by Steven Ross, April 1994, reel 4, for documentary *Black Diamonds, Blues City*, Special Collections, McWherter Library, University of Memphis, Memphis, TN.

153. Tygiel, *Baseball's Great Experiment*, 282.

154. *Commercial Appeal*, March 23, 2013.

155. Justice B. Hill, "Special Negro Leagues Draft," MLB.com, accessed December 27, 2022, http://mlb.mlb.com/content/printer_friendly/mlb/y2008/m05/d29/c2795840.jsp.

156. "Redbirds to Honor Negro Leagues," Our Sports Central, July 9, 2008, https://www.oursportscentral.com/services/releases/redbirds-to-honor-negro-leagues/n-3677782.

157. *Commercial Appeal*, March 23, 2013.

Chapter 7

1. Phil Dixon, *The Negro Baseball Leagues: A Photographic History* (Mattituck, NY: Amereon House, 1992), 20.

2. *Ibid.*

3. Donn Rogosin, *Invisible Men: Life in Baseball's Negro Leagues* (Lincoln: University of Nebraska Press, 1983), 118.

4. Michael E. Lomax, *Black Entrepreneurs: The Negro National and Eastern Colored Leagues, 1902–1931* (Syracuse: Syracuse University Press, 2014), 418.

5. *Commercial Appeal*, July 30, 1922.

6. *Commercial Appeal*, August 7, 1922.

7. *Commercial Appeal*, September 10, 1922.

8. *Commercial Appeal*, August 7, 1922.

9. *Commercial Appeal*, July 3, 1923.

10. *Commercial Appeal*, July 5, 1923.

11. Plott, *The Negro Southern League*, 46–47.

12. *Chicago Defender*, August 11, 1923.

13. *Chicago Defender*, September 1, 1923.

14. *Commercial Appeal*, May 4, 1924.

15. McBee, "They Also Played the Game," 85.

16. Plott, *The Negro Southern League*, 85.

17. *Arkansas Gazette*, June 3, 1931.

18. *Arkansas Gazette*, July 17, 1931; *Commercial Appeal*, July 28, 1931.

19. *Press-Scimitar*, September 3, 1931.

20. Plott, *The Negro Southern League*, 84.

21. *Memphis World*, September 20, 1931.

22. *Commercial Appeal*, September 20, 1931.

23. *Commercial Appeal*, September 21, 1931.

24. *Memphis World*, March 29, 1932.

25. *Commercial Appeal*, April 15, 1932; *Memphis World*, April 15, 1932; *Commercial Appeal*, April 18, 1932.

26. Plott, *The Negro Southern League*, 114.

27. *Ibid.*, 115.

28. "Sioux City Ghosts," Sioux City History, accessed September 12, 2021, http://www.siouxcityhistory.org/art-a-leisure/125-sioux-city-ghosts.

29. *Chicago Defender*, September 15, 1934.

Chapter Notes

30. Anna Hider, "The Bearded Cultists of America's Pastime," *Mashable*, June 9, 2017, https://mashable.com/feature/house-of-david-baseball-team.

31. Larry Tye, *Satchel: The Life and Times of an American Legend* (New York: Random House, 2010), 105–106.

32. Travis Larsen, "Baseball Can Survive: How Semi-Pro Baseball Thrived in Wichita in the 1930s and 1940s," Emporia State Institutional Repository Collection, Kansas (2012), 32.

33. *Bismarck Tribune*, August 15, 1935; *Bismarck Tribune*, August 22, 1935.

34. Jason Pendleton, "Jim Crow Strikes Out: Integration Baseball in Wichita, Kansas, 1920–1935," *Kansas History Quarterly* 20, no. 2 (1997), 88.

35. *Ibid.*, 99–100.

36. *Bismarck Tribune*, August 22, 1935.

37. Larsen, "Baseball Can Survive," 34.

38. Pendleton, "Jim Crow Strikes Out," 86.

39. *Commercial Appeal*, June 4, 1928.

40. Verdell Mathis, interview by Steven Ross, June 1994, reel 57, for documentary *Black Diamonds, Blues City*, Special Collections, McWherter Library, University of Memphis, Memphis, TN.

41. *Commercial Appeal*, July 17–21, 1939.

42. Marlin Carter, interview by Steven Ross, June 1994, reel 1, for documentary *Black Diamonds, Blues City*, Special Collections, McWherter Library, University of Memphis, TN.

43. Clinton "Casey" Jones, interview by Steven Ross, June 1994, reel 28, for documentary *Black Diamonds, Blues City*, Special Collections, McWherter Library, University of Memphis, Memphis, TN.

44. Verdell Mathis, Marlin Carter, Frank Pearson, and Joe Scott, interview by Steven Ross, June 1994, reel 1, for documentary *Black Diamonds, Blues City*, Special Collections, McWherter Library, University of Memphis, Memphis, TN.

45. *Ibid.*

46. *Ibid.*

47. Bob Luke, *The Most Famous Woman in Baseball: Effa Manley and the Negro Leagues* (Washington, D.C.: Potomac Books, 2011), 95.

48. Verdell Mathis, Marlin Carter, Frank Pearson, and Joe Scott, interview by Steven Ross, June 1994, reel 1, for documentary *Black Diamonds, Blues City*, Special Collections, McWherter Library, University of Memphis, Memphis, TN; and James Riley, *The Biographical Encyclopedia of the Negro Leagues* (New York: Carol & Graf, 1994), 572.

49. Verdell Mathis, Marlin Carter, Frank Pearson, and Joe Scott, interview by Steven Ross, June 1994, reel 1, for documentary *Black Diamonds, Blues City*, Special Collections, McWherter Library, University of Memphis, Memphis, TN.

50. *Ibid.*

51. Dixon, *The Negro Baseball Leagues*, 249.

52. Lomax, *Black Baseball Entrepreneurs, 1902–1931*, 166.

53. Mark Ribowsky, *A Complete History of the Negro Leagues, 1884–1955* (Secaucus: Carol, 1997), 98.

54. Rogosin, *Invisible Men*, 123–126.

Chapter 8

1. Roberto González Echevarría, *The Pride of Havanna: A History of Cuban Baseball* (Oxford: Oxford University Press, 1999), 12–13.

2. C.L.R. James, *Beyond a Boundary* (London: Stanley, Paul & Co., 1963), xviii.

3. Phil Dixon, *The Negro Baseball Leagues: A Photographic History* (Mattituck, NY: Amereon House, 1992), 103.

4. Donn Rogosin, *Invisible Men: Life in Baseball's Negro Leagues* (Lincoln: University of Nebraska Press, 1983), 153.

5. Thomas E. Van Hyning, *Puerto Rico's Winter League: A History of Major League Baseball's Launching Pad* (Jefferson, NC: McFarland, 1995), 73.

6. *Ibid.*, 191, and Rogosin, *Invisible Men*, 164.

7. Rogosin, *Invisible Men*, 175.

8. Van Hyning, *Puerto Rico's Winter League*, 10.

9. Rogosin, *Invisible Men*, 162.

10. "Neil Robinson: Negro Leaguers in

Chapter Notes

Puerto Rico," Negro Leaguers in Puerto Rico, March 7, 2021, https://negroleaguerspuertorico.com/neil-robinson/.

11. Van Hyning, *Puerto Rico's Winter League*, 237.

12. *Ibid.*, 140.

13. Jorge Colon Delgado, interview by author, August 7, 2021. Delgado, a Puerto Rican baseball historian, established the "Negro Leaguers in Puerto Rico" website. His insight is invaluable as there are few books on the Puerto Rican winter leagues in English.

14. Verdell Mathis, interview by Steven Ross, June 1994, reel 35, for documentary *Black Diamonds, Blues City*, Special Collections McWherter Library, University of Memphis, Memphis, TN.

15. "Willie Wells: Negro Leaguers in Puerto Rico," Negro Leaguers in Puerto Rico, March 7, 2021, https://negroleaguerspuertorico.com/willie-wells/.

16. Dixon, *The Negro Baseball Leagues*, 292.

17. Echevarría, *The Pride of Havana*, 113.

18. "Negro Leaguers in Cuban Winter League," Center for Negro League Baseball Research, accessed August 4, 2021, http://www.cnlbr.org/Portals/0/RL/Negro%20Leaguers%20in%20Cuban%20Winter%20League.pdf.

19. Echevarría, *The Pride of Havana*, 182.

20. "Negro Leaguers in Cuban Winter League," Center for Negro League Baseball Research, accessed August 4, 2021, http://www.cnlbr.org/Portals/0/RL/Negro%20Leaguers%20in%20Cuban%20Winter%20League.pdf.

21. Echevarría, *The Pride of Havana*, 293.

22. "Negro Leaguers in Cuban Winter League," Center for Negro League Baseball Research, accessed August 4, 2021, http://www.cnlbr.org/Portals/0/RL/Negro%20Leaguers%20in%20Cuban%20Winter%20League.pdf.

23. Rogosin, *Invisible Men*, 170.

24. Gary Ashwill, "1940 Azules De Veracruz," Seamheads Negro Leagues Database, accessed August 14, 2021, https://www.seamheads.com/NegroLgs/team.php?yearID=1940&teamID=VEZ&LGOrd=4&tab=bat.

25. "1941 Tampico Alijadores Roster," Stats Crew, accessed August 15, 2021, https://www.statscrew.com/minorbaseball/roster/t-ta14890/y-1941.

26. Verdell Mathis, Marlin Carter, Frank Pearson, and Joe Scott, interview by Steven Ross, June 1994, reel 1, for documentary *Black Diamonds, Blues City*, Special Collections, McWherter Library, University of Memphis, Memphis, TN.

27. *Ibid.*

28. Larry Lester, *Black Baseball's National Showcase: The East-West All-Star Game, 1933–1953* (Lincoln: University of Nebraska Press, 2001), 280.

29. Riley, *The Biographical Encyclopedia of the Negro Baseball Leagues*, 184, 694, and 803.

30. Peter Marshall Ostenby, "Other Games, Other Glory: The Memphis Red Sox and the Trauma of Integration, 1948–1955" (M.A. Thesis, University of North Carolina at Chapel Hill, 1989), 48–50.

31. James Riley, *The Biographical Encyclopedia of the Negro Baseball Leagues* (New York: Carroll & Graf, 1994), 289.

Chapter 9

1. Kadir Nelson, *We Are the Ship: The Story of Negro League Baseball* (New York: Jump at the Sun/Hyperion Books for Children, 2008), 9.

2. Donn Rogosin, *Invisible Men: Life in Baseball's Negro Leagues* (Lincoln: University of Nebraska Press, 1983), 33–34.

3. *Memphis World*, January 1, 1950.

4. Jules Tygiel, *Baseball's Great Experiment: Jackie Robinson and His Legacy* (Oxford: Oxford University Press, 1983), 35–36.

5. Gary Ashwill, "Memphis Red Sox," Seamheads Negro Leagues Database, accessed June 12, 2022, https://www.seamheads.com/NegroLgs/organization.php?franchID=MRS&first=1923&last=1948&tab=seasons.

6. *Commercial Appeal*, May 6, 1946.

7. *Commercial Appeal*, May 17, 1946.

Chapter Notes

8. *Commercial Appeal*, September 3, 1946.

9. Elizabeth Gritter, *River of Hope: Black Politics and the Memphis Freedom Movement, 1865–1954* (Lexington: University of Kentucky Press, 2014), 176–177.

10. Marlin Carter, interview by Steven Ross, June 1994, reel 1, for documentary *Black Diamonds, Blues City*, Special Collections McWherter Library, University of Memphis, Memphis, TN.

11. *Commercial Appeal*, April 5, 1947.

12. Tygiel, *Baseball's Great Experiment*, 211.

13. James Riley, *The Biographical Encyclopedia of the Negro Baseball Leagues* (New York: Carroll & Graf, 1994), 289.

14. Roberto Echevarría, *The Pride of Havanna: A History of Cuban Baseball* (Oxford: Oxford University Press, 1999), 285.

15. Tom Hawthorn, "Pedro Formenthal," Society for American Baseball Research, August 5, 2013, https://sabr.org/bioproj/person/pedro-formental/.

16. Larry Lester, *Black Baseball's National Showcase: The East-West All-Star Game, 1933–1953* (Lincoln: University of Nebraska Press, 2001), 294–295.

17. *Chicago Defender*, August 2, 1947.

18. *Commercial Appeal*, July 6, 1947.

19. Gary Ashwill, "Memphis Red Sox," Seamheads Negro Leagues Database, accessed June 12, 2022, https://www.seamheads.com/NegroLgs/organization.php?franchID=MRS&first=1923&last=1948&tab=seasons.

20. Rory Costello, "Dan Bankhead," SABR, September 17, 2021, https://sabr.org/bioproj/person/dan-bankhead/.

21. *Memphis World*, August 26, 1947.

22. William Little, interview by Steven Ross, April 6, 1994, for documentary *Black Diamonds, Blues City*, Special Collections, McWherter Library, University of Memphis.

23. *Commercial Appeal*, August 26, 1947.

24. *Ibid.*

25. Costello, "Dan Bankhead."

26. *Commercial Appeal*, August 27, 1947.

27. Tygiel, *Baseball's Great Experiment*, 203.

28. *Baltimore Afro-American*, September 7, 1947.

29. *Commercial Appeal*, September 24, 1947.

30. *Commercial Appeal*, September 21, 1947.

31. *Commercial Appeal*, October 6, 1947.

32. *Commercial Appeal*, October 13, 1947.

33. Riley, *The Biographical Encyclopedia of the Negro Baseball Leagues*, 51, and "1948 Nashua Dodgers Statistics," Stats Crew, accessed June 9, 2023, https://www.statscrew.com/minorbaseball/stats/t-nd13201/y-1948.

34. "1949 Montreal Royals Statistics," Stats Crew, accessed June 9, 2023, https://www.statscrew.com/minorbaseball/stats/t-mr13125/y-1949.

35. *The Sporting News*, July 20, 1949.

36. Costello, "Dan Bankhead."

37. *Commercial Appeal*, May 25, 1950.

38. Costello, "Dan Bankhead."

39. Riley, *The Biographical Encyclopedia of the Negro Baseball Leagues*, 51.

40. Tygiel, *Baseball's Great Experiment*, 259.

41. *Ibid.*, 306.

42. *Ibid.*, 89.

43. *Memphis World*, March 19, 1948.

44. Riley, *The Biographical Encyclopedia of the Negro Baseball Leagues*, 694 and 803.

45. *Commercial Appeal*, May 10, 1948.

46. Leslie Heaphy, *The Negro Leagues, 1869–1960* (Jefferson, NC: McFarland, 2003), 146–147.

47. "Stepin Fetchit," IMDB, accessed July 11, 2022, https://www.imdb.com/name/nm0275297/bio.

48. Larry Tye, *Satchel: The Life and Times of an American Legend* (New York: Random House, 2010), 189–190.

49. Rogosin, *Invisible Men*, 218.

50. Rob Ruck, *Sandlot Seasons: Sport in Black Pittsburgh* (Urbana: University of Illinois Press, 1987), 185.

51. Bob Luke, *The Most Famous Woman in Baseball: Effa Manley and the Negro Leagues* (Washington, D.C.: Potomac Books, 2011), 145.

Chapter Notes

52. Ruck, *Sandlot Seasons*, 185.
53. Gritter, *River of Hope*, 182.
54. Heaphy, *The Negro Leagues, 1869–1960*, 219.
55. *Memphis World*, March 22, 1949.
56. Peter Marshall Ostenby, "Other Games, Other Glory: The Memphis Red Sox and the Trauma of Integration, 1948-1955" (M.A. Thesis, University of North Carolina at Chapel Hill, 1989), 48–51.
57. *Memphis World*, May 6, 1949.
58. *Memphis World*, January 3, 1950.
59. *Memphis World*, January 9, 1950.
60. *Birmingham World*, February 21, 1950.
61. Heaphy, *The Negro Leagues, 1869–1960*, 219.
62. *Chicago Defender*, April 29, 1950.
63. *Birmingham World*, July 7, 1950.
64. *Ibid.*
65. Stew Thornley, "Toni Stone," Society for American Baseball Research, September 17, 2021, https://sabr.org/bioproj/person/toni-stone/.
66. Heaphy, *The Negro Leagues, 1869–1960*, 218–219.
67. Bob Rives, "Bob Boyd," Society for American Baseball Research, September 22, 2021, https://sabr.org/bioproj/person/bob-boyd/.
68. Heaphy, *The Negro Leagues, 1869–1960*, 219, and *Tri-State Defender*, June 21, 1950.
69. Riley, *The Biographical Encyclopedia of the Negro Baseball Leagues*, 457.
70. Lester, *Black Baseball's National Showcase*, 549.
71. McBee, "They Also Played the Game," 266.
72. Lester, *Black Baseball's National Showcase*, 350.
73. *Ibid.*, 360.
74. William J. Plott, *Black Baseball's Last Team Standing: The Birmingham Black Barons, 1919–1962* (Jefferson, NC: McFarland, 2019), 208.
75. *Kansas City Call*, June 6, 1952.
76. *Birmingham World*, May 16, 1952.
77. Lester, *Black Baseball's National Showcase*, 374.
78. Plott, *Black Baseball's Last Team Standing*, 211.
79. Bill Johnson, "Hank Aaron," Society for American Baseball Research, March 24, 2022, https://sabr.org/bioproj/person/hank-aaron/
80. "Playoff Championship Series," Center for Negro League Baseball Research, accessed July 14, 2022, http://www.cnlbr.org/.
81. Charley Pride and Jim Henderson, *Pride: The Charley Pride Story* (New York: William Morrow, 1994), 23.
82. *Ibid.*, 59–60.
83. Riley, *The Biographical Encyclopedia of the Negro Baseball Leagues*, 642.
84. Plott, *Black Baseball's Last Team Standing*, 221.
85. Pride and Henderson, *Pride*, 67.
86. *Ibid.*, 68.
87. *Ibid.*, and Heaphy, *The Negro Leagues, 1869–1960*, 219.
88. "Playoff Championship Series," Center for Negro League Baseball Research, accessed July 14, 2022, http://www.cnlbr.org/.
89. *Commercial Appeal*, May 17, 1954.
90. Pride and Henderson, *Pride*, 69, and Riley, *The Biographical Encyclopedia of the Negro Baseball Leagues*, 642.
91. Plott, *Black Baseball's Last Team Standing*, 241.
92. *Memphis World*, March 8, 1955.
93. *Memphis World*, May 10, 1955.
94. *Memphis World*, March 4, 1955.
95. "Playoff Championship Series," Center for Negro League Baseball Research, accessed July 14, 2022, http://www.cnlbr.org/.
96. *Commercial Appeal*, September 3, 1956.
97. *Commercial Appeal*, June 21, 1956.
98. *Commercial Appeal*, August 26, 1956.
99. *Ibid.*, *Commercial Appeal*, August 7, 1956, and Pride and Henderson, *Pride*, 75.
100. *Commercial Appeal*, August 26, 1956.
101. Pride and Henderson, *Pride*, 81.
102. *Commercial Appeal*, September 4, 1956.
103. Bob LeMoine, "Charley Pride," Society for American Baseball Research, September 17, 2021, https://sabr.org/bioproj/person/charley-pride/#_edn26.
104. *New York Times*, June 8, 1959.

105. *Memphis World,* May 28, 1960, and *Commercial Appeal,* October 6, 1960.
106. McBee, "They Also Played the Game," 279.
107. Vance Lauderdale, "The Russwood Park Fire," *Memphis Magazine,* May 1, 2013. https://memphismagazine.com/ask-vance/the-russwood-park-fire/.

Epigraph

1. Jules Tygiel, *Baseball's Great Experiment: Jackie Robinson and His Legacy* (Oxford: Oxford University Press, 1983), 344.
2. Elizabeth Gritter, *River of Hope: Black Politics and the Memphis Freedom Movement, 1865–1954* (Lexington: University of Kentucky Press, 2014), 211.
3. Shirletta Kinchen, *Black Power in the Bluff City: African American Youth and Student Activism in Memphis, 1965–1975* (Knoxville: University of Tennessee Press, 2016), 22–23.
4. "Tigers to Honor Herb Hilliard," University of Memphis Athletics, February 24, 2017, accessed October 7, 2017, http://www.gotigersgo.com/news/2017/2/24/mens-basketball-tigers-to-honor-herb-hilliard.aspx?path=mbball.
5. David K. Wiggins and Patrick B. Miller, *The Unlevel Playing Field: A Documentary History of the African American Experience in Sport* (Urbana: University of Illinois Press, 2003), 205.
6. John B. Holway, *Voices from the Great Black Baseball Leagues* (New York: Da Capo, 1992), 207.
7. "Now Screening: Black Diamonds, Blues City—Stories of the Memphis Red Sox," On Location Memphis, April 4, 2013, https://onlocationmemphis.org/2013/now-screening-black-diamonds-blues-city-stories-of-the-memphis-red-sox.

Bibliography

Special Collections
Ernest Withers Family Collection
Memphis Shelby County Room, Benjamin Hooks Library, Memphis, TN
SABR Biography Project
Seamheads Negro Leagues Database
University of Memphis, McWherter Library, Special Collections

Journals
The Billboard
Black Ball Journal
Journal of Louisiana Historical Association
Journal of Sport History
Journal of the Cincinnati Historical Society
Kansas History Quarterly
Memphis Magazine
Nebraska State Journal
Time
West Tennessee Historical Society Papers

Newspapers
Arkansas Gazette
Birmingham News
Birmingham World
Bismarck Tribune
Chicago Defender
Chicago Tribune
Cincinnati Enquirer
Cleveland Call-Post
Commercial Appeal
Daily Calumet (Chicago)
Daily News (Chicago)
Dallas Morning News
Evening News (Harrisburg, Pennsylvania)
Hinton Daily News (Hinton, West Virginia)
Hope Star (Hope, Arkansas)
Kansas City Call
Memphis World
Nashville Banner
Nashville Globe
Nebraska State Journal
New York Age
New York Times
Philadelphia Daily News
Pittsburgh Courier
Press-Scimitar (Memphis)
Sheboygan Press
Tri-State Defender (Memphis)
Zanesville Signal (Ohio)

Articles
Larsen, Travis. "Baseball Can Survive: How Semi-Pro Baseball Thrived in Wichita During the 1930s and 1940s." Emporia State Institutional Repository Collection, Kansas (2012).

Malloy, Jerry. "Out at Home." *The National Pastime* #2 (Cleveland: SABR, 1983), 14–29.

Dissertations and Theses
McBee, Montgomery K. "They Also Played the Game: A Historical Examination of the Memphis Red Sox Baseball Organization, 1922–1959." PhD diss., University of Memphis, 2001.

Melton, Gloria Brown. "Blacks in Memphis 1920–1955: A Historical Study." Ph.D. Diss., Washington State University, 1982.

Ostenby, Peter Marshall. "Other Games, Other Glory: The Memphis Red Sox

Bibliography

and the Trauma of Integration, 1948–1955." M.A. Thesis, University of North Carolina at Chapel Hill, 1989.

Books

Biles, Roger. *Memphis in the Great Depression.* Knoxville: University of Tennessee Press, 1996.

Bunche, Ralph. *The Political Status of the Negro in the Age of FDR.* Chicago: University of Chicago Press, 1973.

DeCosta-Willis, Miriam. *Notable Black Memphians.* Amherst, NY: Cambria Press, 2008.

Dixon, Phil. *John "Buck" O'Neil: The Rookie, His Words, His Voice.* N.p.: N.p., 2022.

Dixon, Phil. *The Negro Leagues Baseball: A Photographic History.* Mattituck, NY: Amereon House, 1992.

Dowdy, Wayne. *Mayor Crump Don't Like It.* Jackson: University of Mississippi Press, 2006.

Echevarría, Roberto Gonzalez. *The Pride of Havana: A History of Cuban Baseball.* Oxford: Oxford University Press, 1999.

Eisenberg, *The League: How Five Rivals Created the NFL and Launched a Sports Empire.* New York: Basic Books, 2018.

Farley, Charles. *Soul of the Man: Bobby "Blue" Band.* Jackson: University Press of Mississippi Press, 2011.

Gay, Timothy M. *Satch, Dizzy, and Rapid Robert: The Wild Saga of Interracial Baseball Before Jackie Robinson.* New York: Simon & Schuster, 2010.

Goldberger, Paul. *Ballpark: Baseball in the American City.* New York: Alfred A. Knopf, 2019.

Green, Laurie. *Battling the Plantation Mentality: Memphis and the Black Freedom Struggle.* Chapel Hill: University of North Carolina Press, 2007.

Gritter, Elizabeth. *River of Hope: Black Politics and the Memphis Freedom Movement, 1865–1954.* Lexington: University of Kentucky Press, 2014.

Hamilton, G.P. *The Bright Side of Memphis.* Memphis: G.P. Hamilton, 1908.

Heaphy, Leslie. *The Negro Leagues, 1869–1960.* Jefferson, NC: McFarland, 2003.

Holway, John B. *Blackball Stars: Negro League Pioneers.* Westport, CT: Meckler, 1989.

Holway, John B. *Voices from the Great Black Baseball Leagues.* New York: Da Capo, 1992.

James, C.L.R. *Beyond a Boundary.* London: Stanley, Paul & Co., 1963.

Kinchen, Shirletta. *Black Power in the Bluff City: African American Youth and Student Activism in Memphis, 1965–1975.* Knoxville: University of Tennessee Press, 2016.

Lanctot, Neil. *Fair Dealing & Clean Playing: The Hilldale Club and the Development of Black Professional Baseball, 1910–193.* Syracuse: Syracuse University Press, 1994.

Lanctot, Neil. *Negro League Baseball: The Rise and Ruin of a Black Institution.* Philadelphia: University of Pennsylvania Press, 2004.

Lauterbach, Preston. *Beale Street Dynasty: Sex, Song, and the Struggle for the Soul of Memphis.* New York: W.W. Norton, 2015.

Lee, George W. *Beale Street: Where the Blues Began.* New York: Robert Ballou, 1934.

Leonard, Buck, with James A. Riley. *Buck Leonard: The Black Lou Gehrig.* New York: Carroll & Graf, 1995.

Lester, Larry. *Black Baseball's National Showcase: The East-West All-Star Game, 1933–1953.* Lincoln: University of Nebraska Press, 2001.

Lomax, Michael E. *Black Baseball Entrepreneurs, 1902–1931: The Negro National and Eastern Colored Leagues.* Syracuse: Syracuse University Press, 2014.

Lowry, Philip J. *Green Cathedrals: The Ultimate Celebration of Major League and Negro League Ball Parks.* New York: Walker, 2006.

Luke, Bob. *The Most Famous Woman in Baseball: Effa Manley and the Negro Leagues.* Washington, D.C.: Potomac Books, 2011.

McGraw, Joel, FSC. *Between the Rivers: The Catholic Heritage of West Tennessee.* Memphis: JR Sanders, 1996.

McNary, Kyle P. *Ted "Double Duty"*

Bibliography

Radcliffe: 36 Years of Pitching and Catching in Baseball's Negro Leagues. Minneapolis: McNary, 1994.

McNeil, William. *The California Winter League: America's First Integrated Professional Baseball League.* Jefferson, NC: McFarland, 2002.

Michaeli, Ethan. *The Defender: How the Legendary Black Newspaper Changed America.* New York: Houghton Mifflin Harcourt, 2016.

Miller, Patrick. *Sporting World of the Modern South.* Urbana: University of Illinois Press, 2002.

Mills, Prentice. *Black Ball News Revisited: Interviews and Essays Drawn from the* Journal of Negro League Baseball History. Nashville: Red Opel Books, 2019.

Nelson, Kadir. *We Are the Ship: The Story of Negro League Baseball.* New York: Jump at the Sun/Hyperion Books for Children, 2008.

Oshinsky, David. *Bellevue: Three Centuries of Medicine and Mayhem at America's Most Storied Hospital.* New York: Doubleday, 2016.

Pacini, Mariana. *Photographs from the Memphis World, 1949–1964.* Oxford: University of Mississippi Press, 2008.

Paige, LeRoy "Satchel," and David Lipman. *Maybe I'll Pitch Forever.* Lincoln: University of Nebraska Press, 1993.

Peterson, Robert. *Only the Ball Was White: A History of Legendary Black Players and All-Black Professional Teams.* Oxford: Oxford University Press, 1970.

Plott, William. *Black Baseball's Last Team Standing: The Birmingham Black Barons, 1919–1962.* Jefferson, NC: McFarland, 2019.

Plott, William. *The Negro Southern League: A Baseball History, 1920–1951.* Jefferson, NC: McFarland, 2015.

Pride, Charley, and Jim Henderson. *Pride: The Charley Pride Story.* New York: William Morrow, 1994.

Ribowsky, Mark. *A Complete History of the Negro Leagues, 1884 to 1955.* Secaucus: Carol, 1997.

Riley, James A. *The Biographical Encyclopedia of the Negro Baseball Leagues.* New York: Carroll & Graf, 1994.

Roberts, Randy. *Joe Louis.* New Haven: Yale University Press, 2010.

Rogosin, Donn. *Invisible Men: Life in Baseball's Negro Leagues.* Lincoln: Nebraska University Press, 1983.

Ruck, Rob. *Sandlot Seasons: Sport in Black Pittsburgh.* Urbana: University of Illinois Press, 1993.

Sanford, Otis. *From Boss Crump to King Willie: How Race Changed Memphis Politics.* Knoxville: University of Tennessee Press, 2017.

Stewart, Marcus. *History of Medicine in Memphis.* Jackson, TN: McCowat-Mercer Press, 1971.

Tucker, David. *Lieutenant Lee of Beale Street.* Nashville: Vanderbilt University Press, 1971.

Tye, Larry. *Satchel: The Life and Times of an American Legend.* New York: Random House, 2010.

Tygiel, Jules. *Baseball's Great Experiment: Jackie Robinson and His Legacy.* Oxford: Oxford University Press, 1983.

Van Hyning, Thomas E. *Puerto Rico's Winter League: A History of Major League Baseball's Launching Pad.* Jefferson, NC: McFarland, 1995.

White, Derrick E. *Blood, Sweat, and Tears: Jake Gaither, Florida A&M, and the History of Black College Football.* Chapel Hill: University of North Carolina Press, 2019.

Wiggins, David K., and Patrick B. Miller. *The Unlevel Playing Field: A Documentary History of the African American Experience in Sport.* Urbana: University of Illinois Press, 2003.

Wright, Sharon. *Race, Power and Political Emergence in Memphis.* New York: Garland, 2000.

Young, Darius. *Robert R. Church Jr. and the African American Political Struggle.* Gainesville: University of Florida Press, 2019.

Index

Almendares Club (Cuba) 166–167
Amsterdam News 96, 131
A.P. Martin Barber Boys Baseball Club 16
Atkinson, Elmer 109, 112–113, 115–117
Atlanta Black Crackers 31–32, 38, 85, 87, 93, 99–103, 136
Autozone Park 147
Azules de Veracruz 167–168

Baltimore Afro-American 96, 176
Baltimore Elite Giants 71, 84, 98, 180
Bankhead, Dan 8, 73–75, 136, 142–143, 174–176, 178
Bankhead, Sam 176
Barker, Marvin 131
Bassett, Pepper 140
Beale Street 6, 9, 13, 15–16, 19, 23, 27–28, 30, 35–36, 38, 52–56, 61–64, 68, 71, 83, 109, 130, 180
Bell, James "Cool Papa" 38–39, 139, 167
Bell, Julian 122, 127
Belleville (IL) Stags 129
Birmingham Black Barons 8, 38, 43, 54–55, 73, 76, 78–79, 86, 89–90, 97–98, 101, 132, 144, 154, 172, 175, 177–178, 181, 184–188
Black Diamonds, Bluff City 5–6, 194
Black Sheep Herders (TX) 84–85
Bolden, Edward 3, 26, 49, 71, 89
Booker T. Washington HS 21, 28, 31–32, 113, 122–123, 194
Boyle, Joe "Holy" 109–118
Bremmer, Eugene 89–90, 141
Brescia, Matthew "Matty" 73
Brewer, Chet 157
Bridgeport (CT) Bees 137
Broadway Coal and Ice 21
Bronzeville (Chicago) 124–125
Brooklyn Dodgers 8, 73, 121, 136, 145, 169, 171–172, 175, 177
Brooklyn Royal Giants 13, 123
Brown, Larry, Jr. 144
Brown, Larry, Sr. "Iron Man" 7–8, 22, 34–35, 44–45, 68, 89–90, 94, 96, 102–103, 119–122, 125–127, 129–134, 138–141, 143–145, 148, 160–161, 165–169, 172–174, 177, 180, 183, 187, 192–194
Brown, Sam 72, 84, 135, 187
Brown, Sarah Bell Wood 161
Brown v. Board of Education (1976) 187, 190
Browning, Gordon 68
Bubber, Berry "Bubbles" 101
Buffalo Bisons 90
Buffington Tailoring Company 17
Butts, Thomas "Pee Wee" 100

California Winter League 97, 161
Campanella, Roy 6, 134, 140
Campanis, Al 177
Carter, Audrey, D.D.S. 64
Carter, Marlin "Pee Wee" 8, 45, 64, 67, 87, 102, 158, 173, 193
Cartman, Eva 58, 71, 76, 184
Cecil (Chicks mascot) 18
Chandler, Walter 108–111, 113–115
Charleston, Oscar 38, 96, 139
Chattanooga Black Lookouts 27–28, 34
Chicago American Giants 5, 8, 14, 23, 25–27, 34, 80, 83, 85, 87, 89, 91–92, 95, 126, 129, 131, 138, 140–141, 151–153, 155–156, 158, 161, 181
Chicago Defender 21, 23, 25, 30, 39, 55, 57, 59, 65, 96, 103, 113, 115–116, 124, 135, 138–140, 152–153, 156, 171, 174, 181
chitterlings (chit-lənz) 47
Church, Robert, Jr. 14–15, 25, 35, 53–55, 60, 63, 68–70, 104–109, 112, 116, 118, 192
Church Auditorium 60, 104
Church of God in Christ (COGIC) 105
Cincinnati Clowns 46, 172
Cincinnati Reds 67, 80, 164
Cincinnati Tigers 41, 67–68, 80–81, 97, 132
Clark College 32, 99
Clarke, Vibert 183
Clarksdale, MS 90, 158
Claybrook, John C. 39, 91
Claybrook Tigers 37, 39–41, 68, 80, 87, 91
Cleveland Buckeyes 46, 91, 137, 141, 175, 184

221

Index

Cleveland Indians 8, 75, 123, 169, 172
Cleveland Stars 65, 156
Cobb, Ty 119–120, 157, 169
Colás, Carlos 167
Colás, José 143, 167–168, 174, 179, 184
Cole, Robert 66, 138
Collins Chapel Hospital 51, 59, 71, 76, 142
Colonial Country Club 97, 145
Columbus Blue Birds 82
Comiskey Park 94, 96, 102, 129, 138–141, 168, 174, 184, 188
Commercial Appeal 5, 11, 17, 18, 23, 25–26, 34, 38, 40, 48, 56–57, 64, 72, 75, 79, 84, 87–89, 92–93, 102, 107, 109–112, 115, 134, 145, 147, 152, 154, 158, 175, 188
Cotton Jubilee 172
Crawfordsville, AR 122
Crosley Field 20, 67
Crothers, Dug 12
Crump, E.H. "Boss" 5, 7, 14–15, 21, 35–36, 48, 52, 59–60, 62, 68–70, 72, 75–76, 104–118, 180, 187, 190, 192, 194
Cuba 119–120, 133, 161, 163, 165–169
Cuban Stars 95, 143, 153, 157, 164, 166, 169, 180
Cuban Winter League 161, 163, 166–167
Cummings, Chic 18
Curry, Homer "Goose" 81, 137, 180–181, 185, 187–188

Dallas Black Giants 152–153
Dandridge, Ray 141, 165, 167
Davenport, Lloyd "Ducky" 92
Davis, Clifford 5, 109, 116, 141
Davis, Willie 8
Dean, Jay Hanna "Dizzie" 129–130, 151, 161
Detroit Stars 17, 34, 38, 156, 188
Detroit Tigers 120
Dickey, John "Strong Arm" 126
Dihigo, Martin 166–167
Dismukes, William "Dizzy" 127, 130, 186
Doby, Larry 8, 48, 73, 75, 169, 172, 174
Dominican Republic 164
Double V for Victory 45, 48, 111
Douglass Park 14
Dukes, Tommy 139, 154
Duncan, Frank 119

East-West ASG 35, 39, 42–43, 65, 72, 86, 92, 94–97, 100, 102, 120–121, 132–133, 138–142, 144, 167, 174–175, 179, 183, 188
Eastern Colored League 26, 63
Ebony 182
Eisenhower, Dwight D. 61
Elmwood Cemetery 23
Ethiopian Clowns 101

Fair Employment Practices Commission (FEPC) 173
Fan Appreciation Day 43
Father Bertrand 114
Fay Avenue Park 17
Feller, Bob 123, 135, 151, 161
Fields, Wilmer 166
Fields Park 21
Finch, Larry 93, 191–192
Fisk College 52
Formenthal, Pedro 143, 167–169, 174, 179
Foster, Rube 3, 5, 13, 15, 16, 25–26, 36, 41, 49, 53–55, 62, 66, 80, 87, 127, 130–131, 151–153, 161, 164, 171, 193
Foster, Willie 26, 41, 133, 139, 152–153, 194
Fraternal & Solvent Bank and Trust Co. 30, 56–57
Freedom Train 75, 173
Fuller, Thomas Oscar 106, 113

Gibson, Josh 38, 42, 83, 92, 96, 102, 131–132, 134, 138–139, 141, 144, 165, 167
going around the horn 88, 158, 184
Gottlieb, Eddie 132
Great Depression 38, 56, 62–64, 103, 171, 191
Great Migration 3, 16, 116, 125
Green, Leslie 8
Green, Silas 27
Greene, Joe "Pig" 100
Greenlee, Gus 38–39, 63, 65–66, 82, 90, 132, 136, 138

Hambone 18
Handy, W.C. 35–36, 77
Harlem Globetrotters 178–179
Harlem House 48
Harris, Vic 83, 185
Hayes, Thomas, Jr. 43–44, 69–70, 76, 78, 181, 184
Higgins, Robert "Tobe" 11–13
Hilldale Baseball Club 5–6, 26, 38, 49
Homestead Grays 5, 8, 38, 67, 82–83, 85, 91–92, 95–97, 175–176, 180
Hooks, Benjamin 190, 193
Hooks Brothers Photography 38
Hornsby, Roger 120, 136
House of David 34–35, 88, 155–157
Houston Black Buffalos 79
Hubbard, William DeHart 67–68, 80–81
Hueston, William 56, 131
Hunt, Blair T. 108, 113–114
Hutchinson, Willie 8
Hyde, Cowan "Bubba" 8, 42, 98, 102, 173

Indianapolis ABCs 13, 26, 41, 86–88, 103, 127, 154
International League 11–12, 177
Iroquois Café 53–54

Index

Jackson, R.R. 101, 102
Jefferson, Willie 81, 85, 91–92
Johnson, Judy 38
Jones, Clinton "Casey" 8, 143, 159, 173, 182–184, 193–194
Jones, Reuben 44, 84–85, 123, 128, 133, 143, 156

Kansas City Monarchs 6, 8, 20, 30, 32–34, 38, 41, 44–45, 57, 65, 66, 74, 80, 85, 87, 93–94, 97–100, 134–135, 144, 157, 166, 172, 179, 186, 188–189
Kellman, León 183
Kemp, Gabby 100
King, Martin Luther, Jr. 58, 76
Knoxville Giants 79, 127
Kortrecht Grammar School 122
Kritzky, W.N. 54–55

Lacey, Sam 171
Landis, Kennesaw 125, 161
Lee, George Lt. 25, 35, 52, 58, 62, 77, 111, 116, 180
Leland, Frank 3, 13
Leland Giants 13–14, 41
LeMoyne College & LeMoyne-Owen College 32, 75, 173
Leonard, Buck 83, 95, 96, 144, 165
Lewis, R.S. 19, 21, 25, 30–31, 39, 46, 49–50, 52–54, 56–57, 62, 73, 78, 105, 152–153, 171, 189
Lewis Family Funeral Home 52–53
Lincoln League 14–15, 54, 59–60, 69, 104–105
Little Rock Black Travelers 154
Little Rock Grays 38, 154
Lloyd, John Henry "Pop" 89, 131
Locke, Alain 15
Long, Raymond 159
Longley, Wyman "Red" 8, 99, 173
Louisville Black Caps 38, 103
Lowe, William 123, 127–128
Lyles, Johnny 87

Mackey, Biz 89, 102, 119, 132
Manfred, Rob 4
Manley, Abe 181–182
Manley, Effa 73, 181
Martin, A.P. 16–18
Martin, A.T. 51, 58, 61–62, 113
Martin, B.B. 51, 58, 61–66, 70–72, 76–78, 128, 136–137, 145, 160–161, 175, 178, 183, 186, 188–189
Martin, J.B. 5, 7, 15, 17, 25, 35, 39, 50–51, 54–55, 57–62, 64–73, 76, 80–81, 85, 88, 90, 102, 104–105, 107–108, 110–118, 128, 141, 144, 156, 178, 181, 185, 187, 192
Martin, W.S. 37, 47, 51–52, 57–58, 62, 70–71, 73, 76, 108, 113, 136–137, 145, 159, 179–181, 183–184, 186, 188
Martin Stadium at Lewis Park 3–4, 6–7, 19–21, 23–48, 51–53, 56–57, 63–64, 68, 70, 73, 75–78, 83–85, 87–89, 93, 98, 101–102, 104, 117, 122–123, 127, 133, 136, 143, 148, 153, 155, 158–159, 171–173, 180–182, 184–185, 187–192
Mathis, Verdell 7–8, 28, 42, 44, 46, 71–72, 119–120, 122–123, 125, 127–130, 133–136, 140–145, 148, 159, 165–166, 168, 175–177, 192–194
McCullough, A.M. 15, 57
McDaniels, Fred 8
Meharry Medical School 58, 61
Memphis Chickasaws "Chicks" 18, 20, 24, 40, 78, 124, 192
Memphis Blues (MRS farm club) 76, 181
Memphis Giants 14, 31, 56
Memphis Police Department (MPD) 108–109, 111–112, 115
Memphis Press-Scimitar 5, 34, 48, 76, 110–111, 115–117, 155
Memphis Reds 11
Memphis Tigers 14
Memphis Unions 13, 14, 18
Memphis World 4, 38, 48, 72–73, 75–76, 109–112, 116, 120, 143, 155, 180–181, 187
Mexican Winter League 164–165
Mexico 82, 141, 164–169, 177
Miller, John W. 20–21
Miller, Larry W. 51–52
Milwaukee Bears 25, 147, 153–154
Mineola (TX) Black Spiders 123
Mississippi Boulevard Christian Church 113
Mississippi River Valley Flood (1949) 51
Mitchell, George 87
Monroe, Al 65
Monroe Monarchs 38, 97, 155–156
Montgomery Gray Sox 36, 155
Montreal Royals 176–177
More, Henry L. 98
Morris Brown College 32, 98–99
Moss, Porter "Ankleball" 81, 85–87, 89, 91–92, 95, 101–102, 160, 194

NAACP 15, 54, 60, 69, 104, 173, 190
Nashville Elite Giants 31, 36, 41, 62, 79–80, 154–156
Nashville Globe 13, 185
Nashville Standard Giants 13
National Baseball Hall of Fame 17, 92, 133, 135, 144, 179, 185, 188, 194
Navin, Frank 120
Negro American League 4, 7, 41, 44–46, 66–67, 69–70, 72–73, 76, 80, 86–89, 91, 93–94, 96, 98–103, 129, 133, 136,

Index

139–141, 144, 161, 168, 172, 174, 179–182, 184, 186–188, 192
Negro Leagues World Series 69, 79–81, 83, 89, 91, 131, 133, 161, 180, 184–185
Negro National League 4, 15, 16–17, 25–27, 31–34, 36, 41, 53–54, 56–57, 62–63, 65, 69, 71–72, 83, 87, 89–90, 97, 127, 131, 136, 141, 152–153, 156, 164, 180, 193
Negro Southern League 4, 16–18, 20, 25, 27, 29, 31, 34–36, 38, 40–41, 51–54, 56, 60, 62–65, 68–69, 79–80, 84, 86, 100, 126–127, 130, 152–155, 157, 171, 181–182
Nesbitt, E.E. 15, 57
New Orleans Crescent Stars 64, 79–80
New Orleans Segula Stars 154
New York Age 15, 97
New York Black Yankees 34, 41, 82, 89, 129, 132, 136, 180
New York Cubans 135, 137, 166, 184
New York Giants 14, 176
New York Lincoln Giants 34, 89, 131–132
New York Yankees 24, 145, 165, 176–177, 186
Newark Eagles 71, 97, 141, 166, 172, 174, 180
North Dakota Bismarcks 157
North-South ASG 39, 41, 46, 65–66, 102, 117, 144, 156

Office of Defense Transportation (ODT) 160
O'Neil, John "Buck" 19, 93, 133, 138, 188, 194
Opening Day 25, 30, 38, 45, 51, 54, 104, 134, 136, 144, 172, 187
Orange Mound 93, 180
Organized Baseball (MLB) 4, 12–13, 16–17, 20, 30, 48, 119–120, 122, 126, 130, 133, 135–138, 142–144, 146, 148–150, 164, 171–172, 174, 177–178, 180–181, 184–185, 187, 191–192
Ostermueller, Fritz 176
Owens, Jesse 42

Paige, Leroy "Satchel" 27–28, 38–39, 75, 81–83, 95, 97, 122, 130, 134–135, 139, 141–142, 150, 157, 164, 175, 178–179, 188
Panama Club 52
Parsons, Ell 15
Pasquel, Jorge 164, 166–167
Pearson, Frank "Wahoo" 46–47, 193
Petway, Bruce 17, 119
Phelan, Dick 11
Philadelphia Phillies 20, 47
Philadelphia Stars 34, 68, 71, 84–85, 89, 141, 144, 180
Pittsburgh Courier 26, 55, 64, 83, 86, 91, 96, 98, 111, 115, 119, 122, 131, 138–139, 142, 171, 180

Pittsburgh Crawfords 8, 38, 65, 67, 81–82, 97, 132, 136, 138–139, 156
Pittsburgh Keystones 126–127, 131
Polo Grounds 21, 97
Ponce de Leon Stadium 99, 101
portable lighting system 32–33
Posey, Cumberland 63, 82, 91
Pratt City 121–122
Presley, Elvis 182
Press-Scimitar see *Memphis Press-Scimitar*
Pride, Charley 48, 185–188
Prothro, Thomas "Doc" 46–47
Puerto Rican Winter League 165–166, 177
Puerto Rico 163–166, 177
Pullman cars/porters 18, 58, 151, 158

Radcliffe, Ted "Double Duty" 7–8, 38, 40–41, 44, 67–68, 80–83, 85–87, 89–93, 96, 98–99, 101–102, 119–120, 132, 140–141, 157, 168
Raif, Sam 159
Renfroe, William 11
Republican Party 15, 41, 68–70, 106–107, 114, 117; Black and Tans 15, 68–69, 107, 118, 192; Lily Whites 107
Rickey, Branch 8, 73–74, 136, 142–143, 172, 174–175
Rickwood Stadium 69, 98, 101
Robinson, Bill "Bojangles" 82, 89
Robinson, Jackie 7, 20, 46, 48, 73–75, 97, 121, 143–145, 162, 167, 169, 171–172, 176, 180, 190–193
Robinson, Neil "Shadow" 8, 67, 83, 96, 140, 194
Rochester Royals (A) 97, 145
Roddy, Bert T. 15, 25, 52–56
Rogers, William "Nat" 83, 102, 131, 173
Roosevelt, Franklin D. 62, 70, 106–107, 109, 112, 114, 116–117, 173
Ruppert Stadium 93
Russwood Park 20–21, 23–24, 37, 39–40, 46–47, 65, 78, 124, 152, 172, 189

St. Louis Browns 24, 75, 84, 137
St. Louis Stars 27, 43, 92, 152–154, 158
Santurce Baseball Club (Cuba) 164–165
Saperstein, Abe 178
Scott, Joe Burt 7, 119–120, 123–126, 128–130, 136–138, 143, 145–148, 160, 193–194
Seabrook, Carroll 111–112
Settle, Josiah T. 15, 53, 55
Sharp, Pierre 8
Shotton, Burt 176
Silas Green Minstrel Show see Green, Silas
Silver Trophy 38
Sioux City Ghosts 156
Smith, Maxine 190
Smith, Wendell 98, 139, 142, 171

224

Index

South Memphis 17, 19, 21, 112, 122–123, 128, 193
South Memphis Drug Co. 59–60, 64, 68, 71, 105, 108–110, 113–115
Southern Association 29, 46
Southern League of Colored Baseballists 11
Sparrow, Roy 138
The Sporting Life 12
The Sporting News 12, 177
Sportsman Park 24
Stearnes, Norman "Turkey" 17, 41, 133, 194
Stepin Fetchit 179
Sugarmon, Laurie 190
Sulphur Dell Park 39, 74
Suttles, George "Mule" 96, 140
Swingler, Louis 110–111, 116
Syracuse Stars 12

Tampico Alijadores Club (Mexico) 168
Tatum, Reese "Goose" 179
Taylor, C.I. 3, 13, 26
Taylor, Jim "Candy" 86, 91–92, 95, 140
Taylor, Olan "Jelly" 8, 45, 81, 94–95, 140, 172–173
Tennessee Coal, Iron, & Railroad Co. 121
T.H. Hayes and Sons Funeral Home 43, 59
Thomas, Rufus 28, 47
Tilden Tech 124–125
Time 27, 110, 112

Toledo Tigers 25
Tri-State Mack Distributors 78, 189, 194
Turner, Jessie, Sr. 190

United States League 136

Vargas Club (Venezuela) 165
Veeck, Bill 174
Venezuela 164–165
Verona, Orlando 168, 179

Walker, J.E. 69, 109, 114
Washington, Booker T. 3, 16, 78, 181
Wells, Willie, Jr. "El Diablo" 8, 166
Wells, Willie, Sr. 166, 168
Wichita Eagle 157
Wichita Nat'l Semi-Pro Championship 157
Wilkerson, J.L. 6, 20, 32, 65, 98, 179
Wilkie, Wendell 107, 109
Wilson, Thomas 65, 98
Wilson, Woodrow "Lefty" 87–88, 90
Woodcock, Amos 116–117
Wrigley Field 125, 135, 141

Yankee Stadium 81, 96, 131–132, 189
YMCA on the Paseo 16, 193

Zaharias, Babe Didrikson 156–157
Zorilla, Pedro "Pedrin" 164

www.ingramcontent.com/pod-product-compliance
Ingram Content Group UK Ltd.
Pitfield, Milton Keynes, MK11 3LW, UK
UKHW040052060325
455897UK00006B/41